I0880981

SERIOUSLY FUNNY

Seriously Funny

Mexican Political Jokes as Social Resistance

SAMUEL SCHMIDT

TRANSLATED BY ADAM SCHMIDT

THE UNIVERSITY OF
ARIZONA PRESS
TUCSON

The University of Arizona Press
© 2014 The Arizona Board of Regents
All rights reserved

www.uapress.arizona.edu

Originally published as *Humor en serio* by Aguilar Nuevo Siglo, 1996. A second edition, retitled *En la mira*, was published by Taurus, 2006.

Library of Congress Cataloging-in-Publication Data
Schmidt, Samuel.
[Humor en serio. English]
Seriously funny : Mexican political jokes as social resistance / Samuel Schmidt.
p. cm.
"Originally published as *Humor en serio* by Aguilar Nuevo Siglo, 1996. A second edition, retitled *En la mira*, was published by Taurus, 2006."
Includes bibliographical references and index.
ISBN 978-0-8165-3077-9 (pbk. : alk. paper)
1. Mexico—Politics and government—Humor. I. Title.
PN6231.P6S335 2014
867.009'35872—dc23

2013039489

Publication of this book is made possible in part by the proceeds of a permanent endowment created with the assistance of a Challenge Grant from the National Endowment for the Humanities, a federal agency.

Manufactured in the United States of America on acid-free, archival quality paper containing a minimum of 30% post-consumer waste and processed chlorine free.

19 18 17 16 15 14 6 5 4 3 2 1

To Rosie, Noa, Adam, Eddy, Jack, and Gali:
Thank you for this wonderful life.

Contents

Prologue to the Second Spanish Edition

When I promoted *Humor en serio* (Aguilar Nuevo Siglo, 1996), a true surprise was generated throughout Mexico. It seemed like an act of great audacity: someone had dared to do the unexpected. In a radio interview, I told a joke about the sitting president, and in certain levels of government, a raucous scandal was generated. Someone had shown the audacity to touch the sacrosanct image of the president of the republic, so much so that it seemed that a great act of political transgression had been committed exactly in the one area in which authoritarian power had been under close guard and control: the mass media.

I don't know if it was temerity, provocation, or an attempt to test whether the great accomplishment of the old system of the PRI had been to have people terrified by the threat of horrible consequences upon attacking the presidential image—the old big, bad wolf tale. Here comes the censorship! It was the call that served to disarm critique, and which succeeded in making people themselves cower down. When I approached writing for newspapers, there were three subjects that were clearly taboo: the president, the military, and the Virgin of Guadalupe. We learned to play the game, that of self-repression. The first article I wrote for *Revista de Revistas* (a magazine published by *Excelsior*) criticizing President José López Portillo, was censored, though I don't know if that censorship was a political editorial ploy.

Since then, they have fired me from a newspaper—*Uno mas uno*—due to pressure by a general whose son had gotten the concession to build a military base that I had denounced; I was fired from another paper, *El Universal*, due to pressure from the PRI—and one more—*Milenio*—after having criticized

President Fox. But the director who fired me wraps himself up in the flag of democracy as if he were the epitome of the freedom of expression.

I have never criticized the Virgin of Guadalupe because religious symbols per se don't worry me, though I have criticized pedophile priests and religious hierarchy, which conspires with the political and economical elite.

However, in these years, many political jokes have passed through the ears of Mexicans.

One great pertinent difference between the first version of my book—*Humor en serio* and the second—*En la mira*—is that I pointed out the difficulty in getting political humor onto Mexican television. Today, making fun of the president has invaded every nook and cranny; in fact, the Fox administration stated that a sign of democracy was the existence of a television parody *El privilegio de mandar*, and there is no lack of those who believe that this parody determined the July 2006 electoral result, but it was discontinued when the new administration came into office. As much as Fox may try to take credit for the result of the long, tortuous, and bloody battle for democracy, I would say that the appropriate opening in the media is not the first and it is not a generous governmental concession, but rather the recognition that an escape valve is urgently needed before the explosion of the grave problems the country endures thanks to a government comprised of inept and corrupt individuals. Vicente Fox and the Partido Acción Nacional (PAN) were not able or willing to reverse the old PRI corruption, and PAN members normally aligned themselves on the side of power; for them, the advance of democracy meant their inclusion in elected positions. The television networks—of which two dominate the market, proving the small bit of democracy existing in the country—have opened the doors to political satire because it is commercially viable, not due to a transgressing or democratizing aim.

Why Write a Mexican Second Edition of This Book?

The first reason would be to extend the historical reach of the jokes. The first version of the book was published during Ernesto Zedillos's administration, and it was appropriate to show the jokes in vogue during his six-year term. I formulated the hypothesis that a change in the political system—a defeat of the PRI—would be reflected in the jokes. It was no small thing that Mexicans terminated seventy-one years of power by one political party, and Fox, with great pomposity, has called it the administration of "change."

Since you could barely notice any "change," it behooves us to analyze humor's path at that moment.

Even though this is not an essay on Mexican politics in general, it is important to examine what jokes say when they deny the premise that the PRI is an all-powerful party, and regard a strong president, given the erratic Vicente Fox administration.[1] Zedillo and Fox help us see the meaning in the common mistake we make in believing that presidents used to leave a wide-reaching legacy. They built political groups that preserved their influence and intervened in politics in a mysterious yet effective manner. In addition, they left an indelible mark on the political system and on Mexican society. Nobody in his or her right mind can speak of Zedillism or Foxism, for which reason we have to readapt the analysis to be able to speak of "isms" regarding other presidents. Starting with the suggestion that in this country there was Callism, Alemanism, Cardenism, Echeverrism, and Salinism, the others are there for filler, even though they may be very poor quality filler. Yes, humor is there as an indicator of the level to which society is dissatisfied with all of them. With Salinas and Echeverría, the jokes followed them beyond their presidential terms, while López Mateos and Zedillo were nearly left alone after their terms.

Scholars continue to evade the subject of humor,[2] yet some have continued exploring its analysis; for that reason it was important to introduce a theoretical reconsideration and a bibliographical review, which would be of use to those interested in the study of humor.

It is important to examine how political jokes behave during specific events, or those of great political relevance. As I write this prologue, an enormous demonstration has taken place in the United States, protesting a legal initiative, which would criminalize undocumented immigrants, and very unusual jokes have emerged.

> George Bush went to administer the oath of citizenship to a group of thirty Mexicans, and when he was done he boastfully told them: "You may now kiss the bride."

Many political analysts who have become optimists believe that after the defeat of the PRI, changes have been born for Mexican society and its political culture, yet it seems we are returning to old practices: corruption and society encroaching. Politicians continue to worsen—so much so that the jokes are getting better, and we support the notion that for many people, jokes are the best medium to opine about politics.

As much as I am tempted to update the jokes up to the very last moment, I must end this effort by covering the end of the Calderón administration; however, I included a postscript showing some of the early Peña Nieto jokes, to give a sense of the feeling of the long-expected—for some desired and for some feared—return of the PRI.

Time never stops people from making jokes about long-gone politicians, and they keep laughing about the ones who struggle to get in power. So allow me to end this prologue by introducing one joke that circulated during the 2012 presidential campaign:

Junto al cadáver de un suicida se encontró una carta que decía:

No se culpe a nadie de mi muerte.

Me quito la vida porque dos días más que viviese sería mucho martirio: Tuve la desgracia de casarme con una viuda. Esta tenía una hija. De haberlo sabido, nunca me hubiera casado con ella.

Mi padre, para mayor desgracia, era viudo y se enamoró y se casó con la hija de mi mujer. De manera que mi mujer era suegra de su suegro.

Mi hijastra se convirtió en mi madrastra y mi padre al mismo tiempo ¡¡¡era mi yerno!!! Al poco tiempo, mi madrastra trajo al mundo una niña que era mi hermana, y a la vez era nieta de mi mujer, de manera que era ¡abuelo de mi hermana!

Después, mi mujer trajo al mundo un niño que, como era hermano de mi madrastra, era cuñado de mi padre, nieto de su hermana ¡¡¡y mi tío!!! Mi mujer era nuera de su hija, yo soy en cambio padrastro de mi madrastra, y mi padre y su mujer son mis hijastros, mi hijo es mi bisnieto y tío de su tía. Además, ¡¡¡yo soy mi propio abuelo!!!

Me despido de este mundo, porque no se quién chingados soy, y de repente, hasta podría ser primo del pendejo de López Obrador.

Next to the body of a suicide victim, a letter was found that read:

Don't blame anyone for my death.

I take my life because, should I live for two more days, it would be too much martyrdom.

I had the disgrace of marrying a widow. She had a daughter. Having known that, I never would've married her.

My father, to our disgrace, is a widow, and he fell in love and married my wife's daughter. In such a way that my wife was her own father-in-law's mother-in-law.

My step-daughter became my step-mother, and at the same time my father became my son in law! Soon after that, my step-mother gave birth to a girl who became my sister, and at the same time my wife's grand-daughter, and I became my sister's grandfather!

Soon after that, my wife gave birth to a boy who became my step-mother's brother, and my father's brother-in-law, his sister's grandson and my uncle!!! My wife was her daughter's daughter-in-law, and I am my stepmother's step-father. My father and my stepmother are my step-children, my son is my great grandson and his aunt's uncle, and I am my own grand-father!!!

So I bid my farewell to this world because I don't know who the fuck I am; you never know—I could even be a cousin to that idiot López Obrador.

SERIOUSLY FUNNY

Introduction

A few days after the Partido Revolucionario Institucional (PRI) announced Luís Donaldo Colosio (1994) as its presidential candidate, a joke appeared in a Mexico City newspaper alluding to Colosio's triumph over Manuel Camacho, mayor of the Federal District. A couple of weeks later, a new joke synthesized the opinion about the carrying-out of the Salinas government and the expectations for the new government:

> Este sexenio esta pelón, pero el próximo está en chino.

The play on words in Spanish mean: The word "bald"—*pelón*—which Salinas, the sitting president, was, and in this context that means in trouble. The term "curly haired"—*chino*—which the candidate was, means something approximating the saying, "It's Greek to me."

The play on words refers to the fact that it was assumed that history would repeat itself, and the PRI would take the presidency, and as such, the possibilities of the new government were graded according to the evaluation of the departing president. This didn't only summarize the physical characteristics of both politicians, but also the degree of uncertainty Mexicans were feeling. Some months later, the PRI candidate was dishearteningly felled by a bullet to the head, which humor attributed to Salinas (see chapter 4). The already battered Mexican economy unraveled, and a few months later, José Francisco Ruiz Massieu, former governor of Guerrero, Salinas's former brother-in-law, congressman elect and future speaker of the house, was also assassinated, and the economy continued decaying, hurling the country toward what would be a prolonged economic crisis, which according to many, precipitated the triumph of Vicente Fox's presidential candidacy, which is characterized by being anti-political, and irreverent, and having a nearly chaotic platform (see chapter 5).

Often, political jokes establish the tone of social expectations even before the analysts do so, and in Mexico's case, they express society's sentiments and hopes.

Habitually it is said that Mexicans laugh at everything, even though few ask what they are laughing about.[1] With regard to political jokes we have the same question, even though we are extending it to inquire into why they tell political jokes, instead of participating. The answer has to do with cultural characteristics of the Mexican.

Culturally, Mexicans are more willing to laugh than to actively participate, due to the fact that the authoritarian regime leaves few possibilities to influence or change the reproachable aspects of government. As such, jokes serve to transmit a message of dissatisfaction and are an outlet for frustration.

Citizens regard politics as a system of imposition and manipulation. Politicians are not trustworthy, and democracy can be graded according to the degree of governmental imposition and not according to citizen participation or involvement. By contrast, scholars grade political systems according to an academic paradigm, in which diverse values are chosen as relevant. In the case of political behavior, for Johnson (1980) it turns out to be relevant to study stereotypes in Latin America based originally on the opinions of several experts. The scholars' paradigms don't have to coincide with what society thinks. In fact, academic studies often begin with a preconceived idea, and even when it approximates political reality, the paradigm may exclude relevant information.

A groundbreaking study regarding individual perception of power, referred to as civic culture (Almond and Verba, 1963), found that Mexicans feel reduced by specific political conditions, but it did not touch on the subject of free and uncontrolled opinion of society over government. As with similar studies, this one underestimated the spontaneous and non-compromising sentiment regarding government, reflected in what political jokes express socially.

The idea of the citizen as a product of the State (Torres-Rivas, 1993) creates an academic paradigm under which social opinions are explained, having as a reference, the State and its rules. The majority of books regarding Mexican politics follow this paradigm, attempting to understand the political process through an analysis of the State and the structure of power. Padgett (1976) identifies the creation of the revolutionary credo expanded by the State, and Newell and Rubio (1984) recognize the importance and the role cohesion plays for the government, but both fail to identify what society thinks or feels. Books on philosophy (Ramos, 1934) and psychology (Díaz Guerrero, 1961) explain the Mexican character, but they wrongly characterize the complex relationship between society and the State from a social perspective. Political jokes represent this dimension of opinion as well as social sentiment. In this book, I intend to contribute in the creation of a new paradigm to comprehend the relationship between society and the State.

Political humor is not a minor component in Mexican political culture. Nevertheless, we still lack good mechanisms by which to comprehend its impact. The main purpose of this book is to understand why Mexicans laugh at politics and the impact this has on the political system, and to the extent possible, suggest a new focus to understand Mexican political culture.

I've always liked to tell jokes to entertain my friends even more than usual; on occasion I enjoyed being the funny one in the group, and I still fondly remember that New Year's Eve when I entertained my friends by telling jokes all night. Obviously, I liked to impress others with my ability to remember so many jokes—in addition, the ability to tell them. But I never paid attention to political jokes, until I began studying the confrontation between the State and the bourgeoisie in Mexico.[2] That research led me to consider seriously the role of political jokes.

Treating jokes seriously, as an academic subject, led me from funny joke-teller, to joke-listener. At the same time, my specialty in political jokes saved me from the solemnity and formality of university life, in which if one is not careful one completely loses his sense of humor. Héctor Subirats wisely determined that the university is an imbecile yet generous institution, and this nearly earned him his expulsion from the institution by a Trotsko-fascist who was the dean of graduate studies. To my university colleagues I recommend a boisterous laugh at least once a day to maintain bodily humor at a good level.

Another stimulus to modify my relationship with humor was my son of thirteen years of age (today he is seventeen years older, and editing this book). He has chosen the joke and jest to manipulate his social relationships. Knowing that I collect jokes, he frequently has put me in the predicament of not having one to tell him.

I have written this book with the intention of placing jokes as a social phenomenon within an analytical context. I have avoided sarcasm as much as possible so that it is not said that I have something against the individuals involved. This analysis does not intend to denigrate or offend the subjects of the jokes, and I mention this because he who is the object of a joke feels attacked, especially when the joke is written down, possibly because the written joke becomes part of historical record and affects the future image of the politician. Politicians struggle first for power and then to be pictured favorably in history books; consequently, they take the author of the collection of jokes or essayist who analyzes them as their author, as the cause of the destruction of their image. Since in Mexico it is commonly considered that all is part of a great conspiracy, the one analyzing surely responds to the instructions of some enemy of the politician in question. It is very flattering that it should be attributed to me the genius for the creation of humor included in this book, but I must decline such an honor.

This book does not intend to be an analysis of psychology and political behavior, nor does it intend to resolve the polemics over the same. I don't support discrimination or prejudice involved in the jokes (as much as jokes—and in particular, ethnic jokes—walk a fine line between racism and discrimination and just poking fun at someone[3]). On the contrary, I try to clarify the role that political jokes play in Mexican politics and, by means of this explanation, contribute to the elimination of social stereotypes.

At the same time, if I can make people laugh while reading a political science book, I will have partially achieved my objective in writing this work. I must mention that having showed part of the manuscript to a colleague at UCLA, I received one of the responses that I'd hoped for: "Samuel, I have laughed a lot with your material." I got the same response from Rius (the famous Eduardo del Río)—which was an unexpected compliment, maybe even unmerited.

In this book, I have concentrated on the analysis of several humoristic forms, some dated back as far as the sixteenth century, but the majority from the twentieth century in Mexico—very diverse humoristic forms: nicknames, poems, anagrams, parodies of religious prayers, and more. All of these forms may be considered spontaneous and involuntary expressions, in the sense that they don't create a *client relationship* between the teller and the receptor. The cartoon has been excluded because it establishes a relationship of clientele by means of which the artist influences the reader with a political ideological message (Fultz, 1970). Generally, one looks for one's favorite cartoon artist and predisposes himself to receive the intended message. I am certain that this is the fundamental reason for which Rius became one of the most important and widely read cartoonists in Mexico in the last thirty years. I am one of his devotees, as I am of El Fisgón, Helguera, Pego, Naranjo, Trudeau, and other greats.

The type of humor I analyze in the study includes oral forms, which are easily lost. In the past, few political jokes were compiled. At present, the Center for Media and Public Affairs in Washington, D.C., registers political jokes from American television. Hopefully, contemporary historians and political analysts will routinely record in the future political humor as an additional instrument for learning what society thinks of its leaders and government officials.

Political jokes are an obvious phenomenon, but they have not been able to attract the attention of scholars. Possibly, political analysts have ignored the subject because they prefer to study measurable events, such as the elections. Political phenomena—such as the quantity and quality of jokes—are difficult to quantify, and this is partly due to the impact of political humor being displaced; in any case, it is without a doubt due to political humor being an expression and not part of a formal process. Nevertheless, those positivists who are stuck in the need to know *the number* of existing jokes are unable to see that jokes are a component of political communication, which frequently develops outside of formal channels of communication.

In contrast with political science, psychoanalysis studies explicit and implicit words, and political humor is made up of both meanings and occult symbols, which other disciplines fail to recognize. The search for the real depth of this language has finally expanded into other disciplines. The interesting study of Scott (1990) regarding resistance identifies occult transcriptions, which reflect social resistance, although it doesn't recognize humor's role.

The understanding of political jokes contributes to the interpretation of its hidden political impact. Politics is a subterranean game comprehensible to the initiated, and frustrating for those who are affected by politics yet lack influence because they ignore the game, its rules, symbols, and language. People feel blind trying to see the game that affects their lives. The complexity of this situation can be described with the following Indian parable created to explain the complexity of scientific paradigms and which can be applied to politics.

> Three blind men went to see an elephant, and later on they attempt to describe it. The first one, who saw the leg says: "The elephant is like a great tree."
>
> The second one, who's on the bottom says: "The elephant is like a great container."
>
> The third one, who saw the trunk says: "The elephant is like a great snake."

None of them saw the whole elephant, but each one them described what he saw. Our challenge regarding political analysis is to regard the elephant as a whole, not just one of its parts. Jokes show us another part of the elephant—how society perceives politics and politicians, where society imposes its own rules.

Political development generates and comprises two contradictory processes: the creation of social representative institutions, and social methods and instruments by which to contend with and in its case reject politics and politicians. Political jokes are a good expression of this rejection, yet scientists have failed to explain informal social rejection. These social manifestations reveal another aspect of the relationship between society and the State.

Political science has created theoretical instruments to analyze domination, as a basis for understanding social rebellion (Feierabend and Nesvold, 1969; Gupta, 1990), and to comprehend informal nonviolent resistance against authority (Scott, 1990). We have been witnesses to sufficient instances of nonviolent political rebellion (for example, Gandhi), but we still require a sufficient development of knowledge regarding subterranean confrontation for and against political power. The analysis of political jokes developed in this work intends to contribute to the understanding of this confrontation between society and politics.

Political jokes help us understand the way in which society receives and reacts to political phenomena, such as the nomination of candidates, allowing us to reflect on different forms of political participation. In a certain discussion regarding abstention, I was told "the citizenry no longer worries about politics," which is wrong—people do care, but they have no opportunity on an unleveled field, thus they express their fear of powerful individuals by making fun of them (A.D., 1960).

The argument that different segments of society use different instruments to communicate could come from the high percentages of voter abstention noted in many parts of the world. This does not explain, however, why differing political systems with low voting levels remain stable and record low political conflict. Humor is perhaps the instrument to relieve political frustration. It is an escape valve that society uses to take revenge on politicians without risking political stability.

Political jokes express the confrontation of social wit and that of political power, and they can be the means by which a society emerges, to a degree, victorious in adverse situations—such as when a dictatorship suffocates a democracy, but the people of the democracy are able to retain a sense of pride through political humor, which allows them a means for expressing disrespect for those in power. Differing disciplines base their studies on a variety of social expressions, yet the question of why people accept domination remains unanswered. We certainly don't understand why slaves, or people who live under totalitarian regimes deprived of liberty, do not rebel. But political jokes may be considered a form of rebellion, as they indicate the irritating aspects of politics—their objective being not to overthrow government, but to suggest correcting its mistakes.

Here is an example of a joke from Moscow, related in both Spanish and English.

Berl y Shmerl van caminando por la calle en Moscú en la época pre-perestroika. De repente, ven un policía mirándolos atentamente.

"Estoy en problemas," dice Berl. "¡¡¡No tengo mis documentos en orden, y si la policía me los pide, me llevará preso!!!"

"No te preocupes," lo calmó Shmerl. "Yo tengo mis documentos en orden. Yo voy a empezar a correr, y me va a perseguir pensando que tengo algún problema. Mientras tanto tú te escapas . . ."

Shmerl empieza a correr y, efectivamente, la policía lo empieza a perseguir. Finalmente lo alcanza.

"Mostrame tus documentos," le ordenó el policía a Shmerl.

Shmerl los saca y los muestra al oficial.

"Están en orden. ¿Por qué, entonces corriste?"

"Lo que sucede es que mi médico me mandó correr cada día por mi salud."

"¿Por qué, entonces, no paraste cuando viste que te estaba persiguiendo?"

"¿Me estaba persiguiendo? Yo creía que usted iba al mismo médico."

Berl and Shmerl were walking in Moscow during the pre-perestroika time. Suddenly, they realize a policeman is watching them closely.

"I'm in trouble," says Berl. "I don't have papers, and if the policeman asks for them he'll put me in jail."

"Don't worry, I have my papers," said Shmerl calmly. "I'll start running, and he will follow me, thinking I have problems. In the meantime, you escape . . ."

Shmerl starts running, and the policeman starts chasing him. Finally, the policeman catches up with him.

"Show me your documents," the policeman orders Shmerl.

Shmerl takes the documents out of his pocket and shows them to the cop.

"Everything is fine. Why did you run?"

"My doctor told me to run every day for my health."

"Why didn't you stop when you realized I was chasing you?"

"You were chasing me? I thought you were seeing the same doctor."

Paradoxically, political jokes are an expression of the elite and may be considered elitelore, even when they trickle down to the dominated classes. The elite use humor to correct political mistakes, limit abuse of power, and, if necessary, weaken the power of the governing elite. The "folk," or the dominated, adhere to the same purpose.

In this book, I examine the evolution of several themes surrounded by political jokes since the sixteenth century. Given the ephemeral nature of political jokes, we have limited access to some of them throughout history. Consequently, the majority of the jokes analyzed here have been compiled since 1970, when I began to develop an interest in the subject. Some of the jokes originated before 1970, and others are more recent—even when they refer to historical events.

A consistent compilation of jokes requires interviewing individuals of different ages who have political ties and who are conscious of political humor. These people are difficult to find, and when you find them, they frequently refuse to speak, perhaps because they don't want to risk their careers or their political interests. On several occasions, I attempted to interview a senior Mexican politician who was famous for having recounting and inventing jokes, but he refused to speak to me when he realized I was writing a book on the subject.

I collected jokes from numerous sources (Banc and Dundes, 1986; Flota, 1985; Lukes and Galnoor, 1985; Phillips, 1981; Reyna, 1980; Salgado, 1986, 1986a, 1986b). Most of the jokes cited in this book belong to my collection; others are cited with the appropriate reference. I became a lover of jokes by reading between the lines in newspaper articles, and I began to pay attention to political jokes when these came out in conversation. In one phase of this project, I began a registry of the jokes and their sources, in order to identify the social source of each I used and, if possible, the origin source by social class. This information is irrelevant in explaining a joke's origin; it simply tells me that the joke-teller was a member of the elite, letting me know in a limited fashion about the circulation of the joke. I must add that when it became known that I was working on the theme of political jokes, many people started telling me the ones they knew.[4] This book differs from a simple collection of jokes in the sense that it doesn't retell them, but rather explains them within their political context. I also use them to understand the perception of society regarding the government.

Other humoristic political manifestations, such as poems and anagrams, have occasionally been collected and published (Gallo, 1987). More than one author has published some poems. When there is more than one version of a poem or joke I have given credit to the first chronological source. Compiling nicknames (another manifestation of political humor) presents the same problem as does compiling jokes, but since politicians are generally given only one nickname,[5] the recording is simpler.

My analysis of political jokes does not include the points of view of all Mexicans; it concentrates on urban jokes, primarily from Mexico City, the political and economic center of the country. In Mexico City, ethnicities are mixed; there is a population from the states that might be called in the United States the "melting pot." There, a national culture has generated itself and dominates the country because it has been sanctioned by political economic power; thus, this analysis may closely approximate that which might be made by many urban Mexicans. During 1976, I found the same anti-government jokes and rumors in different regions of the country, though it was difficult to determine their origins. Hypothetically, I suggest that the basic principles of this study may be applied to the urban elite of the entire country, given their interrelations, access to means of communication, and high levels of schooling. Perhaps analysis of this type should be conducted in other regions of Mexico in order to seek out similarities and differences among regions. At this point, my observations concentrating on other parts of Mexico include only the northern border, particularly Ciudad Juárez and Tijuana, and those observations do not reveal major differences.

Analysis of political jokes permits us to see a facet of Mexican society that is frequently overlooked by history. Political jokes offer a distinct perspective for examining the political history of a country, while showing the way in which a society perceives politics, political events, politicians, and government. Perhaps one major correction I would make would be in the official rhetoric. History is written by the victorious, but society, by means of humor, reorganizes the importance of values, symbols, and heroes as they appear in the written history. Political humor is an informal dialogue amongst the elite, and it helps review events and aspects of events often ignored by official history. Political humor often reflects the vision of the defeated, which in the underground reverses the perception of victory, making the defeated become the victorious. The reoccurrence of jokes shows how the defeated elite can attain power and then attack the political elite with these instruments. In the case of Mexico, the government and historians have turned General Lázaro Cárdenas into a revolutionary symbol par excellence, emphasizing the expropriation of petroleum and his agrarian reform but ignoring the opposition that existed against him and his programs—political jokes, on the other hand, revealed the internal opposition he faced.

In this book, I suggest that by means of studying political jokes we can reinterpret history from society's perspective and reveal the internal dissidence ignored by official history. Given the lack of studies regarding political humor, it is too early to generalize and arrive at supposed theories regarding political joke's impact on social participation. Nevertheless, we can correlate economic conditions (among other things) by political jokes' crudity and number.

Even though there is no consensus about the characterization of the Mexican people as a whole, many academicians and writers agree that the majority of Mexicans share certain characteristics. Therefore, we can assume that the basic elements within political jokes reflect the feeling among Mexicans throughout the country based on these shared characteristics.

In literature, the *Mexican* is treated as a universal figure identified basically by negative characteristics (see chapter 1). The lack of historical studies regarding Mexican political jokes makes it difficult to compare the country's political humor from the past to that of its present. Though most of my investigation took place in Mexico City, due to this city's importance and its impact on the rest of the country, I assume that its political jokes are shared by the national elite. Nevertheless, conclusions should be arrived at carefully regarding its jokes' national political impact.

Mexicans are unique in attacking the accomplishments of others. One Mexican will step on his friend's new shoes or will scratch his car to *baptize* it. Mexicans laugh at the first astronaut or at the politician who wins an election, looking to minimize his prominence, destroying his success and thereby theoretically making everybody equal. This is a means by which to achieve equality in a highly unequal society—perhaps an equality that is the essence of the true Mexican democracy. Some indigenous Mexican communities create this equality by means of religion. People take turns as "carriers" (*cargueros*)—those in charge of carrying the virgin or "baby god." The obligation of carrying involves an economic responsibility so great that the poverty of the community is redistributed (Carrasco, 1976).

Mexican humor is unique because the Mexican laughs at everything. He laughs at life and at death, at tragedy, sex, and even the Church. Political power cannot be excluded.

In chapter 1, I offer an attempt at defining the meaning of political jokes. In chapter 2, I examine characteristics of Mexicans in order to understand why they prefer to laugh rather than to participate politically. In chapter 3, I analyze Mexican political humor as a social expression against political power. In chapter 4, I analyze the way in which political jokes treat Mexican presidents, and in chapter 5 I attempt to give an explanation regarding jokes on the last PRI administration and the first opposition administration, or what is called the *alternancia*. Finally, in a postscript, I approach the jokes under the Partido Acción Nacional (PAN) and the return of the PRI.

Humor creates delight and relaxation. This book is analytical and invites critique, but I would like to remind the reader that one good hearty laugh is worth a thousand analytical readings.

CHAPTER ONE

Political Jokes in a Theoretical Context

—Mr. President, what do you think of the Chinese position?
—Well, I like it, but my wife's knees bother her.

Analysis of Humor

It's common to read that books about humor lack the seriousness required to qualify them as a subject to be examined. It is a pity if a reader judges a scholar[1] as spending his time on light or little-respected subjects. When this occurs, it has much to do with the social discourse on laughter. Morreall (1983:88) recounts that the dominant message throughout his educational experience was that "life was fundamentally serious business, and, certainly, serious business is what is important in life. If laughter and humor have any place, it certainly is not in the classroom but rather someplace outside of it." It's possible that because of this, analyses of jokes are rare. If we all laugh daily, surely the subject of our laughter should not deserve our attention and much less our analysis—who can think that a serious scholar should busy himself with the study of something that is not serious? Could he be like the biologist who studies those seemingly insignificant insects?

Many authors frequently refer to Freud's early-twentieth-century study (1973) suggesting that jokes bring to the surface that which is cryptic or hidden, allowing a glimpse at the subconscious. Bergson, also at the beginning of the twentieth century, did an analysis on what is "funny," examining the cause and effect of laughter:

> Laughter needs to be placed in its natural setting, in society; and above all one must determine its useful function, which is that of a social function

> [. . .] Laughter must respond to certain needs of everyday life. Laughter must have a social function. (1973:18)

Provine (2001), Critchley (2002), and Morreall (1983) claim that before them, no one had been able to create an accurate theory regarding humor and laughter. Provine criticizes all authors on the subject for basing their analyses on anecdotes and for writing without a scientific basis, but he concludes that "laughter is the quintessential human social signal. Laughter is about relationships" (p. 44). He affirms that his discovery is a victory for positivists, in that with strong scientific evidence he was able to prove what Bergson was able to prove one hundred years before with what for Morreall was not evidence. Morreall refutes Bergson regarding the social character of laughter to the degree that, a few pages after his refutation, he maintains that this is a social phenomenon. He bases his critique on the fact that nobody can formulate a theory that encompasses all forms of humor, even though one most certainly can't get away from the Freudian motif. Another author who is profusely cited by many authors is Jankelevitch (1982), specifically in his analysis of irony.

Scholarly and specialized treatments are few, because it seems the subject of humor is of little interest to scholars; among those who *do* show an interest are Joubert in his early work (2002, original from 1579), and more recently the Americans Critchley (2002), Morreall (1983), Paulos (1982). Psychologists also show an interest—in fact, they are the ones who have paid the most attention to humor. Though the list of humoristic publications or publications about humor (Fultz, 1970) is quite long, it would include political caricature (Rius, 1984; Pruneda, 1958; A.D., 1960), funny or ironic treatments about politics (Covo, 1987), and even sarcastic newspaper columns such as those by the American Art Buchwald; the Israeli Efraim Kishon; and the Mexicans Marco Antonio Flota, Marco Almazán, Nikito Nipongo, and Catón.

Many authors are confused between humor and expressions causing laughter, perhaps because laughter is often a component of humor—even though, supposedly, laughter alone is not necessarily a sign of happiness. It is undoubtedly proof of a certain state of being, but in some cases it may show a mental problem and in other cases it might even show an illness. Some studies have shed light on different components of humor. Joubert analyzes "the physical and cosmological rationale, the spiritual, bodily in addition to the therapeutics" of laughter (Julian Mateo and Mauricio Jalon, "Prologue" to Joubert, 2002:15) and maintains:

> What excites laughter in us is something ugly, deformed, dishonest, indecent, indecorous and inconvenient. For example: what provokes laughter in those present, is to see how as if by mere happenstance, embarrassing parts are discovered, which by nature or through public honesty we tend to hide because they are indecorous and not worthy of mercy.

Pitchford (1960) explores the social functions of humor, and, for his part, Eastman (1972) explores the different types of senses of humor. Ethnic humor is important for studying political culture and ideology, especially when it comes to discrimination (Telushkin, 1992). Morreall comes to suggest that laughter can theoretically be grouped into three types, even though his analysis suggests that they are really theories on humor: a theory of superiority, which focuses on emotions involved with laughter; a theory of incongruence, which regards objects or ideas that cause laughter; and the theory of relief, whose main point is that laughter frees up nervous energy. Morreall then produces his own single theory of laughter, which is just a combination of the three types he already identified.

Political humor has lately received some special attention. The works of Schutz (1977) offer a new and refreshing perspective on the classics; these works include his comic reading of the Greeks. His analysis regarding politicians' use of humor is particularly interesting—and especially delightful is his chapter on Lincoln. Lukes and Galnoor (1985) collected jokes from all over the world. Banc and Dundes (1986) made a collection of Romanian jokes and re-edited them as a collection of Eastern European political jokes (1990). Both of these studies promise a deep analysis with theoretical advances, yet they leave the reader with a series of unanswered questions. Kishtainy (1985) concentrates on analyzing Egyptian political humor; Beezley (1985) and Schmidt (1990) examine Mexican political humor from folk and elite perspectives, respectively. A few scholarly journals have tackled the topic; among them we find the *International Journal of Humor Research* started in 1988; *The European Journal of Humor Research*, started in 2013; and *The Israeli Journal of Humor Research*, started in 2012.

Notwithstanding these efforts, political humor remains an area little explored. Levine (1968) accepts that there is little interest in scientifically researching humor. Provine (2001), whose work stems from the neurosciences, claims that most studies on humor since Plato are based on anecdotes, and that there has never been such a study with a scientific basis. Banc and Dundes (1990:11) comment that most of the studies available on humor are literally just collections of political jokes "completely devoid of commentary or analysis." There are many questions pending, and with each new study new questions emerge, though most authors would agree with Freud regarding the ability for political jokes to expose, a theme that we will return to further on.

If humor and laughter emerge socially to such a degree that Provine suggests generates social cohesion, one might ask about the social and political circumstances in which political jokes are presented. Who are their audiences, and what are their motivations? In the same way in which many people don't wish to listen to off-color jokes, perhaps many don't want to hear political jokes. And in the same way in which some jokes may be considered inappropriate under certain circumstances—such as in a sexual context, for people of the opposite gender for whom there doesn't exist a level of comfort—perhaps those jokes simply should not be told in those circumstances, or to people of differing ideologies. What are the rules regarding who can tell a particular joke? Is it the highest person or the lowest in a particular hierarchy? Who gains approval to use a joke as a means for breaking the ice?

Provine (2001) says that speech in itself is more important than a joke's content. Paraphrasing him, we could ask if the act of telling a joke is more important than the joke itself. This could explain certain things about power relationships. On the other hand, what comes to our attention might be the point made by Morreall (1983:44) that, based on his experience, humor can be a conceptual conversation that is fun, yet also disconcerting and anxiety provoking. In reality, the same applies to politics. Politics progressed from being an instrument for happiness to a petty game of brotherhood, in which the conceptual conversation causes affliction. Here, the joke becomes a mechanism for the social compensation against politics because it helps society to get even with politicians.

There are many collections of jokes. The purpose of most of them is simply to entertain and be funny, nothing more. In these books, political jokes are few or are not included at all. Part of the problem with including these kinds of jokes in such collections consists in lack of knowledge of political events, lack of interest in politics, fear of repression, and belief that political jokes have no market; the inclusion of topics such as the police are not seen in a political context, as if the police have stopped being the repressive mechanism of the State (the monopoly of the legitimate violence of Weber's dixit). It is possible that in the collective imagination and due to corruption, the police have become an independent body to the point that people believe that they have distanced themselves from the government,[2] or in fact that they are not part of it at all. One must accept the fact that people seek out these books of collected jokes for pure entertainment purposes,[3] as well they should.

We may offer many explanations regarding the lack of studies regarding political jokes:

1. Jokes are common, everyday phenomena. Even though they reflect social reactions to frustrating factors, they imply or create the establishment of relationships, and the conditions in which people confide in each other, functioning as an instrument for social cohesion. Nevertheless, they pass without notice by researchers, as do most of life's daily affairs, because they are subjective manifestations. People experiment with jokes habitually; they live with them, as they are found in the mass media, and they use them rather frequently. But by not being accustomed to focusing on routine, everyday occurrences, such as jokes, individuals—including scholars—ignore political jokes as objects for analysis; instead of analyzing them, they simply celebrate their existence.

2. Laughter, to a certain degree, has been considered malignant. This could possibly be derived from the fact that certain mental illnesses usually produce outbursts of laughter. Much attention has been drawn to a laughter epidemic in 1962 in the village of Kinshasa, some forty kilometers from Bukoba, near Lake Victoria in Tanzania (Provine, 2001:130).

The negative image of laughter may be due to its attack on the solemnity[4] and seriousness with which people treat the events they consider important—politics being a major one of those events. Laughter is frequently condemned[5] and is considered offensive because outbursts are usually presumed to be hostile acts. Consequently, laughter is often suppressed[6] so as not to offend "political dignity."

The Catholic Church attacked humor and laughter for being improper and not a characteristic of the appropriately moderate and good Catholics (Bossuet, cited by Morreall, 1983:87). The Church also denounced Molière's comedies because it conceived of laughter as an instrument of the devil. Baudelaire said that laughter is a punishable element because it is a product of satanic paternity and part of the dark side of human nature. If there was one thing that worried the Church during the Middle Ages, when it gathered its ideological discourse, it was fear of the devil and all that was associated with the devil—such as laughter (Delumeau, 2002). (Fear was commonly directed not only against the devil and laughter but also against women, Jews, and foreigners.)

Even in childhood, adults frequently attempt to stop a youth's laughter by saying, "People are going to laugh at you," which equates laughter with ridicule.

What purpose does it serve, then, to examine something associated and equated with so many negative things? Hopefully, if humor is analyzed in a stroke of bad luck, scholars might discover their social or political dysfunction.

3. Political jokes and other forms of political humor are rarely transcribed,[7] in part perhaps because politics are perceived as something serious and solemn, and thus the political joke is a transgressor, implying an attack against all that is political. Is it that solemnity offers a very thin layer of respectability? Or is it that those people most vulnerable to attack are cloaked within their solemnity, those whose power is fed by an image of them as solemn and dignified are upheld by a frail social base—such as is the case with dictators and political authoritarians? Schutz (1977:189) cites Corwin's "law of political politics": "Never make the people laugh. If you want to be successful in life you must be as solemn as a donkey."[8] Kundera (1986:254) adds, "There is no movement which attempts to change the world confronting ridicule and scorn, because this is the corrosive agent that corrodes all pretentiousness." We cannot underestimate the negative potential of a politician being wounded in or by a joke; in authoritarian and totalitarian countries, this can bring about negative consequences (which we refer to later on) because rulers fear any criticism, whether it be in comic or serious form. In the end, by showing political hostility, jokes test certain degrees of governmental tolerance and confront governmental repression. This is also valid for writing *about* political jokes; writers of such material in many circumstances must be very careful not to offend the wrong people (not to mention being very diligent in working to get their studies published at all).

See the following joke, which applies to diverse dictators:

> A drunkard in Plaza de Mayo (Buenos Aires) is screaming, "The president is a son of a bitch; the president is a son of a bitch!!!"
>
> Quickly, two policemen appear and start beating him for betraying the motherland, and they drag him away.
>
> The poor drunkard starts to implore, "I was referring to the president of the United States!"
>
> To which the policemen reply, "Don't try to confuse us; we know well who the son of a bitch is!"[9]

For politicians to appear as exceptional people is practically an existential requirement; this is why they strive to make myths about themselves to the extent of wanting to appear as demi-gods. The politician presents himself before society as one of the best people in humanity, close to physical and moral perfection[10] almost to the extent of not needing to reveal any emotion. To accomplish this, he needs to distance himself from society. The politician appears to not have the need to publicly accept that he is affected by human passions. Laughter equalizes people, and jokes create a social connection that does not necessarily benefit the politician. When a politician uses humor, it is to improve his image (Gardner, 1986) and to maintain himself above the common citizen. This is yet another sign of his superiority.

Political jokes attack this false myth and destroy the mystery within politics and the life of the politician. They allow us to see that politicians are creatures made of flesh and blood; they have families and lovers; they suffer, cry, age, make love, and even go to the bathroom. In brief, jokes strip away the mystical aura surrounding politicians; they reveal the sanctimony and show the horror they harbor regarding themselves—that they are human beings. We could perhaps play with Jerzy Lec's adage—"I hate my enemy because he looks so much like me"—or in the politician's words, "I hate the joke because it pictures me as I am."

Politicians search for a place in history with the best image possible, but the razor-sharp edge of jokes threatens to cut down that aspiration. When a joke appears in written form, it becomes part of recorded history and may even turn into a platform from which an attack may be later launched toward a once-solid political image. All of these are controversial ideas that scholars frequently evade.

4. There is general confusion about the concept that surrounds humor, and this complicates its analysis.[11] As I have said, humor is often confused with the comical, or with laughter, jest, caricature, comedy, parody, wit, irony, sarcasm, jokes, or satire, because even though these are all parts of humor, it is difficult to classify any or all of them as synonyms for it. It is necessary to explain that these concepts are different because their use implies a certain purposeful way to reflect certain states of being, and even cultural patterns.

Manifestations of humor and their subjects of attack are determined by historical, cultural, and social relations. Political jokes choose objectives with a political, cultural base, a political history and those political elements that irritate society. The science that looks to super-specialize often leaves out complex explanations, to an even further degree when the scientist cannot count on quantitative support to prove his hypotheses.[12] With this in mind, we will attempt to open a path to re-vindicate ourselves before the demanding minds that make positivism a nearly religious belief.[13]

Not all cartoons or cartoon strips are caricatures;[14] there is a position that approaches the matter of cartoons as if some of them are a minor art form, assuming that there are literary works that may be considered cartoons. This position openly contradicts the most conventional definition of *caricature* established by Acevedo (2000:8): "Political caricature is understood as the production of images that express a constant questioning of social relationships, by the use of satire, parody, and symbolic forms, such as allegory." A taxonomy of humor in the arts and graphic humor demands further research—which is far from the purpose of this analysis—however, a point must have to be made to Barajas's claim that the caricature triggered the Mexican Revolution, which refers more to his position as a caricaturist in the newspaper *La Jornada* than to a real proof that a very complex and sophisticated expression motivated an illiterate population to revolt (Barajas 2005, 2007).

In this book, I study involuntary and spontaneous behavior, in the sense that it is indirect, not binding, and not planned, though intentional. With difficulty, these characteristics can be attributed to cartoons or graphic caricature. In these forms of humor, a client relationship is established between author and reader that emerges through the joke. There are readers who follow an author because of a political ideological sympathy or a certain age or race identification, or other criteria, which drives them to agree with the author's message.[15] The reader's agreement with the author doesn't develop in jokes because they establish an ephemeral relationship. The anonymity in other forms of political humor generates a direct relationship precisely at the moment of communication. According to Freud (1973:137), there are three parts to a joke: the person who tells it, the person who listens to it, and the person who is the subject of it. An understanding is established between the one who tells the joke and the one who listens to it. As such, the speaker and listener bring about the subject of the joke, but the relationship between them ends as soon as the joke has been told. The one who tells the joke probably hasn't invented it, and if he has, he surely would have in mind the subject of the joke and not the particular person he is telling it to. In that situation, no clientele relationship emerges.

In some cases, the political joke can be considered a caricature of a person or situation about which the ridicule is taking place, which in itself reveals another characteristic of jokes.

Our attention is focused on political jokes because it is the most common humoristic form, denoting a certain level of freedom. It does not create any ties and permits a certain amount of liberty, even though it may be ephemeral. Political jokes show the gaps in free social opinion, without constraint indicating the themes used as part of social resistance and the limits of social transgression, representing a spontaneous form of political behavior. But, to better understand the jokes, let us first review the different types of political humor.

A Definition of Humor

Refraining from ostentation, we may put forward that basic questions about political humor, and especially about political jokes, are barely being formulated. These suggest certain theoretical and methodological directions at which the general discussion of humor is moving. However, it is the specific aspects of the political slope that should be looked at more closely.

Humor has a primary association with mood. This idea may reflect the physiological perspective and refer to bodily moods,[16] which are believed to determine human health and predisposition (Goldenson 1984:415). Humor has a creative and curative power in that it is "amusing imagination, charming wit" and "romantic irony, equivalent to the triumph of the creative power of the soul of the artist over all form and content," as Hegel affirms in Runes (1983:312); but it also identifies laughter with a pathological symptom (Moody, 1978). The energy released in laughter frees tensions and stress and helps cure personal illnesses and social frustration. Laughter is the result of a joke, satire, or comic reaction against aggression. In humor there is also found aggression and apprehension (*The New Encyclopedia Britannica*, 1990: vol. 6, 144). Freud suggests, in the central aspects of analysis, that jokes are intentional and always have an objective.

The hidden intent of political humor is the correction of unwanted situations and the surpassing of social, moral, and political restrictions, especially those that are a result of political repression. The joke is a logical incongruence in which illogical syllogisms are built. See the following example:

> Man: Hi there, new neighbor, it sure is a mighty nice day to be moving.
>
> Neighbor 1: Yes, it is, and people around here seem extremely friendly.
>
> Man: So what is it you do for a living?
>
> Neighbor 1: I'm a professor at the university. I teach deductive reasoning.
>
> Man: Deductive reasoning? What's that?
>
> Neighbor 1: Let me give you an example. I see you have a doghouse out back. By that, I deduce that you have a dog.

Man: That's right.

Neighbor 1: The fact that you have a dog leads me to deduce that you have a family.

Man: Right again.

Neighbor 1: Since you have a family, I deduce that you have a wife.

Man: Correct.

Neighbor 1: And since you have a wife, I can deduce that you're heterosexual.

Man: Yup.

Neighbor 1: That's deductive reasoning.

Man: Cool.

Later that same day, when our subject is talking with another neighbor:

Man: Hey, I was talking to the new guy who moved in next door.

Neighbor 2: Is he a nice guy?

Man: Yes, and he has an interesting job.

Neighbor 2: Oh? What does he do?

Man: He's a professor of deductive reasoning at the university.

Neighbor 2: Deductive reasoning? What's that?

Man: Let me give you an example. Do you have a doghouse?

Neighbor 2: No.

Man: Fag.

Be that as it may, political jokes not only play with syllogisms but also with the ideal images of politics to establish a new truth or reaffirm an old one. See the following joke, which suggests that corruption, when in the hands of a Mexican, has no geographical limit:

NASA opens a contest to launch a rocket to Venus, and since it is very risky, opens the possibility for the candidates to apply.

The Chinese guy arrives and he is told that the trip is high risk and what does he want in order to go:

"Chinese want a mirion dora."

"Why?"

"Because if Chinese no come back, with a mirion dora famiry opens creaner and rives well."

Then arrives the American, who is explained the conditions and asked, "What do you want?"

"American wants two million dollars."

"Why?"

"With one million family sets up a foundation with the other million, they live well."

Then arrives the Mexican; they go to explain, and he says:

"Buddy, I'm going, save your time; I'm going, it's done."

"But sir, we have to explain, that's the rule."

"Look buddy, it's done, I'm going."

They explain anyway, and they say:

"What do you want?"

"I want three million dollars."

"And what do you want three million for?"

"OK, look here, buddy, one million for you, one million for me, and we send the Chinese guy."

Humor expresses a moral lesson causing a moral correction produced by a positive emotion and the liberating energy of laughter.[17] "In this case, the humorist is a moralist disguised as a scientist such as the anatomist who performs dissections to gross us out. Humor, in the strict sense of the word, is the transference of the moral for the scientific" (Bergson, 1973:107).

In difficult circumstances, humor serves as an instrument to perceive the funny aspect of a situation, or it lightens the spirit's load in an uncontrollable situation[18]—while at the same time, it redefines roles by putting the humorist, or the one who tells the joke, above his objective. One who tells jokes believes to have earned the legitimate right to critique the object of humor.

Political humor confronts situations that bother society, discovering or proposing a truth that may be illogical but in the end serves to bring light to the hidden political game. A joke need not tell the truth, but by attacking the official truth, it establishes reasonable doubt that questions politicians.

Jokes help reduce the distance that government has established in society between people and politicians. The State becomes autonomous from society, and those who govern develop a political project to represent themselves even when this pits them against society or even against the immediate interest of the ruling class (Schmidt, 1988). Against this autonomy, the elite try to limit politicians' power without destroying the system, preserving a façade of national unity behind which humor works as a confrontational instrument. With humor, the elite can participate without compromising themselves and without jeopardizing the stability of the political system. And humor is transmitted from the elite down to the people,[19] providing a jubilant way of the people confronting the leadership, cutting social tensions and relieving political stressors without putting the government in danger. The political joke is not pleasant for the government, but it turns out to be better than a revolt. Political humor is an instrument used to attack the political leadership that oppresses society, or because it violates political and moral values, norms, rituals, or symbols generated and imposed to defend those who govern. Both the transgression of the rulers and that of the joke must be public, and though they might not be communicated directly, the transgressing acts should produce awareness of themselves. Imagine a society that rejects its government, but never lets it know—and juxtapose this with a society that paints walls, organizes marches, and even sets off bombs to show its discontent. In the first case, the government may assume that harmony exists on its terrain, while in the second case, the government knows that it faces problems. Jokes are a social event; never remaining private, they therefore always transcend outwards. Even in systems in which an individual knows that he's being spied on, jokes are a transgressor because sooner or later the government will become aware of their ridicule.

A political joke adapts to circumstances and interests that model the moral order by means of which society organizes values and symbols to ridicule norms and rituals established by politics; this is inherent in a joke's transgressing character. For example, consider the joke my brother, a doctor, told me, which attacks a supposed pompous event:

> The first Jewish president of the United States was being inaugurated. His mother was seated next to one of the secretaries of the new cabinet. Very excitedly, she said: "Do you realize what's happening? The first Jewish president of the United States is my son!"
>
> The secretary turns and patiently says: "Yes, ma'am, I am very aware of it."
>
> After a few moments she turns to him again and says: "But understand my son is the first Jewish president of the United States and he is . . . the brother to the doctor!"

This joke attacks the seriousness of a presidential inauguration with reference to the stereotypical image that Jewish parents (especially in the United States) want their sons to turn into the epitome of success as a member of one of the most prestigious and most well-paid professions: that of the physician. The social value is transmitted through the political joke to reduce the value of the politician's position and the importance of the political event, emphasizing that the doctor's profession is actually the more socially accepted. After all, the supposed most powerful president in the world ends up in second place after his brother the doctor.

Political jokes look to denigrate and ridicule politicians and their image. Other forms of humor have the same role when applied to politics, though each genre has special characteristics that affect its circulation. Before getting into that, however, let us look at the taxonomy of humor to clarify our analysis.

Toward a Taxonomy of Humor

Morreall's thesis (1983:47) can be accepted thus: the essence of humor consists in the enjoyment of incongruence, and the psychological change that laughter brings is an emotional change—although it can also be sensory, perceptual, or conceptual, and on the latter terrain we must consider culture, history, and geography. In this section, we identify three elements and eight types of humor commonly recognized in the literature on the subject. The three elements—comedy, laughter, and wit—are general elements found in humoristic situations. Tricks, caricatures, comedy, parody, irony, sarcasm, satire and jokes are all the eight types of humor. The form and frequency of these types depend on cultural determinants and historical context. Comments regarding each one are limited, considering that my purpose is to present a taxonomy that will allow the organization of humoristic expressions to facilitate the analysis of humor. I look to various authors, assuming that their definitions are sufficiently precise.

General Elements Contained in Humor

Comedy

According to Bergson (1973:50, 64), what is comical can be defined as "all incidents that call our attention to something physical in a person when what is moral is important" and "all combinations of comical acts and occurrences which produce in us the illusion that life and the sensation of a mechanical disposition," as both are invested in each other. As Goldenson (1984:159) says, *comical* is "a word which means funny or laughable but as a concept . . . is not easy to define." Goldenson also points out that "Kant emphasized the element of surprise. The sudden transformation of a forced expectation to nothing."

Comicalness is something unexpected that shouldn't happen but does, at which point it creates a ridiculous situation. Take the case of the person whose pants fall down while he is dancing, or a person whose supermarket shopping bag suddenly breaks, or someone walking down the street who steps on a banana peel and slips and falls.[20] When such events occur, it is comical and provokes laughter.

Laughter

Speaking mechanically, laughter may be defined as "convulsive and pleasant sounds which serve to free intrinsic tension when we listen to a funny story or see a fun event." Eidelberg says that "laughter should also be used as a defense against crying and against shame'" (*Encyclopedia of Psychoanalysis*, 1968; Goldenson, 1984:415). Morreall (1983:20) adds that laughter is like the release of nervous energy, and says, "Laughter has a social function because it is a natural expression of entertainment. We can use laughter before others, to seem in front of others as if we weren't bothered but rather as having fun in the situation we find ourselves in" (1983:56). And with hysterical laughter, according to Morreall, by "reacting with laughter the hysterical person denies the reality of a traumatic situation" (1983:57).

Eastman says that people use any excuse to gratify themselves with laughter, since it serves to unify society (1972:4), while Bergman says, "It's not a pure pleasure, I mean a purely aesthetic pleasure, totally disinterested. It carries with it a second intention. Within that pleasure goes the unconfessed intention to humiliate by which to correct." Bergson's perception (1973:88) can help explain why laughter was historically excluded from religious rites, temples, and most formal events.

For his part, Provine (2001:44) says that "laughter is the quintessential human social sign. Laughter is about relationships." But, he adds, it is also "a sign of domination or submission" (p. 30).

Finally, in Kundera's words (1987:96), we find the following sarcastic perception regarding laughter:

> Things that suddenly are deprived of the sense that is attributed to them, of the place that has been assigned in the pretended order of the world a Marxist raised in Moscow believes in horoscopes, provoke our laughter. Laughter then belongs, originally, to the devil. There is a bit of malice in it [things appear different that what they pretend to be], but also a bit of benevolent relief [things are lighter than they appear,

they allow us to live more freely, and stop oppressing us with their severe austerity].

Wit

Wit is "a certain predisposition to portray quick sketches[21] or such quick and subtle comical scenes that we have barely started to perceive what happened and it is already finished" (Bergson, 1973:91–92). Goldenson (1984:798) believes that "it is a mental function which consists in the ability to make entertaining and incisive commentaries that enlighten a subject or a person. In psychoanalysis wit represents a biting verbal replica, or a play on words, that suddenly, and with a punch, frees a repressed or hidden feeling or attitude."

Wit entertains but also embarrasses its victim. A typical example might be the short joke known as the *one-liner*, or a joke that is based on stereotypes. But anecdotes can also be witty. For example, here is an anecdote describing Eva Perón as a prostitute:

> During her trip throughout Europe, groups were protesting in Milan the high price of exported food charged by "fascist" Argentina. While stones and tomatoes hit her limousine, Eva addressed the admiral general who escorted her and complained:
>
> "Do you hear that? They call me a whore!"
>
> To what her escort responds:
>
> "I understand perfectly; I haven't been in the ocean for fifteen years but they still call me admiral." (Wilkie and Menell-Kinberg, 1981:106)

The admiral's wit is an important component of the anecdote because it creates an unexpected and illogical turnabout by attacking Evita's reputation even when his military discipline *should* impede it.

Jest

With jest, "the apparent primary goal is the satisfaction in having carried out what critique forbids and also foremost is the tendency to like and be content, that its expression should not seem to be off the mark, or lacking in content" (Freud, 1973:121).

Jest is "a fun commentary or one that makes fun of" something (*Webster's Dictionary*, 1955:786), which can be found in childhood games or humorous comments about attire, haircuts, or even something supposedly important—see the following example (Nikito Nipongo, 1985):[22]

> "What is the definition of idiocy?"
> "A serious and ingenious idea coming from the finance ministry."

Caricature

According to Freud (1973:195), caricature is based on the "exaggeration of certain features that normally go unnoticed and constitute degradation." Put another way, it is

> artistic expression about people, ideas or situations, which is brought about by sculpture, painting or drawing, sometimes with the purpose of ridiculing and other times with the purpose of emphasizing to a grotesque, ironic or funny degree, the physical features of a figure or peculiar scene. (Pruneda, 1958:11)

Goldenson (1984:126) describes caricature while including the theme of authority—without diverging from the above definition:

> A drawing or description of an individual whose peculiarities or defects are exaggerated with the purpose of ridicule. Psychoanalysts compare caricatures with *a* play on words, where repressed impulses such as hostility elude the censor in order to be expressed. For this reason caricatures often deal with authority.

Caricatures or cartoons have been the most exclusive form of humor, because to be transmitted, they must be printed skillfully. And after being printed, their dissemination excludes certain social groups, such as the illiterate, though more than one author suggests that in fact the graphic nature of the cartoon served to spread its revolutionary effect in Mexican society at the beginning of the twentieth century (González Ramírez, 1974). This assertion must be questioned because it includes a certain condescension toward the illiterate, suggesting that their political consciences might be considered easy to manipulate.

From this point of view, it may be inferred that illiterates are able to better understand graphic statements, but the cartoonists are so sophisticated that their work cannot be easily understood by those with less education, and on occasion even by those who consider themselves sophisticated. Take, for example, several cartoons of Porfirio Díaz at the beginning of the twentieth century, in which there appear razor blades that represent flattery: in Spanish, *hacer la barba* means "to kiss ass," and this would likely be unintelligible to someone who lives in the countryside and doesn't use a razor. Other cartoonists make allegories out of Greek myths, which must be virtually unknown to the illiterate population.

Cartoons served as a pedagogical instrument for some immigrants to the United States at the beginning of the twentieth century, but even so, we must consider that the cartoons were made under the sieve for the interests of the owners of the newspapers in which they appeared.[23] Thus, we should examine whether the immigrants in question were altogether illiterate, or on the other hand consider the thesis that they were only illiterate regarding English. Perhaps we could accept this thesis, for those in Mexico, and assume that the cartoons served to educate people—but from there, to affirm that they were a creative medium of political conscience might be an exaggeration. If we were to discuss this thesis about the political elite, we should handle it with care. Part of this elite were revolutionaries, while another part criticized the regime—and yet another perhaps might try to change its political opinion due to what a certain cartoon was communicating. One despicable fact is that the regime attacked political cartoonists with all that it had. Many were jailed, and some died from diseases they contracted in jail, which could have turned public opinion against a dictator as he gradually lost his good image. What is certain is that historians have not shown evidence for any of these arguments; instead, they have tried to assume that political cartoons feed a movement of the masses that unleashed a revolution.

Unlike with other forms of humor, the cartoon creates a relationship with clientele that can help mold ideas and opinions, such as with the present case of Rius, who has helped educate a generation of Mexicans, or of the cartoonists of *La Jornada* (Magú, El Fisgón, Helguera, and Hernández), who have comprised an important part of the left-oriented discourse in the latter part of the twentieth century and the beginning of the twenty-first.

Comedy

"Comedy can only begin where we are not moved by the person of the other and begins with what we can call rigidness toward social life" (Bergson, 1973:112).

Following Aristotle, Runes (1983:75) says that theater comedy

> is a work where main characters behave worse than people do in everyday life, contrasted with tragedy, where the characters behave more nobly. In Plato's *Symposium* Socrates argues that a writer of good comedy is capable of writing good tragedy.

Runes adds, in relation to its philosophical aspect: "Metaphysically Hegel's comedy consists of looking at reality as a unique and exhaustive category."

Parody

"We accomplish parody if we portray what is solemn in a familiar tone" (Bergson, 1973:104). Manipulation in religious prayer offers a good example of parody, such as in the following case that was circulated in anonymous copies of single sheets of paper that were picked up in downtown Mexico City:

> OUR FATHER
> Father José López Portillo, you who are always away on trips, your name has been greatly celebrated, bring us your government, do what you desire, be it in the school or in the textbook, make our bread more expensive each day, please let us have it today, and forgive our taxes the way we forgive your trinkets, do not let us fall within the free election of your police and inspectors. Amen.

The following is an American parody of "Our Father":

> Our Father, who are in heaven, hello! What be thy name?
> Give us this day our daily breath.
> Our Father Who art in heaven, Hollywood be thy name.
> Our Father Who art in heaven, Harold be thy name.
> Give us this day our jelly bread.
> Lead us not into creation
> Deliver us from weevils.
> Deliver us from eagles.
> (Phillips, 1981:20)

Irony

In some ways irony is unexpected. For Jankelevitch (1982:31–69):

> It is something that we would call a simulation more than a dissimulation, a behavior full of tricks and retractions, an insidious and complicated intrigue [. . .] it is improvisation and paradox. [. . .] And once it

> has happened there is more truth and light. [. . .] it could be called in the true sense of the word, allegory, because it thinks one thing and in its own way says another.

Eastman (1972:49–52) considers irony to be the humor of the little emphasized. For Bergson (1973:107), it is transposition in two diverse directions. Sometimes it enunciates what should be—making believe that it's precisely what it is—and it is in oratory form. Runes (1983:312) adds: "Socratic irony is the profession of ignorance over the part of a question, which in itself can in fact be very judgmental."

For his part, Cioran (2004:34) notes:

> Irony is derived from an appetite of frustrated unsatisfied naiveté, which must by means of failure become bitter and poisoned. Inevitably it has a universal reach and if by preference it attacks religion and undermines it, it's because it secretly experiences the bitterness of not being able to believe.

A joke about the end of Porfirio Díaz's dictatorship proves to be a good example of irony:

> It is said that when Porfirio Díaz resigned, he suffered a very strong toothache and in those days it was difficult to find a dentist. It seems there were only two, and they were both foreigners.

One of the complaints against Díaz is that he permitted foreigners to expand their business interests, hurting local interests. The irony lies in that people's complaint about foreign economic intervention was one of the leading causes for the common opposition to his rulership. The joke illustrates the feeling amongst the people regarding a set of unjust governmental actions.

Sarcasm

Perhaps the most sarcastic comment I ever heard was when a newly appointed high-level official was congratulated in the following manner: "My condolences, Mr. Secretary." "Sarcasm is a caustic and derisive comment, it is a form of verbal aggression" (Goldenson, 1984:652).

Satire

Satire is "a written composition in prose or verse, whose objective is to bitterly censure or ridicule people or things. It is a hot, biting, sharp saying or discourse" (*Universal Hispanic Dictionary*, 1964). For an example, see the following poem from the Mexican colonial era:

> "Virrey Marquina"
> For perpetual memory
> Viceroy Marquina left us
> A fountain in which people urinate
> And that is where his story ends.

Joke

The quintessential joke is the most widely used form of humor. It engages in provoking laughter and the comical. Its laughable content usually creates a syllogism that distorts reality, creating a "logical incongruence" (Morreall 1983:74) through which a joke can easily in fact transform reality to fit itself, because it establishes truths about what people think. Jokes don't necessarily turn all politicians into fools in the public mind (much less actually *make* politicians fools in reality)—but they do manifest in people's thoughts that politicians may not be the most intelligent people in the world. Here precisely resides political jokes' destructive ability.

Different analysts bring different definitions of the joke. For Freud (1973:9), it depends on "the ability to find analogies between the uneven, this is hidden analogies." For Goldenson (1984:415), "a joke allows us to, albeit temporarily, leave adult reality and return to the dominion of simple childish pleasure." Meanwhile, Howe (1951:217) asserts that "a joke usually involves an attack against someone."

In any case, a joke certainly allows the ignoring of rules, and it usually has a hidden intention focused on judging something or someone unusual or unexpected. The following example emerged at the end of the Mexican Revolution:

> One day, during the administration of Plutarco Elías Calles, an Indian peasant walks by the National Palace in Mexico City. At that time they were adding another story to the palace and so he found himself surrounded by scaffolds. The Indian went up to ask what was happening and he was told that they were building a third floor. The Indian answered:
>
> "I can calm down."
>
> "Why?"
>
> "I thought they were taking it apart to take it to Sonora." (Aguilar de la Parra, 1971:29–30)

This joke alludes to the extreme corruption that allows politicians, including the legendarily corrupt revolutionary leaders (Fuentes, 1962), to take anything they want—in this case, parts of a building—back to their homes—in this case, Sonora. Many stories in Mexico support the opinion expressed in this joke (see chapter 4). However, more than anything else, political jokes reflect that which most troubles society, a population frustrated by the changing nature of politics.

Politics stops being a means for providing happiness to society when it instead becomes a tool for satisfying politicians' appetite for power and wealth. And since corruption seduces, it gains legitimacy in society's expansion (Le Bon and Boyes, 2005:45), especially in the expansion of those in society whom corruption directly benefits. But through telling jokes, which can evade the rule of law, one can exorcise the negative impact corruption creates. In the end, with corruption, there are shared gains, someone can break the law and pay to evade the punishment; from there results popular wit, such as the case of José López's campaign theme, which was changed from *The solution is all of us* to *Corruption is all of us*.

Each one of the concepts described and analyzed in this section possesses its own specificity, yet because they are all found in the same intellectual and discursive arena, and they all have the same purpose, it is easy to generate confusion and to use them indiscriminately.

To confuse matters further, we must recognize that societies cultivate different varieties of humor according to the unique characteristics of certain historical periods, meaning that specific forms of humor may have different degrees of importance depending on the historical period. Still, it cannot be doubted that even though expressions of humor change, all expressions have a highly defined place within a society's social lingo.

Political Humor as Iconoclasm

Humor not only serves to free us of something that frustrates us—it is also a transgressing instrument through which we can overlook certain social norms and values, as well as put down certain symbols. As we saw above, through humor, we can parody religion, representing a rebellion against the dogmatic; we can satirize public figures and the pompousness of their acts; we can mock those situations that are vital to the life of politicians; we can create irony to express the incongruence of political decisions; we can make public discourse into a comedy, as we turn it into the object of our sarcasm; and finally, we can develop funny critiques and tell jokes to diminish political ostentation.

Equipped with the tool of humor in all its forms, society can assail political values and symbols, taking the heroism out of political history—as it did in the case of the young girls who made fun of child heroes and other boys distorting the national anthem (see chapter 3)—because at the pace at which history moves, reconstruction of official discourse is very difficult. Whether it is a critique recovered from the past and validated for use in the present, or a newly generated critique projected toward the past to degrade the present, the attack against political icons through humor is a response to a general discontent, aimed at what contemporary politicians feed on. If, with humor, we establish that our politicians are more fools than heroes, the heroic base—which the establishment adopts—loses validity.

The importance lies not only in the fact that political humor may degrade the politician—even if he is president of a republic—but also in the fact that it may generate a devastating effect in attacking an iconic symbol and transforming it into a caricature. This is evident in the razor-blade cartoon work of Porfirio Díaz that we discussed earlier (González Ramírez, 1974: illustration 43).

Being a free and liberating medium, humor destroys symbols. It engulfs moral considerations and puts the validation of symbols under the axe, never halting in the destructive, clandestine objective of weakening the dominant iconography. Nevertheless, the possibility also exists that the government will react or that society will destroy this system. As an old Mexican saying goes, "Once the dog is dead, the rabies epidemic will end," in which case certain values and symbols will recover their place, though renovated, and humor restarts again.

Political Humor and Participation

Different forms of political participation characterize different political systems, reflecting the relationship between society and the State. In a democratic system, people participate in a wide variety of institutions that together legitimize the system as a whole, and not just the government. That is why democratic governments can fall without creating major damage to the system. Citizens involved one way or another in the complex decision-making process can support or oppose different projects with relative effectiveness because the government has the power to impose its decisions on society. The more open and democratic the system is, the more power society has to limit the degree of governmental imposition. The limits on social action come from a complex combination of factors to which the government, politicians, civil associations, and citizens all contribute. What is remarkable is that there is no formula that can synthesize all forms of action, limitation, and repression.

The limitation of social actions in a repressive system points to what the government considers—because it has so determined—to pose a threat to the system, even though these are social demands that may be taken care of without major complications in another system. In fact, the State feeds its great power with its ability to determine the origin and make-up of "evil"[24] that assails the sociopolitical and economic system as a whole, or any of its parts. One interesting example occurred under Roman law, in which the crimes of *laesa maiestas* were those that hurt the security of Rome, the emperor, or the Roman provincial governments (Cohn, 2004): The definition of these crimes was so extensive that it included jokes about the emperor.

Within authoritarian systems, participation tends to be controlled and manipulated by the State. Elections hold a ritual and symbolic role, since the results are predetermined. Society has little power to influence the deciding processes, and some groups opt to participate within the margins or outside of institutional political processes. Authoritarian regimes have a certain level of tolerance with respect to marginal participation, even though they support open systems of oppression that hold capricious and arbitrary repression of liberties as an essential characteristic.

In totalitarian systems, society practically and essentially lacks any influence in the decision-making process because there is no liberty. Elections, if they even exist, play no role in the making of decisions, since these are made at levels of power that are out of the reach of average citizens.[25] Marginal participation is forbidden, and is risky for any person who does assume it. Systems of repression openly repress any expression that the State considers inadequate. The Nazis, for example, created courts to judge those who made jokes about Hitler or who named their dogs or horses Adolf. Hermann Goering instructed the German Academy of Law to sanction these types of jokes as acts against the Führer, the State, or the entire Nazi system (*Weltanschauung*).

One of the challenges of political participation is *creating* room for dissent when there is no such room. In democratic systems, society finds ways to organize itself and tries to limit any insidious elements of domination. These elements complicate matters within authoritarian systems due to two factors. The first is that, according to Detlev Peukert (quoted by Le Bon and

Boyes, 2005), resistance implies that reservations of a regime originate from a personal code of beliefs and behaviors that are expressed through a lack of enthusiasm, or a person withdrawing from the collective life, restricting, as much as possible, social interaction—or becoming a dissident. The second factor has to do with governmental action meant to limit the spaces and time of free and independent political expression, and therefore resistance.

If all political systems have a certain level of tolerance for this resistance, some social and political groups differ from using unconventional or underground methods. Because of this, we can identify different types of resistance that depend on a society's level of political liberty and governmental tolerance, but also its level of political frustration.

Political resistance can be defined as the refusal to cooperate[26] with the structures of political power and authority. We can distinguish between passive and active political resistance. Active resistance can be both violent and not violent.[27] Violent forms include guerilla movements and invasions of lands. Nonviolent forms include rallies, marches, and strikes. Passive political resistance encompasses electoral abstention, civil disobedience, and political humor. Let us now go on to explore the manifestations of political humor.

Manifestations of Political Humor

Political humor is a complex phenomenon. It is a manner of public participation in politics as reflected in jokes, nicknames, caricatures, and parodies. In Mexico, there exist anagrams and satirical poems written specifically for one person or one occasion, or adapted to create a special political impact.[28] Each one of these manifestations varies in its intensity, content, and usage, according to the historical period in which it circulated, though some continue in their popularity. (There are jokes that have existed for nearly a century and have crossed borders, as we will later show.) In a study on humor, it is important to identify the type of humor that prevails in jokes, parodies, satire, and other forms. Even if we know that the joke is the most common type, it is worthwhile to analyze all of humor's themes and tones.[29]

Some manifestations of political humor do not lend themselves to wide use. Nicknames, for example, are usually based on a certain characteristic of an individual, and thus they are used in only one situation—and they are not always able to be transferred from one culture to another, being perhaps of the most culturally restricted type of humor. This can be seen with the nickname "Tricky Dick," given to Richard Nixon after he manipulated the results of an electoral investigation, whose phonetics are very difficult to achieve in another language. Or consider "The Dog," the name given to José López Portillo after declaring that he would defend the peso like a dog—just before the peso was devaluated (along with "The Dog"). Similarly, the ex-Bolivian president, Víctor Paz Estensoro[30] was nicknamed "IncaPaz" (with *incapaz* meaning "incapable" in Spanish); such a play on words is impossible to imitate in other tongues.

It is similar with anagrams made out of names, which consist of small changes in the order of letters in a name to achieve a comical and satirical effect. For example, an anagram for Álvaro Obregón is VENGO A ROBARLO ("I COME TO STEAL IT").

Parodies of religious prayers are few and far apart and scarcely in circulation, probably because they are not very versatile and they tend to brush up against the sacrilegious, possibly offending certain listeners. On the technical side, it may be difficult to learn them when they are very long, and circulating them is not easy because they demand prolonged attention. The following is an example of this type of humor adapted to politics:

> CREDO
> I believe in the all-powerful PRI, creator of candidates on Earth. In de la Madrid, his only son. Our Father. He was born from the Bank of Mexico and appeared surrounded by his army of technocrats. He was made up, photographed, enlarged, and televised, and on the third day believing to be dead he came back to life among the dead. He went up to the presidential mansion (Los Pinos), he re-built it, he changed their street, and he is sitting with the International Monetary fund to the right of the PRI. We believe in his stone face, in the holy institution of taxes, in the fiscal deficit, in the public debt, and in the terrible life of the future world. Amen.

The same difficulties are found in political humor in the form of oral poetry, since it ends up being long and difficult to communicate and demands a greater effort, factors that cause the loss of humor.[31] When the narrator utilizes the elements of oral poetry to transmit his humoristic message, the attention of the listener may likely vanish,[32] and the humor will be lost.

Beyond needing brevity, political humor needs a comic effect, sarcastic or ironic, to be transmitted and make an impact. For an example, let's look at the following fragment of a poem:

Gorillas

Soy un gorila, tengo mi fusil	I am a gorilla, I have my rifle,
por la consigna me he de morir	For it is my duty to die,
y si me dicen que habrá democracia	And if they tell me there will be democracy,
a fuerza de bombas lo he de impedir.	By means of bombs I will stop it.
Me sostiene el Chase Manhattan	Chase Manhattan supports me,
y también la Wall Street.	And Wall Street too.
Si ordena la Casa Blanca	If the White House orders it,
yo doblaré la cerviz.	I will bend over backward in submission.

(Gallo, 1987:256).

In the historical context of this poem, written during the 1968 student movement, the police were called gorillas. The allusion not only degraded the president, whose physical ugliness had won him the emblem of monkey, but also exploited the image of the gorilla as an ugly and aggressive animal. On the other hand, a typical political attack in Mexico was (and is) accusing someone of working for the United States,[33] and that year's conflict was no exception. Word spread around of a hoax that the student movement stemmed from CIA and KGB conspiracies.[34]

The diversity and wealth of humor reflects, in part, social complexity, because we can assume that diverse groups have preferences for different types of humor. These groups' social, historical, and cultural characteristics determine the prevalence of any certain form of humor—though as we've expressed, jokes are the predominant humoristic manifestation because they are brief, easy to transmit, favor social relations, circulate better than other forms of humor, and, presumably, are more effective in having their message reach politicians and others in power.

Political Jokes

The joke is the most important manifestation of political humor because it is intentional, it is hostile, and it can be obscene due to a tendency to produce figurative nudity—at least, says Freud, "those jokes that have a tendency to run the risk of tripping up against people who find them undesirable to listen to" (1973:79). The political joke's obscenity consists in denuding politicians, bringing them down from their pretentious superiority. In the following paragraph taken from a book of Freud's (1973:87), I decided to replace the word "sexual" with the word "political" to demonstrate the value of denuding in humor:

> Smut is like an exposure of the *political* differed to whom it is directed. By the utterance of the obscene words it compels the person who is assailed to imagine the part of *politics* or the procedure in question and shows her that her assailant is himself imagining it. It cannot be doubted that the desire to see what is *political* exposed in the original motive of smut.
>
> It can only help to clarify things if, at this point, we go back to a hypothetical primary desire to touch the *political* parts. As, so often, looking has replaced touching.[35]

As with politics, sexuality is repressed in everyday communications and must be expressed within accepted social norms. The knowledge of politics is hidden from social perception, forcing people to accept politicians' decisions. Politics, as a public matter, hides from society and becomes something private. This is a fundamental distortion that reinforces humor's effect: politicians have stripped society of public representation and have turned it into a private game that evolves exclusively among politicians. Politicians in fact turn to secret negotiations and yet demand legitimacy and the social acceptance of their dealings.

Sex and politics are hidden from the common person's eye, and this causes frustration to the people. One of the risks of democracy consists in substituting the people for politicians, which tends to happen when political maneuverings are handled in secret. Within these lies the process for the nomination of candidates, congressional negotiations, and even the negotiation of electoral results. The average citizen does not usually confront the resulting decision of such negotiations. Sometimes he is asked to ratify them with his vote, but that occurs when he has little or no capacity to influence the political process, which further frustrates him. The nomination of Dan Quayle as vice presidential candidate of the United States in 1988 is a classic example. It is very possible that the revelation of the impact of Quayle's economic position angered many Americans because it destroyed the image of democracy as an open game with equal opportunities. This, in part, explains—in addition to his proverbial ignorance—the great number of jokes that were made about this character. The same can be said about Vice President Dick Cheney (2000), who was the head of Halliburton, a business that has benefited with big contracts in Iraq and that is enveloped in a serious suspicion of bad management and economic abuse. As the saying goes, history repeats itself. In this case, the history of the power of money repeats itself, and the humoristic response is that the one who really governs was Cheney, and not George W. Bush.

Sex and politics must be attacked and unveiled to overcome frustrations. Jokes help in the following manner:

1. The joke is a spontaneous manifestation, an involuntary behavior, and even though its effect is immediate, it can be considered ephemeral. It's most valuable feature is that it produces pleasure; it is a hilarious expression that produces relaxation. In this manner, the joke has a great advantage over politics, since its serious nature cannot generate a socially gratifying effect.

2. The gratifying effect[36] of the joke is short lived, but within a social context this effect is magnified because it is transmitted and generalizes, making room for a prolonged social response, while the pleasure that politics produces is restricted only to those who can extract a benefit from it. If political pleasure becomes lewd, it is very different from that which humor allows, because it is selfish, while the pleasure of the joke, though ephemeral, is social.

3. The joke is a means of dealing with reality, especially in its most crude form. It is a cathartic expression and an act of self-defense against the abuse of power.

4. What is funny is in large part determined by cultural context (see Freud's discussion about the word *famillionar* and its connotation in a capitalist society). The joke is based on cultural values and symbols that are not often shared by other cultures. As a result, when we speak of "British humor," the frequent experience is that if a joke of that country is told in a different cultural or social context, rather than laughter it might be greeted with expressions of surprise. The political culture determines the funniness of political jokes.

5. The joke in general has its cycle: It goes from blooming into decadence and then into oblivion (Eastman, 1972:31). Most jokes follow this pattern, though some tend to have a longer lifespan than others and move both geographically and culturally. Following Bergson (1973:72–73), one could say that a joke has a dynamic effect: "an effect that propagates, growing in such a manner that the cause, insignificant in the beginning, reaches throughout a necessary progress, a result as unexpected as it is important." The political joke is often short lived when it is personalized against the head of state, but its life can be extended if the joke's essence is drawn out and transported to another era or culture to be expressed in a different context. The joke can allegorically emphasize the repetition of an event and make us incessantly remember its comical aspect; this is why, when dealing with a systemic circumstance, such as a people having a lack of freedom,

the situation that the joke critiques is preserved and is easily transmitted to other cultures with similar problems. Jokes about lacking freedom are easily understood because they deal with a universal value that is trampled on. The oppression being joked about is what awakens sympathy in us. Banc and Dundes (1986) followed the path of jokes in communist countries and found them to be repeated often and long lived, since those societies suffered from the same political vicissitudes, and if politics frustrates individuals, political jokes acquire universal value for them. The question is how to find common values and concerns among different cultures. When this happens, the same joke with minor corrections is applied in several countries. Such is the case about a Republican banker in the United States at the beginning of the twentieth century, about President Echeverría in the 1970s, and an Egyptian general during the Six Day War in 1967 (Lukes and Galnoor, 1985:167):

> An Egyptian needed a brain transplant, so he went to the store to see what was available. The salesman showed him the brain of a mathematician who died at fifty-nine years old and said because of the mathematician's advanced age the Egyptian could have it for $500. The Egyptian thought that the brain's age could be disadvantageous, so he asked for a different brain. They showed him that of a peasant who died at 25. The Egyptian shook his head; it was improper for his social class to have the brain of a peasant. At that moment, he saw a brain in a very well lit display and asked, "What's this?"
>
> "Well, this is our best product," said the salesman. "It is the brain of an Egyptian general who died fighting against the Israelis. It costs $100,000.
>
> "Why so expensive?" asked our customer.
>
> "*Well,* it's never been used!"

The essence of this joke survived more than seventy years since its original American version, even though the Mexican and Egyptian jokes are more recent (the Egyptian one being from 1967 and the Mexican one from 1971 to 1975). As it is told in the United States, the most expensive organ in the joke is the heart (which has never been used) of a Republican banker, while in Egypt it is the (never used) brain of a military leader and in Mexico it is the (never used) brain of a political leader. There is no cultural relationship among the three country's societies to explain the ways in which this joke was transferred. Perhaps the proximity of Mexico to the United States helps explains its transmission in that case, but not its long-lived subject matter—unless we accept our frustrations with our leaders as a common denominator among societies. In the United States, the thing most desired in the joke comes from a stony-hearted banker; in Mexico and Egypt, it is the intelligence—or lack thereof—of a politician and a general. In all three cases, the person in society listening to the joke is meant to react strongly against the person in the joke who boasts power, as well as the failure that this character's behavior leads to. In one joke, the powerful character fails in the arena of financial interest and wellbeing, in another, the military man fails at leading a war, and in the third, the powerful politician fails at leading a nation.

6. The joke serves to subtly criticize the character in power, and it has a small chance of causing a strong reaction by virtue of the fact that it leaves no room for polemics or debate.[37] When a joke criticizes, it is a categorical, rotund, and determinant criticism, since opposition to political debate isn't open for discussion—nor does the joke pretend to convince.

Even when the joke intends to be synthetic, it is explicit enough to leave no doubt as to what it is attacking. For example, in the following joke about Luis Echeverría, there is no doubt that what is being criticized is his lack of intelligence:

> Echeverría finds himself looking for a scuba-diving wetsuit in a sailor's berth. The sailor comes in and, surprised, he asks, "What are you doing here, Mr. President?"
>
> "I'm looking for a wetsuit."
>
> "Why?"
>
> "Because the captain told me that, deep down, I'm not an asshole."

Here is another joke, which comes from the era during which Poland was under a communist regime; it criticizes the country's lack of freedom as a result of Soviet domination:

> A genie appears to a Polish laborer and grants him three wishes. Three times, the laborer wishes for China to invade Poland. The genie asks why he chose the same wish three times.
>
> The Pole responds, "Can you imagine how the Russians are going to end up after the Chinese go back and forth six times?"

7. The political joke works as a contradiction to achieve its humor. For example, in the case of a joke about a politician, it is assumed that the politician will be commonly shown as intelligent, moral, and honest[38]—but

when a joke makes the politician assume the opposite attributes, the character becomes funny and causes laughter:

> Bush asks how the Jews know it all: "If Saddam Hussein plans to invade Kuwait, they know it; if Assad plans to invade Lebanon, they know it; if the PLO plans to attack, they know it. How do they do it?"
>
> "Well, Mr. President, they go to synagogue, they speak Yiddish to each other, and they ask what's new. And that is how they get a hold of the information."
>
> Bush responds, "I want to learn Yiddish."
>
> They teach him Yiddish, dress him like an Orthodox Jew, beard and all, and on Saturday they send him to synagogue. He sits down and asks in Yiddish to the man sitting next to him, "What's new?"
>
> "*Shhh*, be quiet," says the man. "Bush is coming today."[39]

8. The political joke has strength because it is logical. It builds syllogisms strong enough to destroy the image of a politician; its logical consistency makes it funny, though perhaps unrealistic. In the above joke, it's obvious that Bush's helpers weren't going to tutor Bush in accelerated Yiddish to be able to pass as a Jew in the synagogue. Normally, Orthodox Jews know each other, and they know if an outsider will be arriving. But, believing, after all, that he is Jewish they also reveal that they know that the president is going to be in the synagogue. The result is that the president of the United States, who controls the most powerful intelligence institutions in the world, actually has to rely on going to a synagogue to find out what is going to happen in the future. This is how the syllogism serves to turn the politician into the victim. See the following example:

> Echeverría is digging at the base of a tree when his helpers ask him what he's doing.
>
> He answers, "I'm looking for the square root."

According to the syllogism established in the joke, for Echeverría the tree has a root, there exists a square root; therefore, the square root must be under the tree. This syllogism classifies somebody as ignorant who should not be; as such, the incongruence and contradiction make it funny.

9. The political joke has a liberating energy because the individual citizen temporarily abandons his social responsibilities and recovers his freedom by abandoning his identity with the symbols and obligations imposed by the politicians who govern him.

The citizen doesn't attack the motherland, even though he may degrade its national symbols. With the joke, he confronts politicians to strip them of their power, a power that is used by experienced politicians in such a way that the common citizen cannot understand. For this, understanding would imply that access to power is open, and control would be lost over society, as well as the ever-present project of governing society.[40]

The secrecy in politics helps the State to maintain its autonomy from society. The joke looks to diminish that autonomy, and though ephemerally, to limit the power of politicians.

10. Power is managed from an underworld hidden from the eyes of citizens, even though its effect is felt on a daily basis. The following joke illustrates this distortion:

> A telegram arrives for a mayor in the Guerrero mountain range. It reads: TELLURIC TREPIDATION MOVEMENT RECOGNIZED IN YOUR AREA. SEND INFORMATION.
>
> Two, three, and four weeks go by.
>
> Finally, in the sixth week, a telegram comes in response: MOVEMENT SUFFOCATED. TELLURIC IS DEAD. TREPIDATION AND FIFTEEN OTHER BASTARDS TOOK FLIGHT, BUT WE FOLLOWED THEM CLOSELY. IN THE MEANTIME WE DIDN'T SEND INFORMATION BECAUSE WE HAD ONE HELL OF AN EARTHQUAKE.[41]

This joke shows the government's attitude towards dissidence and can reflect society's fear. I have found evidence of a telegram sent by the dictator Porfirio Díaz to the governor of Veracruz (nicknamed "The Panther"), where per a revolt by a lieutenant in a steamship, he ordered his men to "capture the vessel, shoot the officials and ten percent of the crew, all people involved in this campaign, and then inform." The governor ordered the detention of nine people; they were executed, and when faced with a national uproar, the governor said that he "was only following superior orders and had a quiet conscience." At the same time he was being protected by the dictator, who appointed him senator of the state of Hidalgo, the governor of Oaxaca, and made the judge presiding over his case declare himself incompetent. According to Barajas, "Popular voice interprets the sense of instructions well and summarizes them with a solid phrase: 'Kill them on the spot! !*Mátalos en caliente*!'" (2007:172–183). It is possible that the joke has evolved since this event in 1879, taking on a more recent topic.

There are key words that dominate communication between politicians and society. With these words they mask their intentions—it is what Scott

(1990:52–55) defines as "euphemizing or stigmatizing actions or people who seem to question official reality." In Mexico, a movement usually represents a political protest. This joke reveals politicians' obsession with fighting dissention, and that is why the mayor reacts with all his might to accomplish what is expected of him: disarm the movement, at all costs. The joke expresses the citizen's rejection of this persecutory mentality. The citizen knows that politicians are always loyal to power, on the side of the State, even if this implies stomping on individual, civil, or human rights. The local politician's reaction is supported by this principle of submission before the higher spheres of power, which establishes another logic—that power emanates from power, and not from the people.[42] In Mexico, and perhaps in other countries, a politician's career depends on his capacity to pull strings in order to influence the political game; it doesn't stem from specific actions representing the people's interests.

With humoristic attacks, the citizen takes revenge by turning the image of the politician into that of a silly and aggressive macho. In this way he gets even because in the political arena the politician controls legitimate violence and the rules and methods of the game. The citizen plays at a disadvantage for he doesn't know those rules or real politik. With the joke he levels the playing field.

With the joke, the confrontation between civil society and the politician remains in the realm of the symbolic, without personalizing or going against the citizen. This is in some ways the history of democracy. Governments define themselves according to the level of representation in the population as well as the degree to which they impose themselves on society. They use methods that are more or less democratic, with relative social acceptance and representation. From there, the use of humor should be an important component in the democratic game. Within this scope and within democracy, for once, perhaps society wins. It unmasks power and denudes politicians, stripping them of their larger-than-life image, criticizing what it wants to criticize, and destroying established symbols. Meanwhile, neither fools nor the invisible hand of legitimate violence can reach it. Nor can anybody be deprived of liberty, because it is society in the abstract that is transgressing, and because of that the common citizen enjoys the opportunity for freedom.

The following example criticizes the politician's false honesty and juxtaposes honesty with feminine virginity. One is a fundamental value of the democratic system, and the other is a fundamental principle of social morality in many religions. The objective of this riddle is to symbolically destroy the truth:

What is the difference between a virgin and a politician?

Answer: When the virgin says "no," it means "maybe"; when she says "maybe," it means "yes"; and when she says "yes," she is no virgin. On the other hand, when the politician says "yes," he means "maybe"; when he says "maybe," he means "no"; and when he says "no," it means he is no politician.

11. One of the most important questions surrounding the political joke consists of determining the relationship between the type of political system portrayed and the political humor being used.

Conventional thinking suggests that there is a negative correlation between humor and democracy, assuming that with less freedom comes greater humoristic expression. There is no evidence to prove this affirmation—but we may modify it, suggesting that less freedom elevates the role of humor to that of liberator. Nevertheless, different problems emerge when analyzing this affirmation. For starters, democracy[43] doesn't consist only of the realization of effective and honest electoral processes. Rather, it has to do with the existence of equality and freedoms; for the purposes of our study, I put in first place the freedom of expression.

We may suggest that democracy is a system in which liberties are extensive and guaranteed; in authoritarian regimes the government and the State have an arbitrary management of liberties, and in totalitarian systems liberty is completely absent. Nevertheless, we must be careful with two aspects. First, we must be conscious enough to not get into any discussion regarding the preference of ideologies that distract from rigorous critical analysis. Second, we must be careful not to fall into quantitative traps. We may suggest that to prove the relationship between jokes and democracy would require a rigorous and workable definition of the democratic concept, which in itself is problematic to obtain. Busey (1985), Russell H. Fitzgibbon, and Kenneth F. Johnson in Tomasek (1966) and Gupta (1990)—to mention but a few—present the limitations of the definition that quantify the characteristics of democracy. Their work shows the need to generate an index that will establish a scale for political systems, but these types of indexes have great shortcomings due to a strong ideological component in their elaboration. This, no doubt, can be accomplished by means of models that measure phenomena. However, we can also move in another direction, such as in one that proposes measuring the quality of the democracy.[44] Such a task elevates the analysis to a different dimension because not only are elections quantified but also we must consider the citizen's control over political systems and the degree to which the society is politicized. Still, many scholars criticize this approach as biased.

In any case, we find the need to formulate a taxonomy and typography of universal political humor and quantify them adequately to correlate both variables. To begin, we must accept that it's not possible to quantify all jokes: a possible methodological obstacle. The lack of *exact numbers* in humor doesn't nullify the analysis because numbers may be replaced with a qualitative, semantic, or semiological analysis of humor. This may help us understand the mood of a specific part of society, and here we must insist that no one may assume that political humor represents the opinion of *all* of society. The analysis of humor is a subjective expression of certain social segments. We should not lose sight of this aspect and continue with the objective of overcoming methodological obstacles that could become metaphorical straightjackets that would simply deny the development of a new focus of political analysis.

Even if we were to resolve this problem, we would still require the correlation of the type of political system with the qualitative aspect of political humor. Measuring jokes is a monumental task, especially because, as we've already mentioned, they are ephemeral and not always recorded. We must calibrate the *sharpness* or *crudeness* of a joke, and this can vary historically and geographically even within the same country—a clear indication of its complex character. We may conclude that analyzing jokes implies analyzing subjective expressions contained in the greatly inexact area of social values.

Political jokes indeed have to do with democracy. We find different types of political jokes in different types of political systems. Take, for example, the difference and impact of the role of television in the United States and Mexico. The Center for Media and Public Affairs in Washington, D.C., registered in just one year (1990) 3,025 televised political jokes, including those about the president. Up until the twenty-first century, it was ridiculous to think that we would one day see presidential jokes on Mexican television. There are several instructive anecdotes about the level of censorship that existed—and exists—in this medium.

Using a collection of jokes as indicators, we can compare political systems even when they are not similar. Let's take the Romanian collection of jokes from Banc and Dundes (1986) as an example of those developed under a totalitarian regime, those from Schmidt (1996) as an indicator of jokes from an authoritarian regime, and those from the Center for Media and Public Affairs (1990) as an example of jokes from a democratic regime. This abbreviated comparison test demonstrates that there are more political jokes in a democratic system and that that number is drastically reduced in the totalitarian system. If we add in the factor of mass media, we find that while in democracy it is not unusual to find jokes on television, in the other two systems they are rare or nonexistent. The number may turn out to be irrelevant because the impact of the jokes may be greater in a totalitarian regime, in which criticism is persecuted. Here, the joke can turn into the only form of political critique. Such was the case during the Nazi and Soviet regimes, for even though they successfully silenced criticism, they could not put an end to jokes.

Hypothetically, we suggest that jokes have a relationship with economic development and the consequent urbanization. Political power is concentrated in capital cities, and in cities in general, where economic power is centralized. This phenomenon is exacerbated, since most countries are predominantly urban. Consequently, the concentration of human populations that are found near the sources of power experience political fallout in a more significant manner because they are more exposed to formal and informal information. Certainly, in these populations, given the effect of mass media, jokes are more easily spread because people are familiar with the governmental elite and they are more sensitive to "bedroom secrets," which are also a source of rumors and jokes.

The amount and the sharpness of jokes vary according to the *juncture* as well as the quality of democracy even though there are certain topics that remain from the past. Examining the Mexican case turns out to be very useful in shedding some light on this point. Mexico is a country that has some basic democratic components, such as systematic elections, political parties, and organizations. Nevertheless, in the literature, Mexico is considered to be an authoritarian system (Stallings and Kaufman, 1989; O'Donell, 1986). Political jokes circulate widely around such themes as corruption, and their sharpness varies; however, even when the political system is very open, humor doesn't reach the masses. A good example of this can be seen in the case of Héctor Suarez, a popular comedian who told a joke about President Carlos Salinas and was fired by the station on which it was aired.[45]

12. The discussion about the usefulness of relating a number of jokes with a political system, to identify characteristic and thematic differences in political jokes, according to a specific system, has been insufficient. The superficial analysis of political humor, which is based on collecting jokes from a specific period, has led to mistaken conclusions, such as the negative correlation between humor and freedom. This allows us to suggest that to understand this type of humor it must be examined in relation to sociopolitical elements, such as with research into how society perceives itself.

If we accept Almond and Verba's (1963) definition of political culture as the way in which the individual sees himself before power and the government, we can conclude that different forms of political participation exist in a given political system. In all systems, there are jokes, and these jokes derive from the political culture; a symbiotic relationship is created in which jokes and political culture feed off each other. Let there be no doubt—no matter the attitude of politicians—that political humor has a great importance in the political system. I thus put forth the idea that political humor represents a social opinion regarding politics and is an important component of political culture.

Political culture also determines the forms of participation within a political system. Voting is one of the most important, because it nourishes the creation of a consensus, and it is verifiable. This facilitates the approval of society as a whole and generates legitimacy for the system. That is how legal legitimacy is attained: The fact that a candidate is elected by a majority in an honest election gives the system legitimacy.

Nevertheless, beyond voting, the level of influence a given society has over politics can vary. Society in general has a limited influence on certain political events, as with, for example, the selection of candidates, because even when the process is an open one, society is faced with a limited number of options to choose from. A typical case is the selection of the candidate for vice president of the United States, since he is selected by the presidential candidate through a secret process. Therefore, to counteract society's lack of say in certain decisions, other forms of political participation—from electoral abstention[46] to political humor—develop. Through these means, society demonstrates the channel through which it prefers to send differing messages to communicate its opinion.

On another level, we have citizens who are able to participate in labor unions, civil associations, nongovernmental organizations, professional groups, and interest or pressure groups. By means of the same activity, they can reinforce the system, but abstention only weakens it. It is paradoxical that those in power, who require for their legitimacy an increase in political participation, might try to manipulate the very political process but thus end up supporting electoral abstention.[47]

In Mexico, neither presidential re-election nor consecutive congressional re-election exists, except regarding labor, peasant leaders, and other positions such as university presidents. In this manner, the system supports its leaders in different organizations that—even though they are often corrupt—exercise iron-like social and political control. While citizens continue to participate in social organizations, the political system is legitimized in general, since society lives its daily life according to the established order. This allows a political stability that is complemented by the efficiency of the administration and the electoral system.

When people are frustrated with the political imposition on their lives, different social and political reactions occur, among which are electoral abstention and attacks on politics by means of jokes.

13. In nondemocratic regimes, jokes facilitate an underground political participation comparable to the power's exercise of police methods. To confront and attack power, one should situate one's self on the same grounds that those of power stand on. Obviously, the confrontation is still unequal because while politicians count on efficient instruments to act when they feel that there are threats against their system, the citizens have weaker weapons, many of them informal, such as political jokes. Those who tell jokes are not expecting to overthrow power, but rather to ridicule the powerful and what they represent.[48] Jokes are one of the means that society uses to defend itself from the excesses of power. Society makes up damaging anonymous revenge through humor without provoking a backlash; they are a form of resistance that avoids the "open confrontation with the structures of authority which it resists,"[49] and in democratic systems they are a balancing mechanism in the hands of society.

Political humor destroys the seriousness, solemnity, pomposity, and ritual that surround politics. Losing respect or fear regarding politics reduces one's obedience to power and promotes society's mobilization. On the other hand, a individual who only has humor left as a form of expression possesses very limited—almost *no*—formal participation. Politics stops being of interest to him because the access routes to power are closed off. That is why a demagogue's lies and secrecy gain him favor in a society that has to keep quiet in front of their government's lack of transparency.

Jokes don't lie, they don't fool, nor do they use subterfuges; they are beyond party logic and beyond the calculations of a system's need to reproduce itself. Political humor allows an individual to confront politics and politicians, without violence and all while relatively safe from retaliation. Political humor is a form of free political expression[50] and doesn't follow a set course. It has no predetermined constructive or destructive intention. Contrary to the dynamic of political discussions, political humor lacks specific themes and regularly takes unexpected turns.

Finally, the humoristic recourse is more effective than the political. The joke only requires people to listen, and they are aplenty. It could even happen that they are in the audience, even if they don't realize they are the object of the joke. Formal political process requires legitimacy, consensus, and other resources that can be difficult to obtain. Naturally, politicians react in different ways to humor. It is said that several heads of State have collected the jokes about them. A student told me about having seen a collection of jokes in the private library of Luis Echeverría, even though during his administration there was a rumor that whoever told jokes about him would be jailed.[51]

14. The political joke focuses itself against what characterizes the political system and what most irritates society. Until recently, in ex-communist[52] countries, the irritation emerged as a result of the lack of freedom under the Soviet regime. Consider the following examples:

> Two dogs run into each other in the old Warsaw plaza; one is very well fed, the other is very weak. The well-nourished one says that he has just arrived from Prague, where there is an abundance of good food and beautiful girl dogs.
>
> The other dog says, "So what are you doing here?"
>
> And the first one answers, "I just came to bark."[53]

> Once, Khrushchev and Ulbright were walking around Moscow, and they found a child.
>
> They asked him, "Who is your father?"
>
> "Khrushchev."
>
> "Who is your mother?"
>
> "The Soviet Union."
>
> "What would you like to be?"
>
> "A cosmonaut."
>
> Some time later, Khrushchev was visiting East Berlin, and as he was walking with Ulbright, they saw a child and asked him, "Who is your father?"
>
> "Ulbright."
>
> "Who is your mother?"
>
> "The Democratic Republic of Germany."
>
> "What would you like to be?"
>
> "An orphan."[54]

The economic situation in socialist countries is spoken of in much the same way. In a joke about Fidel Castro, the economic situation is very well outlined:

> Vladimir Putin visits Cuba, and when he notices that all of the Cubans have broken shoes, he asks Fidel how it can be possible that after fifty years of *improvements* the Cubans have been walking around with broken shoes.

Fidel answers: "And in Russia they're better?"

Putin answers him yes, and that if he wanted to he could go to Russia and he had his permission to kill all of those he sees with broken shoes. They get on Putin's airplane, they get to Russia, the first person he sees has broken shoes, and so according to their pact he pulls out his pistol and kills him.

The next day the Russian newspapers had the following headline: CRAZY BEARDED MAN KILLS CUBAN AMBASSADOR IN THE AIRPORT!!!

Before its disappearance, in the USSR there was also concern about the country's economy. The following joke alludes to the subject, and in a very sought-after comparative game, it synthesizes what would happen in three countries:

President Francois Mitterrand has one hundred lovers, and one of them has AIDS, but he doesn't know which one.

President George Bush has one hundred bodyguards and one is a terrorist but he doesn't know which one.

Mikhail Gorbachev has one hundred economists but only one has a brain, but he also doesn't know which one.

The main targets of political jokes are usually power symbols and those political elements that most bother society. Thus, in the Soviet countries, jokes' subject matter was often freedom; in Mexico, given the great impact of the federal government and the chief executive in power, the subject is often the president. When jokes refer to local issues, they tend to attack governors and even municipal presidents, but always as representatives of the pyramidal and authoritarian political system.

In the United States, even though there is a wide choice of subject matter for jokes, the jokes tend strongly to concentrate on the president, his politics, and his decisions. During 1990, the ten subjects most covered in jokes recorded by the Center for Media and Public Affairs (1990:4) were the Persian Gulf War, the USSR, the environment, crime, business, the savings-and-loan scandal, the economy, and the presidential figure. In the case of jokes about George W. Bush, they have often ridiculed his apparent ignorance of speaking the English language properly.

Political jokes attack principles related to power that the citizen is supposed to respect. It destroys the general consensus while stripping powerful people of their aura. Within the underground world of power and humor, the joke has greater power because it can refuse to recognize political rules while establishing them, and when their effects rise to the surface, it's undermining job is such that it is uncontainable. It denudes the politician, and it shows him the way society wants to see him, not the way he wants to be seen. It is a distorted version of the story about the emperor's clothes; for the political character nothing is worse than the joke because it allows for no disguises. Political jokes clothe the politician against his will. With this new wardrobe, society can view him in its own way, leaving him with no other option but to hide his shame (see the following examples):

> They call that politician "Mr. Synchronized," because every time he opens his mouth, he sticks his foot in it.

> They call that politician "The Fish," because he opens his mouth and says nothing. (Salgado, 1986:45).

The essence of the joke is not to elucidate, but to ridicule. Nevertheless, once it exists there is more light and truth. The people win for the first time, expressing preferences without associating themselves with certain influences or political ties and ideologies. By means of the political joke, the people struggle against defeat and political immorality, though its path may have violated conventional political norms and rituals. When politicians fall in the path of the joke's ambush, they lose respect and legitimacy.

Certainly the confrontation between humor and politician is unequal. Humor has the advantage of attacking with weapons that are little understood by the political system, since politicians trust that the people will continue to be satisfied with the imposition of the system's rules and abuses. For politicians to be able to make their own jokes, there would have to be a change in rules and rituals, because in principle they would have to question their own formality and solemnity.

When politicians use the joke, their objective is different than that of societies. John F. Kennedy used to make jokes to enrich his image. Gardner (1986) attributes this use of humor to the value attributed to candidates after Kennedy, who took advantage of jokes to improve their images, to make themselves seen like the common man—or, on the other hand, to insult other politicians—but by no means did they use jokes to attack social values. Ronald Reagan's use of jokes is a classic contemporary example. Politicians in general don't tell jokes that denigrate the nation or the political system; political jokes can be guerilla weapons—but not in the hands of politicians.

Humorists are free to attack anything, but politicians, are limited by morals and values,[55] especially consensual ones.[56] In contrast to what Pitchford (1960:46) thinks, political humor is not an instrument to produce a consensus, even though it originates within the society and destroys its adversary as well as any consensus. The political joke always has a subjugating intention.

For a joke's narrator and creator, there exists a certain dual type of values. In his life, he surely defends traditional values, symbols, and verbal expressions, while with humor he destroys these with impunity. Similarly, in the area of political discourse, he must show an immense amount of earnestness and seriousness to convince, whereas humoristic discourse circulates easily in the opposite way—with powerful jokes and jests.

15. The political joke has the ability to synthesize opinions, which gives it an enormous advantage over other forms of communication, which usually require long dissertations. As we have already seen, brevity is one of the joke's main characteristics.

Here are some examples of jokes showing an ability to synthesize many opinions into a single public opinion:

> What colors destroyed Mexico during the presidency of López Portillo?
>
> They were green, black and bright pink; green because of the great leak in dollars and the elevated national debt. Black because of 'black' Durazo's childhood friend and ex-chief of police of the Federal District, who was famous for the levels of corruption he reached; and bright pink for the rumored romance he had with Rosa (pink) Luz Alegría.[57]

The next joke is isomorphic:

> What are the colors of the past three presidents of Mexico?
>
> Echeverría, bright red for his purported communism; López Portillo, rat grey, for his reputed corruption; de la Madrid, medium ochre (mediocre) for his ineptitude.

16. The political joke can represent an act of optimism through its intention to generate change—because, as we have already seen, if an individual doesn't have the capacity to influence the political system by means of formal channels, then he may try to better it by means of humor.

Who Makes Up the Jokes?

The etiology of political jokes seems to be a mystery. But knowing who invents them, or at least in which social circle they originate, can help us understand which segment is the most unhappy with the political situation because that is the segment most motivated to use jokes to send political messages.

Some jokes originate outside the political sphere and are later adapted to fit some political figure, and some jokes may come from other countries.[58] Often, anecdotes are invented or told and then converted into jokes because they display a certain degree of incongruence. Even some political jokes originate as anecdotes, despite most of them being anonymous. Given the difficulty of determining the exact origin of jokes, let us for now be satisfied with the analysis of their propagation.

Among those who tell jokes are comedians; others are simply natural joke tellers when they participate in social events but are not necessarily interested in political jokes.[59]

In Mexico, political jokes are disseminated among different sectors of the elite: politicians, academics, comedians, leaders of opinion, and citizens concerned about politics. Businessmen generally tell off-color jokes, as well as some political jokes. The same happens with academics. But political and off-color jokes can even circulate among politicians. Those who are not part of the elite most often share sexual and non-political jokes. The collections of jokes contain a reduced amount of jokes—of the ones that are of concern here (Salgado, 1986, 1986a, 1986b; Rojas and Esparza, 1985; Phillips, 1981; Canar, 1974)—and generally, they refer to the police as if that wasn't a political subject, and they avoid real political issues. Political jokes can even be considered part of the elite;[60] they circulate in places that the elite frequent, such as cafés, restaurants, and bars. They often come up in the conversations of politicians, businessmen, managers, and scholars. Among scholars, the type of conversation consisting of political jokes is usually recorded in universities. In contrast, among the non-elite groups, not a single political joke seems to have been produced. Thus, we can say that evidence supports the following affirmations:

1. Most of the flow of information is recorded among the elite, where there is knowledge and incentive to make up jokes about subjects that very often don't reach the public arena. The elite may develop a joke as a quick response to a political or governmental administrative action. The joke sends a message of correction to the government, and of transgression for the rest of the society.

The following joke refers to the economic measures applied by President Clinton:

"What does it take to ruin the U.S. economy?"
"One Bill."

This joke was made up at the beginning of Clinton's administration, and it shows the discontent among some segments of the American elite regarding the economic measures his government had adopted.

2. The elite know the bedroom secrets of functionaries, which is one of the main reasons political humor is so powerful. The people want to air the dirty laundry of political personalities.[61] Because of that, intimacy acquires a great weight, such as was the case for Fouche in France, whose spying system caused the downfall of Napoleon (Zweig, 1958).

3. The nonpolitical elite want to know—in the strictest of confidence—the secrets of power, as well as how politicians are able to exercise it. Those who exercise power ignore society, and—even though all of society resents it—the elite make up the social segment that can best use this information to promote their interests. The elite are sensitive to the immediate impact of political decisions and know how to send messages to the government and politicians. Politics and political jokes are part of a hidden political game, but jokes are the political weapon used by the elite in the face of their conflictive relationship with power.

4. Here, we should add a comment about the exercise of power in general. We know that there is scarce inside information about power from those who have exercised it, and there are few politicians who write about it; nevertheless, there exists a category of participants in power who are educated and talented social climbers. When these people leave their positions, they are free from political or moral pressure to keep secret their knowledge of how power functions. Thus, they constitute a valuable source of information with respect to politicians' secrets.

5. The economic elite enjoy the privilege of travel and communication with people of other elite groups in the world, enabling one nation to adapt the ironies, parodies, and jokes of other nations. This explains why there are long-lived jokes that are told in many different countries and cultures. Possibly what is important is not affinity between cultures, but rather that between different elite groups belonging to those cultures.

6. The long lives of some jokes lead us to assume the existence of a historical memory that belongs to the elite. In fact, the elite do have access

to formal information through educational institutions and publications through which international contacts are established. Informal information is also readily available and circulates in the various networks of the elite.

As we have suggested, some jokes have similar structures, though parts have been adjusted to fit different regional and time situations or various important personalities. These jokes may appear in different cultures at different times. Consider the following example:

> President Chun of Korea, President Reagan of the United States, Pope John Paul II, a young boy, and a captain are all in a submarine. The submarine starts to sink, and there are only four oxygen tanks. The Pope mentions the importance of his responsibilities in the church, takes a tank, and disappears. Reagan says that he needs to lead the free world; he takes another tank and leaves. Chun says that forty million South Koreans depend on his leadership and decides to take the third one; he also leaves.
>
> The captain then turns to the boy and tells him to take the fourth tank because the captain is going to go down with his ship.
>
> But the boy says, "It isn't necessary, Captain. President Chun took a fire extinguisher."

There is an isomorphic joke about the president of France, Giscard d'Estaing; instead of in a submarine, it takes place in an airplane, and instead of taking the parachute, he takes a hippie's backpack.

Another interesting joke is shared by Yugoslavia and Mexico. In the first, Tito is nominated for the Nobel Prize in chemistry because he made crap out of the dinar. In the Mexican version, López Portillo is nominated for three Nobel Prizes: the one for physics because he made the peso float and then he sank it; the one for chemistry because he was able to make crap out of the peso, and the one in biology because he converted man into dog. Obviously, the idea of the prize is repeated, and the part of the joke about chemistry is the same, even though the Mexican version was expanded to include other subjects—especially the unfortunate underlying declaration that López Portillo would defend the peso like a dog. This joke was also adapted to Carlos Salinas.

Jokes about de Gaulle, Khomeini, Zia, Brezhnev, and other world leaders also share similar themes, in their case a visit that the leaders pay to God. Here is a version including Brezhnev, Nixon, and Ceausescu:

God receives Brezhnev, who is crying, and he asks him why he is crying. Brezhnev responds: "The Americans have a better standard of living than us."

God says: "Don't worry, you are ahead in the space race."

Then he receives Nixon, who is crying, and he asks why he is crying. Nixon answers: "The Russians are ahead in the space race."

God says to him: "Don't worry, you have a better standard of living," and Nixon is consoled.

Then God receives Ceausescu, who is crying, and he sits down to cry with him.

Similar jokes appeared in Mexico during the foreign debt crisis in the eighties.

In some cases, the colonial or post-colonial condition explains the transference of jokes, which has prolonged their life. However, in other cases, without cultural similarities or direct economic connections among countries, the transmission of jokes can be explained by the movement of the elite, as we discussed above, as well as their access to mass media.

7. The elite are generally better educated and have experience managing large amounts of information, which allows them to create jokes and understand the messages they involve.[62] As has been mentioned, this turns out to be important because a joke that has to be explained loses its comic effect. Nevertheless, the elite have sufficient information to make funny, comprehensible jokes even in a transcultural environment.

8. The elite can benefit from the use of jokes;[63] in sending messages to politicians, they can even use them to threaten the government (Schmidt, 1991b). They can then use political humor to seek a new and more convenient agreement with power.

9. The non-elite sector is influenced by the elite and internalizes its values and opinions. We don't know exactly how the transference between the elite and the common folk occurs, but we can appreciate that there is a mutual influence. The dominant language prevails, and the dominated assume it as their own. Furthermore, jokes can be transferred more surely and quickly than a political critique, and through jokes, whoever does not want to be identified as a critic of a regime may do so without declaring a political preference. Jokes are not usually created to motivate the dissention of other social groups, yet for the dominated, laughter can sometimes be the only instrument to incite dissent.

10. Politicians can be considered part of the elite; all the same, they develop their own system of linguistic codes and behavior that might be

known as political lore: a system of symbols, written and unwritten rules, and a concept of the world and life that regulates public and private conduct. In this way, political lore can help the elite communicate with other social sectors.

Conclusion

Humor has different forms and manifestations that are determined by historical and cultural conditions. Some cultures may prefer a certain form during a particular period. Nevertheless, jokes seem to be the most profuse humoristic manifestation. They are easy to transmit, don't require explanation, and don't create annoying conversations. They are hedonistic and help to free energy; consequently, they are an important instrument for the freedom of expression.

There is sufficient evidence to associate certain types of political humor with certain types of political regimes. In fact, democracies tend to be more tolerant of political humor. The paradox is that political humor, as a critique of power and its symbols, is a conservative instrument for participation whose final objective is to simply correct and not fundamentally change the political system.

Jokes don't truly correct problems in themselves, but they do send messages about problems that must be corrected. In authoritarian systems and even in totalitarian ones, they can even, in a way, substitute elections as a means of allowing political expression. Political humor can synthesize public opinion and manifest political critique even when formal participation is nonexistent.

It's difficult to determine who makes up jokes, but we can more easily discover who tells them. Political humor originates and circulates within the elite, trickling from that circle of society downward to the rest of society, as well as moving across borders to the elite of other countries to be adapted for fitting into certain local contexts. The elite is the social segment that most benefits from political humor's use.

Mexicans are famous for using humor widely and for laughing at everything, seemingly even death. This is some of what we will explore in the next chapter, together with inquiry into what makes the Mexican laugh and what role political jokes play in Mexico.

CHAPTER TWO

What Does the Mexican Laugh At?

> *Perhaps the aggressiveness with which the Mexican avenges himself, in the most innocuous manner, or the expression of our secular dissatisfaction; or the revenge that any given Mexican takes in exchange for his enormous capacity for patience and resignation toward what he is avenging; maybe it is the expression of resentment or perhaps the only method of political opposition he has at hand.*
>
> —JUAN LOMAS (1975)

Why Laugh?

In general, Mexico's humoristic culture transgresses norms, traditional values, and established symbols. Mexicans, like all people of course, laugh and make fun of taboos and moral restrictions, but there is much literature on Mexicans' humor in particular; some say their psyche is saturated with humor even in the most desperate of circumstances. Homero (1974:13) says that "happiness, misfortune, religion, politics, marriage, friendship, the cost of living and even sex make Mexicans laugh."

But Mexico, contrary to what some may think, doesn't have a monopoly on humor when looking at tragedy. Just a few hours after the spaceship *Challenger* exploded, the same joke was told on both coasts of the United States:

> When the teacher who was aboard the ship said goodbye to her husband that morning, she said to him, "You feed the kids; I'll feed the fish."

To protect themselves, many people laugh at disaster. Through humor, they overcome the psychological impact of tragedy: jokes exorcise them. Howe (1951:211) says, "This people of such a tragic fate [the Jews] chose laughter as the main path to its folkloric expression." The cathartic power of humor is obvious when, for example, after the 1985 Mexico earthquake, humor responded in this way to explain why it took so long for jokes to emerge:

> Jokes took a long time because Pepito [a young impertinent boy who is a staple of Mexican jokes] was buried under the CONALEP [a school building that collapsed in Mexico City].

Díaz Guerrero (1961:35) asserts that the laughter of Mexicans is part of their need for personal interaction and of their irreverent attitude toward everything, especially toward taboos. Jokes about sex get to such a point, according to Linares (1976), that the Mexican turns into a *sexolatrist, sex maniac, sexophile, sexaholic, sexologist, sexopath,* and *sexophagist*. But no one people has a monopoly on laughing at sex—just as none has one on laughing at tragedy—and Mexican humor encompasses much more than sex, including family, marriage, religion, and, of course, politics.[1]

As we've now touched upon the Mexican's tendency to laugh at politics, we might again bring up his tendency to likewise laugh at tragedy (and other negative or solemn subjects)—highlighting that the former, naturally, may be the *cause* of the latter when it does not support the Mexican's happiness and wellbeing. We might first ascertain the popular opinion that the Mexican laughs at, or at least makes light of, the ultimate tragedy: death. This is reflected in the celebratory skulls brought out during the Day of the Dead holiday and results in a superficial reading of Posada's work. It can't be denied that one may not see people laughing hysterically at a burial or at a graveside wake during El Día de los Muertos. However, the jokes that are told on such occasions have a deep psychological explanation involving the need to free stressful energies, being that death causes great emotional stress and psychological conditions that are difficult to manage.[2]

The same is true when the Mexican laughs at politics, which may also cause great stress and other adverse emotions. Besides perhaps causing a tragedy like financial strife or being driven from one's land, politics might even result in death (his own or loved ones') in the case of war or revolutionary struggle.

It is now certainly relevant to ask why the Mexican reacts to tragedy and politics with humor, when he could confront such things, especially political ones, in another manner. For example, for a long time it seemed as though Mexicans didn't care about the radical discourse that diplomats used outside of Mexico; nevertheless, the subject didn't escape humor, as can be seen in the following joke:

> Two representatives of the Organization of American States were nearly put to sleep by the boring discourse that they were hearing during a meeting, when all of a sudden they heard, "We demand social justice for workers and a higher standard of living!"
>
> One of them said, "Who let the communists in?"
>
> And the other responded, "It's only the Mexicans, go back to sleep."

As a component of authoritarianism, Mexican political culture makes the public fearful of political consequences in almost any activity that may have a political impact. Perhaps because of this, Mexicans prefer anonymity or to work underground[3] instead of expressing opinions and influencing politics.

Why don't they use formal political means, which they have at their disposal? Part of the answer is found by checking the general attitude of the archetypical Mexican: apathetic, servile, and subordinated by power, which translates into a very limited participation, motivated by humor, yet risking nothing. Through humor, the Mexican expresses his opinions, takes on a political position, and saves himself from possible unwanted consequences.

But *is* there an archetypical Mexican? Scholars ask themselves: *What does it mean to be Mexican, and why does the Mexican behave as he does?* Whatever the result of this inquiry, the author will be criticized—whether in his time or later—because he will end up saying something that the dominant forces will not want to hear. If, for example, someone analyzes the reason that Mexicans allow themselves to be led to a political rally for which they are compensated with a sandwich and a soda and the promise of future well-being, that person will be disqualified by the appropriate political forces, since such revelations knock down the supposed popularity of those politicians.[4]

Trying to define the Mexican can lead to an epistemological error, as would be an attempt to define the native of *any* country, assuming that there exists national homogeneity. Geographic differences, or differences in education, gender, and social class, are important distinctions among Mexicans. The lack of homogeneity makes people from other parts of Mexico reject inhabitants of Mexico City, better known in Mexico as *chilangos*. Nevertheless, it is interesting to state that the jokes that are generated in Mexico City can be applied to any Mexican in the country; no matter how much it is said that inhabitants of the northern city of Monterrey are *chilangos light* (as in "diet" *chilangos*, like Diet Coke), jokes about them[5] are not at all like those with reference to residents of the capital.

The analysis of the Mexican as a lone subject is also erroneous, and perhaps unfair, as we will see further ahead. The culture does not speak with one voice, and specifics must be recognized in each examination of a group of individuals—but where political humor is born is in still more complex quarters. Booth and Seligson (1994) suggest that the Mexican culture is a mixture of history and political regime; Bartra (1987) argues that the capitalist exploitation of Mexicans is a manner of differentiation, and we are inclined to recognize that social economic and geographic differences among Mexicans are determinants for the culture, notwithstanding that some characteristics are common to many Mexicans and are reflected in their humor. To support this analysis, we will examine characteristics that are shared by Mexicans as they are recorded by scholars, essayists, writers, and humorists. This will allow us to become familiar with the attitude of the Mexican.

Characteristics of the Mexican

There exists a great yearning to understand the Mexican, or what it means to be Mexican—that is to say, the philosophical essence of the Mexican and his identity. Some authors (Basave, 1992:145) assume that the Mexican is not aware of his own identity. Apparently, this problem originated with the Spanish conquest, when the cult of the worship of Mexican Gods was destroyed. At that time the native nobility was terminated, customs were violated, and the population was decimated. Furthermore, there took place a long and painful racial integration in which a caste system relegated the indigenous population to the lowest social scale.

The present-day Mexican, not withstanding his being *mestizo* (a person whose ancestors are both European and indigenous), resents this affront of the past. He lives with the idea that being mestizo implies accepting the Spaniard's superiority over his native indigenous roots. Basave (1992:144) tries to resolve this identity crisis by promoting mestizo domination over the aggravating factor of the internal conflict suffered by the Mexican. When authors refer to this conflict, they generally assume a position of eurocentrism, with the exception of Campbell, who wrote a paternalistic description (1994) of the struggle of the Zapotec Indians (perhaps because he is not Mexican and sees with different eyes, those of an American married to a Zapotec).

The usual portraits of the Mexican or about Mexican attitudes create oft-ignored debates because some people find them offensive. Ramos (1934) analyzed the Mexican in the 1930s and concluded that he suffers from an inferiority complex. The Mexican demonstrates immaturity, he wrote, because his society has stalled in adolescence, and Ramos hopes that his analysis will help in the maturing process. For Díaz Guerrero (1961:45), the Mexican's inferiority complex is due to a lack of self-esteem as a result of unmet self-value. Paz (1986), following Ramos, concludes that Mexicans hide behind a type of "mask."[6] Bartra's contribution (1987) makes reference to a lack of capacity for change and metamorphosis and introduces a class-based analysis to show the complexity of the Mexican identity. Rodríguez and Ramírez-Buendía (1992) make note of certain differences, yet arrive at the same negative conclusion regarding the characteristics of the Mexican. Norman Martin, a non-Mexican, differs in opinion because he feels that the Mexican suffers from a "complex of defeat," which causes psychological underdevelopment (Le Clézio, 1992:62).

Overall, psychologists haven't had much success in defining the Mexicans. Philosophers and humorists, likewise, have searched for peculiarities, but frequently don't go beyond compiling lists full of adjectives lacking meaning. Part of the problem could be that Mexicans tend to reject questionnaires, whose results are therefore frequently inaccurate or lacking in representation.[7] Let us not, however, overlook the fact that part of the problem is the previously mentioned reductionist idea that there is only one type of Mexican, for which adjectives provide a comfortable path, albeit not a trustworthy one, to build a simple typology, since it excludes part of the population.

Octavio Paz (1986) uses more than forty adjectives in his analysis of the Mexican, including "impassible," "untrusting," "underhanded," "ironic," "patient," "nihilistic," and "contemplative." Torres (1984) concentrates on resigned and satirical. Among Linares's sixty adjectives (1976), we find "aggressive," "boaster," "erotomaniac," "sponger," "offensive," and "sex-crazed." For Lomas (1975), the Mexican is abusive, jealous, corrupt, and spiteful. Salgado (1986a and 1986b) calls him rustic, blasphemous, hypocritical, cynical, and indolent. To Bejar (1968) he is untrusting and flees from himself. To Monroy (1967), the author who uses the most adjectives, he is a prisoner of his own dwarfism; he is an impostor, solemn, full of hatred, and slanderous.

There is nothing inherently wrong with using adjectives to characterize someone if and when we are aware of the risk involved in creating stereotypes. In the case of stereotypes about the Mexican, the number of adjectives is overwhelming, prejudiced, and contradictory, and so we must take care to select the most significant ones, accepting the risk that they might not reflect reality. The analysis of adjectives helps us create a close portrait of what can be called "Homo Mexicans" (Hernández and Narro, 1987); in analyzing adjectives, it is useful to count on a list of the ones that help us maintain a certain objectivity and help us create a constructive analysis of the Mexican's attitudes, culture, and political behavior. Most of these adjectives involve self-disapproval stemming from the frustration inherent in the Mexican's perceived inability to change the system, yet this must be incorporated into the analysis of the Mexican elite, since amongst Mexican intellectuals it is held that an important part of their job is to transform society.

To better understand why Mexicans laugh at politics, we must look at historical, sociological, and psychological determinants of being Mexican, which we will do in the following excerpt; for now, let's look at the idea that joke books escape censure with great ease, and that they reach a greater number of readers than, say, essays. Let's admit that it's easier to read a book of jokes than it is a philosophical essay,[8] even though the reader of the jokes loses the depth of the analysis and historical perspective given in the essay, and the author of the jokes evades the greater responsibility involved in writing the essay. For the writer, to offer a serious analysis could imply confronting Mexican censure,[9] at the same time teaching Mexicans constructive criticism. The effort involved in writing such an analysis requires the acknowledgement that Mexico City can act the equivalent of the U.S. "melting pot," and in so doing eliminate the idea that even when the Mexican from Mexico City is a refined product, he doesn't represent all Mexicans. It must be emphasized that official history doesn't necessarily reflect national life, and many times a society becomes actively engaged in the rewriting of its past. This is not for the purpose of creating fiction, but rather to try to re-create what really took place instead of what the government wants to make known or believed. For this reason, like many other authors, I will begin my explanation of the characteristics of the Mexican with his historical origins.

A Historical Perspective

There are, on the one hand, those who believe that the characteristics of the Mexican originate during the precolonial period, affected by "the pain of one hundred generations of subjugation through enslavement by royal warriors who pushed them toward cruelty and assassinations" (Torres, 1984:36). On the other hand, there exists the ample point of view that what most influenced the make-up of the Mexican was the traumatic mixing of native cultures with the Spanish culture.[10] "During the colonial period the smile of the Mexican symbolizes his passive rebellion against the conquistadors, his growing hatred toward the victorious invaders" (Homero, 1974:19).

Considering the adjustment required by the mixing of races, the combination of indigenous cultures with Christianity led to the adoption of a language with many modalities: "expanding the repertoire of Spanish refrains to sayings, jabs, proverbs, *(albur) play on words,*[11] *sizing up, fodder, mocking and fooling around*, disfigured the language to mask embarrassments and insolence" (Torres, 1984:36). *Albur* is a game of words that is uniquely Mexican in which, verbally, two men try to figuratively sodomize each other; it ends when one of them shows verbal superiority, leaving the other battered and defeated: sodomized. *Tanteada*, a game whose name may be roughly translated to "sizing up," is a form of joking around in which an individual tries to explore the attitudes or states of mind of the others involved. *Carnes* ("fodder") are jokes that fool another person. *Choteo* ridicules the victim of a practical joke, though the game also carries a warning to not take a particular situation or person seriously. *Vaciladas* games simply play around with the person subjected to the joke. In fact, this type of cultural employment, a product of Spain's colonial period, continues to our day. Acknowledging this situation implies an understanding of the way the indigenous population met with the costly and painful process of the crossbreeding of the white and Indian races. By the seventeenth century, the Europeans had decimated the indigenous population (Borah, 1977) and finished by squashing their knowledge of their own languages, Gods, and customs, leaving those things a mere niche in the folklore, today, such things whose traces might be found at a tourist attraction such as the Guelaguetza, at the Day of the Dead festivities in Mixquic and Pátzcuaro, and in the flyers of Papantla, among other places.

The cultural clash between the indigenous and the Spaniards also assumes a linguistic battle,[12] in which the already defeated indigenous population transforms its language in a defensive manner against the imposition of the conquistador. This distortion implies a victory, though a pyrrhic victory, for the conquered. Idiomatic expressions, such as slang,[13] mine the cohesive capacity of language and perhaps represent an attempt at social differentiation by means of private languages. "Slang is a literary phenomenon and a social product [. . .] it is the language of misery [. . .] all labor unions, professions, and even accidents of social hierarchy, as in all forms of intelligence, have their slang [*caló*]" (Hugo, 1989:622).

The idiomatic expressions of hostile slang cause the ostracizing of social groups and prevent social uniformity. This confirms the existence of local cultures or subcultures within immediate boundaries. It is similar to the nostalgia and the wish to return to the world that was destroyed by the conquest. The mestizo society lives in a paradox when it denies its hidden desire to recover or re-create a grandiose image of the indigenous world that was lost in a traumatic conquest;[14] in this struggle between defeated (former) grandiosity and the detested victor, the Mexicans end up hating a part of themselves that might otherwise give them pride.

It is very possible that the Mexican's nostalgia gives rise to a severely confused nationalism because it tries to build its symbols and heroes on the elevation of Creole characters (characters of people born in the New World of European parents)—who in another context one would learn to hate—and in a buried past, whether it be due to the lack of feasibility to defend themselves in this past or because they were defeated with a certain ease. Mexican nationalism has poorly rewritten its national history because it has preferred to leave out the narration and interpretation of uncomfortable facts. Furthermore, the return to that poorly told past eliminates the modernity contained in the nationalism. The Mexican lives in an unwanted present, dreaming of a grandiose past he didn't have because the great majority of Mexicans are mestizos; neither do they have a future, since they have not been able to solve the paradoxes of the past. This colonial heritage illustrates one of the main characteristics of Mexicans: the avoidance of speaking straight while using idiomatic pretexts. Maybe because of this, Cantinflas[15] was so popular and the albur, the play on words, became such a frequently used mode of communication.

Mexicans play with language; they twist it and transform it to subvert it and communicate with their friends or family, creating initiating rituals that isolate them. Fuentes (1993:193) refers to the albur while saying that "language helps more to defend than to communicate, it helps more to mask than to reveal. The game of the *albur* aids one to withdraw, disguise oneself and hide."

The historical resentment of the conquest provokes in Mexicans the pleasure of ruining victory for others.[16] Somehow, Mexicans continue avenging themselves for the oppression, deception, and the excessive abuse of the Spaniards,[17] aiming their weapons against themselves. In the year 2000, the National Action Party won the Mexican presidential election, pointing their munitions against the seventy years of PRI governance; however, unless we can prove that the vote that year had a historically correcting effect, we will continue to resort more to a humoristic exit in the face of the country's history of frustration rather than joke about moral and political values and political symbols.

A Behavioral[18] Perspective

One can also use a behavioral analysis regarding the Mexican character in order to complement the information obtained from a historical perspective. If we observe common behavior and the current tide of Mexican public opinion, we can observe some of the Mexican's basic characteristics.

Of course, we don't want to generalize nor analyze the peculiarities of a specific type of Mexican, but rather the generic behavior inferred from the stereotype. I admit that the stereotype can be prejudiced or incorrect, but it serves as a guide for the analysis.

In this section, we build the image of the Mexican, following the characteristics that several authors consider representative. They all refer to the Mexican of male gender, even when there are minor references to women. Among the values and symbols most subscribed to as relevant, we have blame, trust, patriotism, uncertainty, a very particular concept of time, responsibility, credibility, power, and solidarity.

Mexicans behave as if nothing affects them. They let things slide off of them, and nothing touches them, especially when it comes to confronting a situation that makes them feel guilt. For a people with deep religious convictions—whose religion, such as those of many others, is based on reward and punishment surrounding guilt—recognizing guilt becomes an important part of daily behavior.

Nevertheless, the Mexican doesn't *himself* feel guilty about anything, because the guilty party must always be the other. As Lomas (1975:141) says:

> Parents blame their children and children blame their parents. We blame destiny, bad luck, bad education, women, bad friends, but we never admit our own fault. Furthermore, the Mexican never feels guilty, and consequently considers it unfair that he is believed guilty, he is very clever at finding scapegoats.

Salgado (1986:11) completes this picture, saying, "The Mexican will never admit his mistakes; he therefore invents a series of excuses that exonerate his thoughtless behavior in nearly all of his actions."

Looking again at the subject of religion, we must consider that a sense of guilt lasts only as long as a person decides it will. He may free himself of guilt simply by going to confession, though this method is a difficult one to use socially or politically, not only because there is separation between church and state but also because there is no process to free a society from its presumed guilt. On the other hand, if Mexico's six-year presidential period has any value at all, it lies in the fact that when we bring in new politicians we are allowed to blame everything on the past, even though the incoming political group may be equally at fault in the creation of great national disgrace.[19] The absence of a mechanism to cure social or political guilt reduces the number of possible scapegoats, possibly leaving only the State—but neither can the State use religion to wipe its sins clean. Nevertheless, the

State punishes whomever it considers threatening the whole social system as guilty or evil, in such a manner that the great acts of repression have released heavy social and political pressure. This is a dead-end road for the Mexicans, because religion allows them to resolve their individual guilt, but it makes it difficult for them to do it collectively. It is a matter of one of the paradoxes resulting from their social, political, and cultural development.

All of this leads us to the following subject: mistrust. The Mexican (male) mistrusts everything, especially women, and for that reason he constantly insults them, nicknaming them and degrading them whenever the opportunity arises. It means a lot that the worst insult for a Mexican man—who will kill because of this insult—has to do with one's mother.[20] This fact transformed Malinche from a goddess to the prototype of betrayal, and for that very reason the word most used in the Mexican language is *chingar* ("fuck"), which implies above all to violate, sexually degrade, and establish an attitude in front of life and society based on chingar or to be *chingado* ("to be fucked"). The Mexican mistrusts his friends, the government, and those who govern him in non political ways. And the government, for its part, mistrusts those it governs. Perhaps for this reason, the Mexican confronts and regards its nationalism by making jokes about the institutions and symbols that represent it.

One of the possible consequences of this mistrust is the immediacy of the Mexican and his concentration on the tangible present, being that the future is somewhat distant and intangible, inaccessible and full of uncertainty. As has already been mentioned, the weight of the past causes the present to be filled with uncertainty, and to depend on the future brings with it a weight that is overwhelming and cannot be managed. In a study, 70 percent of Mexicans interviewed agreed with this idea. "They see the future as uncertain" (Hernández and Narro [1987:23]).

There is no reason to think that the political and cultural elite should be exempt from clinging to the past, since they are responsible for generating a made-up history,[21] made up so as to serve the needs of the regime. An official history is made up for and by the victors, even though the people have ruined it,[22] replacing solemnity with irreverence and humor.

The resulting living condition can explain the humoristic attack against national symbols, heroes, nationalism, and anything having to do with politics. But here again, the Mexican finds himself at a dead end. He doesn't manage to achieve national cohesion to be able to conquer the future, and he sees no advantage in retrieving a history that is completely traumatic.

The Mexican constantly lives in a situation of great uncertainty with unpredictable results,[23] in which things can occur or not occur, or be one way or another,[24] even when various results may be juxtaposed. Two jokes help illustrate this point:

> A man in a bar asks for a small shot of tequila and they bring him a mug full. Surprised, he asks for a mug of beer and they bring him a small shot. Now completely disconcerted, he asks for a napkin and they bring him a tablecloth.
>
> This bothers him so much that he asks for an explanation from the bartender, who responds, "In this bar, everything is backward."
>
> And the man says, "Oh, in other words, the one that is going to *chingar a su madre* [the one fucking his mother] is me, right?
>
> ~
>
> A man says to a psychiatrist that he is very confused because he has a trilemma.
>
> The psychiatrist says, "Look, there are dilemmas but not trilemmas."
>
> So the man begins to tell him, "The other day, I went to my buddy's (my compadre's) house to collect some money that he owes me. I got there and the door was open, and because we are very close I went in and went upstairs, and his bedroom door was open. I peeked in and I saw his wife (my *comadre*) naked. Since his wife is very hot, I went in and made love to her. While I was in the act, my buddy came out of the closet and made love to me. When it was over, I left, and I forgot to collect the money that they owed me. A week later, the same thing happened. I went to collect, the door was open, my buddy's wife was naked, I made love to her, my buddy came out, and he did it to me. And that's how things have gone. The trilemma is that I don't know if I'm going to make love to my buddy's wife, if he should do it to me, or if they should pay me the money."

There are many elements that influence the way the Mexican lives. Muñiz-Huberman (2005:190) synthesizes them brilliantly:

> The advantage of living in Mexico is that Mexico doesn't exist. Mexico is what each person invents. Mexico is Mexico. All of the Mexicos you could want, the present, the past, the future. The one that will be perfect the day of its inaugural. An imaginary country.

Perhaps here is the crux of the Mexican's concept of time: It practically has no importance in daily life. Hall (1973:87) divides time into three categories: technical time used by specialists; formal time, the kind that everyone knows and everyone takes for granted, and informal time, which has to do with imprecise situations such as: *luego* ("later"), *al rato* ("in a while"), or *en un minuto* ("in a minute"). Mexicans have converted formal time into something imprecise, or they live within the third type, always used as an imprecise reference that doesn't relate to productivity or discipline.

The calendar is a guide for celebrations. One can say that the dates most respected in the calendar are saint's days and/or commemorations of political events, and this is perhaps because they are mandatory days of rest that usually make "bridges" of three-day weekends.[25] It has always caught my attention that the union for workers of the Universidad Nacional Autónoma de México (STUNAM) was able to achieve as a union victory that the twelfth of December, the day of the Virgin of Guadalupe, would be given to workers as a holiday. This occurred even though its leadership, since its inception, had a leftist orientation to the degree that when this conquest was recognized, it was characterized as a communist and guadalupano labor union,[26] which is without a doubt a strong ideological contradiction. The workers would make fun of the union's victory, but they never rejected it because it represented an additional day off in the collective contract. We can't ignore that this type of victory is also related to the defeat of authority. The union triumphed over the university's administrative authority (see "The Mexican and Power" section below), which should be more important than an extra day off.

The Mexican protects himself when he evades the responsibility of setting a goal regarding his activities. In this way, nobody can tell him that he failed, because he may never have had the intention of fulfilling what he promised from the beginning—but surely he leaves his options open if he wants to claim a goal achieved. Evasion is a defensive instrument with considerable flexibility. It is very difficult to hire an independent worker to perform a service and expect that he will give one a date when the work will be finished for sure.[27] One often hears stories like the following: A person hired a construction worker to install a tile floor. The construction worker said it would take a few days. The first day, he requested an advance for his labor. He took it and never came back. He of course sent somebody else to say that he couldn't finish the job because he found another job.

Often, foreigners laugh and make fun of the fact that in Mexico work can be, and essentially is, always "done *mañana* [tomorrow]." The astute observer understands that *mañana* is an imprecise reference, that it doesn't literally mean the day after today.[28] On the contrary, it means someday after today—for sure not today, and probably not tomorrow, either. Building upon this transitory uncertainty, we must understand that when somebody says an event will take place *ahorita* ("right now"), it means that the event has the probability of occurring; but if he says *ahoritita*, it means that the event surely will never take place. If we confront the uncertainty of the event occurring at all with the unexpected results we face, we must see that it's possible the Mexican will always arrive late and/or never will produce the desired results. Frequently the person waiting receives a phone call saying, "*Ahí voy*" ("I'm coming"), or "*Voy para allá y llegaré*" ("I'm on my way over there, and I'll be there"), meaning wait for me the time necessary because I'm assuring you that I will be there. Political promises fall within this category. Demagoguery is not only to promise something that will never take place, but rather, the imprecise promise that something will take place, for example, *justicia revolucionaria* ("revolutionary justice") promised by postrevolutionary regimes, or the "change" promised by governments previous to and after the year 2000, when Mexico inaugurated an "alternative" government.

The Mexican is also incredulous. Bejar (1968:120), citing Ramos, says, "If he is a businessman he doesn't believe in business; if he is a professional he doesn't believe in his profession; if he is a politician he doesn't believe in politics." The incredulity regarding his profession launches the Mexican toward introversion to the point of living in a fictitious world—a lonesome place where he is not questioned, a world that Paz framed with the metaphor of the masks because, furthermore, the Mexican doesn't admit superiority, although he demands veneration, respect, and discipline. In fact, he disguises his lies to achieve recognition. To make matters worse, he applies his talents toward taking away the value of the accomplishments of his neighbors.[29] If someone buys new shoes, a friend will step on them to "initiate" them. If he buys a car, someone will scrape it with a bottle top or a piece of metal to take away his delight at its perfection. So, it is not surprising that the Mexican mistrusts his peers, his political leaders, electoral results, and political processes—and not necessarily in that order.

The Mexican seeks to degrade the achievements of his peers. From there evolved the concept of the *pendejo*.[30] A pendejo, according to his peers, is simply a person who has something that others lack. You hear this definition on the street when someone says, "Did you see that car that that pendejo has?" or "Did you see the gorgeous woman that that pendejo is with?" In this manner, he transfers his frustration, turning the world upside-down, in which it is the fools who are driving the nice cars, are with beautiful women, or have political power. There are two aspects used to destroy the presidential image to brand him as pendejo: one is the censorship that qualifies his accomplishments, and the other is jealousy. Surely, both are part of the reasoning that motivated the following joke told at the end of Miguel de la Madrid's tenure in government:[31]

> A man arrives at Los Pinos [the presidential residency].
>
> He knocks on the door, and when it is opened, he says, "I'm here for the job of president that they are offering."
>
> The surprised doorman says, "*What* do you want?"
>
> "I am here for the job of president that is being offered," repeats the man.
>
> "Just a minute," says the doorman. "Are you a *pendejo*, or what?"
>
> "Why? Is that a prerequisite?"

Many authors agree that the Mexican lies. Lies are an innate practice of the daily activities in the country. De Mora (1985) believes that this, in Mexico, "is a game of understood values: lies are told, everybody knows that they are lies, but everybody—and especially the media—proceed as if they were the truth." The entrepreneur lies when he pays his taxes, the worker lies when he doesn't complete his job, the bureaucrat and the politician lie nearly systematically—the country seems to be covered in a dynamic of lies.[32]

"The average Mexican is a liar by vocation. He doesn't consider the lie as an embarrassing act. [. . .] He lies continually. He practices it as a sport. He enjoys lies. Furthermore, he specializes in inventing enormous exorbitant ones in order to hide insignificant details. And when he is caught in a lie he invents a second one, even more complicated and unlikely in order to cover the first one" (Morones, 1980:65).

There is a joke in Mexico that is so common I call it a saying:

> Which are the three lies of the Mexican?
>
> "I'll pay you tomorrow," "It's not going to hurt," and "We'll get married soon."

This mockery rebels against trust. It puts into doubt the *palabra de honor* ("word of honor")—so important to the functioning of the system—and destroys even the basic premise of the opportune payment of commercial transactions or loans. Perhaps this would be a world in which a notary public must certify practically all important commercial or credit transactions. On the other hand, in this world there would be no responsibility regarding sexual relationships and their reproductive consequences. The promise that there won't be any pain refers to deflowering, and the reference to the marital pledge is the argument used by a man at the beginning of a relationship. In a Catholic society such as the Mexican one, the above three lies exist throughout society's moral values. A chauvinist principle says that for a man to be a man, he must deflower a woman; nevertheless, he must marry only a virgin. This is yet another situation with no way out for a man, morally speaking. When a man lies to a woman in order to deflower her, he fools her and the man who will want to marry her (thinking her a virgin)—thus possibly destroying the life of that woman and the man who might want her as a wife. Thinking about this sets us up for Paz's (1986:21–22) statement that "the Mexican lies in order to fantasize, out of desperation or to better his sordid life." Francisco Zarco's lapidary phrase (cited in Solares, 2005:175) seems to express the idea without beating around the bush: "In Mexico all that is authentic and noble is weak and ephemeral. The only thing that lasts is the power of the lie."

The lie is part of the mechanics of social interaction, but it ends up imposing itself as a general factor that affects activities that, by definition, should be based on trust—the assumption of truth. Lomas (1975:50) adds to this conversation:

> The avowed use of the lie is not only assumed to exist, but rather, it is considered basic and necessary to the functioning of professions. We have the example of the legal profession, which in our country represents the biggest juggling of the consistent use of the lie in multiple and diverse forms. There is the lie between the lawyer and his clients, between clients and their lawyers, between lawyers and judges or stockbrokers and vice versa, et cetera.

Carlos Monsiváis, on one occasion, defined lawyers as the professionals who quickly forget the one book they've read (referring to the Constitution). This reveals a very serious outlook if we take into consideration that after the 1940s, Mexico began to be governed by lawyers[33]—who haven't lost their preeminence, though they haven't been elected to the presidency since 1982.[34]

The fact that the country was governed by lawyers for such a lengthy period of time has two explanations: (1) given the condition of the lying Mexican, a union remains in power even though, as Lomas states, it has made the lie his profession, or he has used the union to victimize the public; (2) the prolonged dominion of lawyers helped institute the lie as an everyday practice. As a result of this situation, the political joke is desired because it unmasks the lie and challenges the base of power based on it.

The Mexican lives imprisoned in a world of constant mistrust, jealousy, and envy. He mistrusts others' virtue, perhaps because he has none. And of course he mistrusts women for the same reasons—he is jealously watchful of what she may have done before meeting him. He requires chastity and innocence, which he desires her to have guarded for him like a treasure, even when he has already embarked on a crusade to deflower a long list of women to affirm himself as a man, or better yet, as a macho man. Or he may even have led a life of complete dissipation. And take all of this into account without questioning women's rights—because in Mexico, these are still subject to debate.

The Mexican holds a grudge. Lomas says (1975:20):

> The Mexican is one of the most rancorous individuals on the planet. Sometimes he seems to forget the offenses but he remembers better than an elephant. The Mexican finds it nearly impossible to forgive the Spaniards, because he remembers the Mexican conquest as if it had been yesterday.[35]

More than a decade after Lomas wrote this line, González and Ronfedlt (1986:30) comment:

> The rematch is a concept present in all cultures, but seems to prevail in Arab and Latin cultures, maybe in part due to the great importance these cultures place on pride, respect, and dignity and their relationship with justice and injustice.

Some authors (Ramos, 1934; Díaz Guerrero, 1961; Linares, 1976) think that the Mexican suffers from an inferiority complex, which is evident when he attains positions of authority and becomes aggressive, abusive, and intolerant. The moment that he puts on a uniform, he feels he has power, and he abuses it. The following anecdote[36] shows this argument (Linares, 1976:56):

> On one occasion, an automobile that was carrying the congressman Francisco Galindo Ochoa parked momentarily on the street of San Juan de Letrán. In the car there were the generals Rodolfo Sánchez Taboada and Gabriel Leyva Velázquez, as well as the congressman Teófilo Borunda.

At that moment, a traffic policeman arrived and said to Galindo Ochoa, "Hey, friend, can you see that you are not stopped well?"

He responded, "You think I'm not stopped well? Look at the general"—and he pointed at Sánchez Taboada. "He's president of the PRI, and this other man"—he pointed to general Leyva Velázquez—"is the governor of Sinaloa. And this one," he said as he took Borunda by the arm, "is the next governor of Chihuahua. And I'm warning you, I'm a federal congressman. So, it looks like the one who is poorly stopped is you, idiot."

Note that in this anecdote, "stopped" refers both to being parked and to being in a powerful political position.

The Mexican likes to pretend that he is powerful. Nothing is worse for the Mexican than confronting another Mexican who carries some sort of credential, be it that of a reporter or of a policeman, or even that of an aide to a congressman—whether the credential be real or fake, because even fake credentials open doors in Mexico.[37] Certainly, even carrying a business card showing one to be somebody influential works. A sociologist friend of mine, who has now turned into a businessman, told me that at the beginning of each presidential period he writes to the president—and the president invariably responds. Even though the content of each letter may be irrelevant, this friend frames the letter from the current president and hangs it in his office. This has yielded much business because inspectors get scared when they see the presidential seal on a letter hanging on the wall. Nevertheless, there's something else that is important, and that is that there is always someone more influential than oneself. Thus, in the Mexican political culture, bad luck is always possible in the threat of one man encountering a different man with more influence than he has.

The Mexican takes hold of power and influence over his close friends and acquaintances as if he truly *possessed* these people—and he does this, of course, with the very clear intention of benefiting himself by committing excesses. There is an anecdote in which a viceroy does a favor for a petitioner. The petitioner says, "Mister, when you go to your office, you always pass by a certain street. The only thing I ask is that if you see me there, you acknowledge me with a wave of the hand." The viceroy accepts, and every day when he passes by that street, he sees the man and he waves at him from his carriage. Very soon the man becomes rich because the people think he is in the viceroy's favor.[38] In the political milieu, it is known that photographers take pictures of politicians who are close to the president and sell those photographs to the people photographed; these people hang them in their offices to give the illusion that they are close to the head of state.

Even when Mexicans abuse power, in the people's mind, the police are the ones who are the most abusive people in power. For this reason, the majority of jokes about powerful people abusing their influence have to do with the police. Here is an example:

> There was once an international contest among law enforcement agencies, the point of which was to see which agency could find a rabbit in the least amount of time. When it was the FBI's turn, the group of men went out into a field, and ten hours later they came back with a rabbit. Then the KGB went out and came back with a rabbit in twenty-four hours. Finally, the Mexican police came back in only thirty minutes—but with a dog.
>
> The contest judges were perplexed about the dog . . . until they heard it say, "Yes, I'm a rabbit, but please stop beating me."

We have mentioned the impact that urbanization has had on political humor and political culture. Mexican society has urbanized quickly. The rural population went from 64 percent in 1940 to 28.7 per cent in 1990 (Lorey, 1993:22, table S100). Between these years, nearly all of the sixty-five most important cities of the country grew at a faster pace than the rest of the population (Schmidt, 1986: appendix I). The relationship between the urban and rural populations has inverted in only forty years, turning the country into a predominantly urban one in which information is shared more often—but which also has more problems. In this situation, the self-employed Mexican peasant has no choice but to earn his wages and suffer the rigors of discipline, real time, and time as it is interpreted by the boss. The understanding of influence is modified, since the individual has to confront these changes daily.

Migration patterns propelled by social networks (Lomnitz, 1987) create points of arrival to cities, and though there are proven petitioners that assist recent relatively well-off immigrants with work and shelter in these cities, migration patterns also show channels for aid to the poor. This has promoted urban growth without destabilizing the system, and it has also contributed to the reproduction and preservation of political culture.

Paradoxically, Mexico has become very urbanized in one generation, creating for itself a hybrid society in which many of the old rural values remain intact, combined with the new needs of modernity. The recently urbanized segment of the population has great expectations, which, without being grandiose, are new for the political system. These "new" Mexicans are rural in many senses, but their life's requirements are urban. One of these urban requirements is the political life; this fact has brought forth a new political culture that mixes old and new political values and reformulates others, such as loyalty. While paternalism doesn't disappear, it's manifested differently—for example, it's not the same thing to obey a labor union president as it to obey a tribal chief (cacique). For the immigrant, there is a modification of the elite, and consequently the creation of a new subordinating relationship.

Throughout the process of economic and social maturity in Mexico, there also occurred a political change regarding values. We may see one example of this attitude change in the social response to the earthquake of 1985, in Mexico City, when the government became immobilized and the first to react were the ex-guerilla groups, which taught society a lesson regarding solidarity and a sense of community. We must also consider that the expectations and experiences of those newly arrived were added to the frustrations of those already used to urban life. When immigrants prosper and become acculturated to urban values and participate in the disdain for politics, abstaining from voting and eventually taking part in the political humor of their urban surroundings, they begin to overcome their fear of the government. The continuance of this phenomenon could be one of the greatest indicators of the future political culture, resulting in one of the greatest challenges of the Mexican political system.

The Mexican and Power

The Mexican respects and fears, power, and authority. His figurative mother (La Malinche, the native mistress of Cortés considered the mother of the first mestizo) supposedly gave in to the wishes of the conquistadors, and the Mexican lost his figurative father when Moctezuma was defeated. In modern times, Mexicans in rural areas continue to lose their fathers, since men are increasingly abandoning their conjugal homes in search of better economic opportunities, including foreign ones. This results in the absence of a paternal role model. The mother is very important because she takes care of the family, but the absence of the father causes a chauvinistic response that sets Mexicans against their mothers and power. When a leader appears, he fills the place of the father, and easily becomes a guide. The need for a father figure is understood by politicians, and instead of filling in for that father in a constructive process, politicians may use the situation as a basis for the abuse of power. For this reason, the lack of a stable and functional family and the feeling of a nonexistent primordial father leads to the Mexican's rejection of all forms of power.[39] This is—or may be seen as—reflected in his daily behavior: contempt for the boss, irresponsibility at work, and a general negligence and lack of discipline. The following segment exemplifies an employer's view of the "work ethic" of Mexicans (Salgado, 1986a:13):

> When Johnny Come Lately went to see the office manager where he "worked" and demanded a raise in pay, he received the following response:
>
> "Look, Mr. Lately, the year has 365 days, out of which you theoretically work only eight hours a day, or a third of that time, which means 122 days of actual *labor.* Out of this take 52 Sundays, and this leaves 70 days of real work. From this you also have to subtract 25 weekday holidays, which leaves a balance of 45 active days. Then, from these you must subtract 20 vacation days, which leaves 25 workdays. From these, take out 10 days that you don't work because of sickness, or because your grandmother died, or because of any number of crude reasons (such as you being hungover). In addition to all of this, you also have personal matters for which you ask for 10 days off to tend to. There are 5 workdays left, out of which you lose 3 due to tardiness, going to the bathroom, going to the water cooler, making jokes, laughing at jokes, making telephone calls, gossiping with your coworkers, or getting a visitor here and there—among other things.
>
> "So, my good friend, for only two days of supposedly prolific and creative work, you dare come and ask me for a raise, a promotion, and additional benefits?"
>
> "Wow boss," said Johnny. "Looking at it that way . . . you name how much I have to give back to the company."

Naturally, the boss is one of the targets when Mexicans confront power through humor. Griselda Álvarez (1992:70), the first woman governor of Mexico, said, "Whoever makes up jokes uncover their irony by disrespecting the boss, to devalue him, specifically because our systematic rebelliousness against authority is an essential part of our way of being."

Salgado (1986:9) adds: "Let's make reference to the classic boss, the bald one with the look of a fierce dog, forever a grouch, the one who waits, watch in hand, at the office door." Better yet is to let humor exemplify the image that Mexicans have of the boss, which is not at all pretty, as this humorous poem shows:

"The Boss"
If he is friendly, he is a common politician.
If he is quiet, he is a first-class petulant.
If he makes quick decisions, he is arbitrary.
If he is slow in his decisions, he is stupid.
If he makes plans, he is like a vulture.
If he doesn't plan, with this guy we go straight to bankruptcy.
If he tries to simplify paperwork, he is an enemy of the system.
If he adjusts to the formula, he is a simple bureaucrat.
If he requests big budgets, he is a big spender.
If he requests a small budget, he is an insect who doesn't think big.
If he is old, he is out of touch with reality.
If he is young, the squirt lacks experience.
If he is late, he is ungratefully taking advantage of his position.
If he routinely arrives early, he's a damned slave.
If everything is in order, he's a dictator, the ass.
If everything goes wrong, he is a worthless incompetent.
If he agrees with his fellows, he needs new ideas.
If he doesn't gather the group, he doesn't appreciate the group effort.
If he talks a lot with his superior, he's a kiss-up.
If he is seldom seen, he is in disgrace.
If he goes out on assignment, he is an abusive wanderer.
If he doesn't go out on assignment, he prefers to stay to annoy me.
If he requires more personnel, he wants to make himself seem important.
If he doesn't require more personnel, he is stuffing us with work, the scoundrel.
If he has an attractive secretary, he is bastardly hogging her.
If she is ugly, he should take that fright home.
If he takes work home, he wants to impress.
If he doesn't take work home, he has time on his hands and he has too much fun.
If he is successful, it is pure luck and he exploits us.
If he fails, it makes sense, no matter how much he bugged us.
If he asks us to change, he is a damn slave driver.
If he can stand us, this, buddy, is a dumbass.

When the rejection of the boss is applied to politics in Mexico, its focus is the president, because he is the country's topmost person of political authority. The Mexican attacks local authorities as well, and has an attitude of respect and fear toward other politicians, because he views them as power factors.

The president is power, and in an authoritarian system such as Mexico's, he is the source of good and bad. He helps build or destroy careers. The Mexican tendency to reject power and politics can be explained by circumstances of bad luck, yet this tendency often puts him in political situations from which there is no easy way out. Thus, always before him is the government as the cause and effect of his bad situation.

The Mexican Revolution may be taken into consideration within this context. The current government, which defines itself as the continuation of the revolution, is paradoxically synonymous with the failure of the revolution, since it hasn't delivered on promised benefits.[40] If someone tried to defend the government by emphasizing the benefits the revolution did cause, that person would actually only be able to highlight injustice and the way it is handed out.

In the repertoire of the Mexican's complaints, the government is always the main target, with few opportunities to vindicate it. Political jokes are one of the only sure and pleasant instruments with which to remain at an even keel with the government and with politicians.

Part of the Mexican's complaint is that political culture follows a blind loyalty to those in superior positions, which causes great abuse of power. Remember the joke about the earthquake in chapter 1 and read the following joke, which can be considered sophomoric and which illustrates the unconditional quality mentioned:

> The head of an insane asylum says to his assistant that three crazy people have escaped and they need to be caught.
>
> The next day, he calls his assistant and asks, "What happened with the three crazies?"
>
> The helper responds, "We blew it, sir."
>
> "Why?"
>
> "Because I thought there were thirty-three and they are already all inside."

One of the mechanisms used by politicians to distance themselves from society consists of the creation of symbols and of politicians' own visual and verbal language. The Mexican detests the pompous attitude with which politicians present daily activities; therefore, he acts in every way possible against the politicians' ostentatious language, thereby allegorically diminishing the excesses of power. But the Mexican citizen lacks a democratic credo, which could reduce the crude reality of the imposition of power, so he turns to humor in order to disguise this reality and overcome the frustration derived from his indefensible relationship with politicians. Political jokes do their part when they destroy the image of these politicians. Even as a simulation, the joke is a powerful instrument to tell the truth

In Mexico, with or without justice, the political system and the citizen have both been characterized as corrupt[41] and as liars. The following joke shows the social opinion regarding corruption—that some politicians regard it as positive:

> The president sends one of his trusted colleagues to the first world championship of corruption.
>
> The colleague calls him on the telephone and says, "I have good news, Mr. President—we ended up in second place."
>
> "That's not good news," the president responds.
>
> "Well, we were in first place," says the colleague wistfully, "but at least we arranged to end up in second."

It is almost routine for politicians to enshroud the political process in mystery and secrecy, ignoring society and creating a pattern that keeps feeding the political system. It's precisely when the process is kept secret that social action by citizens in the dark is no longer significant. Society has very few ways in which to influence the fundamental decisions about which politicians have power because political parties have already secretly determined their positions.

The process of systematic exclusion thus explains why society can't get involved in politics and why the absentee electoral rate is so elevated. As our readers have probably seen, it all also explains clientelism, paternalism, and corruption. Equal opportunity exists only as a myth.

Regarding the mystery of politics, Mexicans fantasize about the nomination process of the candidates, perhaps because they do not try to penetrate the shroud encircling the process by which the PRI chooses its presidential candidate. This process has been crucial in Mexican politics, being that from the 1920s until 1994 the candidate from this party invariably won the election—his nomination was, in essence and in fact, the designation of a new president.

Humor helps Mexicans make obvious what everybody imagines, simultaneously helping the Mexican overcome the frustration caused by not knowing how the nomination of this semi-God—who will govern his country for six years—works. The following anecdote attempts to expose this mystery (Homero, 1974:83–84):

Lázaro Cárdenas and Plutarco Elías Calles run into each other.

Calles says to Cárdenas, "We have focused on you to become the president of the republic by virtue of your solid revolutionary heritage [*cepa revolucionaria*]."

Cárdenas, with an imperturbable expression, responds, "Pardon my ignorance, General— what is 'heritage [*cepa*]'"?

Calles is surprised by the question and, scratching his head, says, "Well, *cepa* is . . . *¿Sepa la tiznada?* [Who the hell knows?] The important thing is that you will be the next president of Mexico."

Actually, until the end of the twentieth century, Mexican society was apparently aware that no matter how it voted, the PRI candidate would be president. Citizens were called to vote only after the crucial nomination had been made. And the party politicians, apparently not satisfied even with this basic farce, tried to disguise it by turning the electoral process into an extremely serious ritual. Citizens confronted the seriousness of the elections—and the politicians' insult to their collective intelligence—with humorous mockery of their own:

A Mexican and an American show off to each other about their respective political systems.

The American says, "Our electoral system is so advanced that we know who won the presidential election within just 24 hours of voting's culmination."

The Mexican responds, "And so what? Our system is much better. We know who's going to be president a year beforehand."

In the political environment, jokes tell the truth because in presenting subjects plainly, they annihilate the lies inherent in politics—even while Mexican citizens lie daily.

At this point in our analysis, it is worthwhile to ask why the Mexican looks for ethical behavior in politics while he avoids it in his everyday life. The answer is that this contradiction is derived from his rejection of power rather than from what he thinks he can possibly gain from telling a lie.

Laughter as a Remedy

We began this chapter discussing the way that Mexican people laugh about politics and tragedy as a defense mechanism. What we have found is that political strife is a true tragedy for Mexicans, and in its face they have turned their aggression, dissatisfaction, desire for revenge, and resentment into a critique against power that combines passivity and humor.

As we have suggested, politics can be tragic for Mexicans both literally—by affecting their physical lives—and emotionally—because, while they know politics as a means toward mobility, prestige, and the acquisition of wealth, they also know that there is no equal access to politics. Power—and specifically political power—has turned into a type of family inheritance (Schmidt and Gil 1990; Schmidt, 1991a; Gil, Schmidt, and Castro, 1993), where loyalty comes out of the revolutionary family (Alcántara, 2000)—*la familia revolucionaria,* which emerged in the politics of the 1920s. By the 1980s, the control of power was clearly a question of endogamy: the cabinet of Miguel de la Madrid included the descendants of many politicians, including his successor—and of the six politicians that the PRI presented as pre-candidates for the 1988 candidacy, three were offspring of politicians; of the six candidates, two were offspring of politicians, and one was the son of an ex-president. Also, as we have suggested, the elite themselves form a kind of family simply through their exclusive knowledge of politics. Like any Latin American family, it is a closed unit (Adler and Pérez, 1987), which makes Mexicans who are not a part of the elite feel alienated and underrepresented by their leaders. Thus, while politicians may frequently turn to democratic discourse to fight this breach in democracy and representation, society itself applies what is possibly its only recourse, *laughing at politicians*.

Nowadays, Mexico confronts an elite that has access to the good life (*la buena vida*): the best schools in the world, travel without limit, and ample material comforts. The advantages enjoyed by this select group are the result of a country's terrible distribution of economic rewards and a monopoly on political opportunity. Normally, it is expected that politics will be a means of social mobility, that even when it doesn't produce wealth, it rewards with social gain, which produces prestige and recognition, and therefore, by association, possible wealth. But in Mexico, the doors are normally closed to the common Mexican, and "miracles" like gaining these elite privileges occur only in soap operas—not in real life. In modern Mexico, another Benito Juárez[42] is not only a fantasy, but also possibly an impossible feat (see this book's postscript regarding López Obrador).

The segment of the elite that protests against the privileges of politics and their families does believe that these are unmerited, since they are obtained by means of political corruption such as that via the improper handling of public funds or an unacceptable route to the world of recognitions.

This group's supposed refusal to accept sharing said privileges implies that Mexicans should ascend the social ladder as a result of public posts. This particular segment of the elite degrades the political system with jokes and mockery as protest against corruption and the abuse of power, even though it may benefit from that same corruption.[43] The joke is its best instrument for opposition because it doesn't want to destroy the political system—only to criticize it so that politicians understand that corrections are expected. The political joke, with the reduced risk it imparts through anonymity, offers the most secure form of political opposition in a society where repression prevails. Since the economic elite is an accomplice of politicians, it is obvious that it doesn't want to ruin its business nor its privilege, especially in a country like Mexico that has maintained a closed system for so long, to protect entrepreneurs who have often taken politicians as silent partners. Furthermore, the joke offers pleasure under difficult circumstances. In this way, the economic elite may abuse power and selfishly use any opportunity to exploit the system.

Politics and power have created a rationale of impunity in Mexico, where the powerful may protect each other in order to commit their excesses and occasionally make fun of society. With knowledge of these circumstances, we needn't be surprised regarding society's angry and stupefied reaction when President José López Portillo named his son as undersecretary (noting that this was his favorite act of nepotism). He chose one of his sisters as his private secretary and named another sister the general manger of the country's radio, television, and cinematography—as well as naming one of his cousins as another undersecretary. Finally, though he may not have wanted this action to be seen as sarcastic, he named one of his childhood friends, El Negro Durazo (of questionable reputation) as chief of police of the Federal District. The scandalous rumors of corruption regarding all these individuals' appointments circulated very rapidly. As a result, subsequent jokes about López Portillo were very pointed, as we will discover in more detail in chapter 5. The traffic of influence reinforces the dominant political system with impunity because, as we've seen, the powerful abuse their power, making the average individual feel completely unprotected and forcing him to search for some sort of balance.

Wisely, perhaps, the Mexican thus mistrusts the justice system and practically evades the legal process. He prefers to fix problems by means of morally questionable intermediaries called "coyotes," who can resolve things rapidly.[44] Collective Mexican wisdom dictates that everything and everyone has a price; the problem is taking care of each price as necessary without serious ethical or other consequences. As Lomas asserts, "The ultimate in bad luck for a Mexican who has committed a misdemeanor is to offer a *mordida* ["bribe"] to a decent man" (1975:54).

Miraculously, even when the Mexican understands the practical value of corruption, he is able to laugh at it and maybe exorcise it from his thoughts. Perhaps he feels less guilty giving than receiving, and for that reason he criticizes officials who spread their hands to get a handout. He knows that corruption makes things easier, though it makes obvious the differences in social status. Though not laudable, corruption *is* an adequate method for getting services or privileges that are difficult to attain if one lacks political weight or the ability to manipulate the established rules. After all, for many, the end justifies the means. Lomas (1975:55) believes that General Calles had a pragmatic political outlook that was reflected in phrases such as, "There is no official or senator who can resist the caress of the general treasurer." This cynicism is rejected by means of jokes.

The attack of political corruption goes hand in hand with the attack of politics in general. The Mexican laughs at both, because he has no other means of fighting against them. In fact, he characterizes politics by using humor. Years ago, there was a sign displayed in the House of Representatives that defined politics as follows:

> Politics is a shitty art,
> Which by my observation alone, is based on
> Offering your ass to the ones on top,
> and giving it in the ass to the ones on the bottom. (Linares 1976:39)

The Mexican laughs at the government and at the president because he is tired of playing the game of Mexican democracy, in which he can say what he wants or expects, and the government simply continues to do what it pleases. It has become saturated with discourse, campaigns, and empty promises while the country deteriorates to no end. Surely the Mexican must suffer a laughing attack when he becomes aware of how bad the situation is and that it will probably only get worse.[45] Furthermore, he will count on the government's help to indeed make it worse in reality.

Mexicans have many reasons to be politically frustrated and few risk-free opportunities to be politically active. They possess a pessimistic mentality within situations that force each one to confront acute social and economic differences. The cliché perception of the Mexican has crossed over the U.S.-Mexico border, making him vulnerable to being cast as a stereotype even in his neighbor to the north. Indeed, a collection of jokes making the rounds in the United States includes ethnic jokes about the Mexican that are in very bad taste and show a few of the prejudiced ways in which Americans view—and ridicule—Mexicans. Here are some examples:

What do you get when you cross a Mexican with an octopus?
I don't know, but it sure picks tomatoes fast with all those arms.

~

Why are scientists breeding Mexicans instead of rats for experiments?
Mexicans multiply faster, and you don't get as attached to them.[46]

~

What do you get when you cross a Mexican with an Italian?
A guy who makes you an offer you can't understand.

In the United States, the Mexican can't help but be discriminated against and be relegated the lowest rung on the social scale;[47] thus, he has no choice but to bear the ridicule. In Mexico, on the other hand, when one laughs at oneself, he disarms others who would criticize him. And this might be one of the few options he has to overcome a traumatic past and an oppressive present. Transgression and humor help him rise above his frustration and stress, as if they really free him from political oppression and from the all-encompassing blanket of political power. And so what better action to take than to laugh at politicians in order to laugh at one's own misfortune?

CHAPTER THREE

The Role of Political Jokes in Mexico

One day on the news they announce that two Parralenses *[people from the city of Parral in the border state of Chihuahua] have shown up dead, shot to death while trying to flee from U.S. customs officials. The Mayor of* Parral *sees the news during his early breakfast, at 11:30 a.m., while trying to get over a horrible hangover with very spicy* chilaquiles *[a special tortilla dish] and a very cold beer.*

He leaves his house in a fury and skidding he arrives at town hall and he says to his secretary:

"Mr. Secretary, get a hold of the Pentagon immediately."

"Where, Mr. Mayor?"

"The Pentagon, dummy! Those damn gringos are going to pay for what they did to our people."

The secretary gets a hold of the Pentagon and asks to speak to the secretary of war of the United States, telling him that the mayor of San Francisco del Oro, Parral, is on the line:

"Listen to me, you son of a bitch, I'm calling to let you know that the independent and sovereign municipality of Parral, Chihuahua declares war against the United States for the death of our fellow citizens who were assassinated by your customs officers."

"Excuse me, I don't understand, who's calling?"

"Don't play dumb, you asshole, the elected Mayor of Parral says you're going to go to hell, you assholes."

"Excuse me, well, where's Parral? I don't know what you're talking about."

"Look, you son of a bitch, don't play dumb. I know that you have CIA agents infiltrating my government to destabilize me. Parral, if you don't remember, is south of the capital of Chihuahua, Mexico."

"Oh, you don't say. So you're declaring war?"

"Yes, asshole. And don't chicken out. We're going to beat the hell out of you."

"Excuse me, do you know to whom you're talking?"

"You want to make me mad, asshole?"

"Do you know that you're declaring war against the most powerful nation in the world?"

"Well, you son of a bitch, we don't give a shit, asshole. We're going to beat the shit out of you."

"Oh yeah? You have an army?"

"Well, of course, we have the one from town hall that already has policemen on bicycles and some other buddies who deal with bud; they have their guns, but we don't need more asshole. We're men, asshole, and you're going to go to hell this time."

"Well . . . you do know that the United States of America, in less than three hours, can launch a thousand missiles, send three hundred combat and bomber airplanes over there, seven hundred armed helicopters, and in addition, three hundred thousand soldiers supported by ten divisions of tanks and four of heavy artillery?"

"Oh shit, excuse me, how many soldiers did you say?"

"Three hundred thousand, what do you think?"

"Oh shit, wait a sec, I'll call you right back."

A little while later the phone rings again at the Pentagon:

"Well, listen, you know, we give up."

"Didn't you say you were very manly?"

"We are men, you asshole. It's just that they cut our budget, the harvest hasn't been very good. Only a little corn sprouted and with the drought some cows died and there are no more hens, so how the hell are we going to feed the three hundred thousand prisoner soldiers that we're going to take? But fuck you anyway!"

Introduction

If one analyzes the different forms of political humor in Mexico, one finds that jokes and cartoons are predominant. In June 2004, in Mexico City, the Consulta Mitofsky found that 38.6 percent of those surveyed remembered having heard a political joke in the recent past, and 38.5 percent of the jokes they heard were about Fox. Jokes are created and adjusted constantly, even though some disappear when the politicians they involve leave the limelight; occasionally, these jokes are revived and adapted to fit other politicians.

There are some jokes that last longer than others because they have to do with certain "appropriate" themes, and this might be true for the political joke. Schutz (1977:26) says, regarding the cycle of political humor, "Political humor has something of the nature of folklore; the same joke will appear in different forms with different characters over the years, but with the same principle." The joke assures itself a lengthy existence and is recycled, recreated, and adapted to new politicians because they can't keep from making the same mistakes as their predecessors. Some jokes are adapted and converted into political jokes; others are made up specifically for a certain character and disappear along with him. Consider the following versions of the same joke (here, all appearing together):

> It is said that Cárdenas (1934–1940) receives the Nobel Prize for mathematics because he divides land, multiplies problems and subtracts in the capital. Forty years later, Echeverría (1970–1976) received the Nobel Prize for chemistry for making *crap out of the Peso*. Some years later, López Portillo (1976–1982) received three Nobel Prizes: one for physics because he made the Peso float, one for chemistry because he made crap out of the Peso, and one in biology for turning man into a dog.[1]

The political joke is a communicative metaphor in which society tells the government what bothers it, with the hopes of fixing what is ailing. When a joke says that the president is an asshole, it doesn't mean anything against the president personally; rather, the joke truly expresses disagreement with a decision or decisions he has made. When a joke is about the government, it implies a double challenge: first, for the government to listen to society's complaints in an area of discourse outside the conventional; and second, for the government to correctly interpret its messages. It is easy to fall into the paranoia of Echeverría, who believed that jokes were made up by the Grupo Monterrey—which, by the way, had good reason to be offended due to the lack of presidential warning regarding the possible kidnapping of Eugenio Garza Sada, a kidnapping that culminated with his assassination. That doesn't imply that entrepreneurs use humor as an instrument for political struggle, though they do use it to undermine the government.[2] This is congruent with the centralization of power and a political culture that assumes that there lies somebody powerful behind all actions. The president concentrates political decisions, which doesn't exclude the possibility of someone making up jokes to destroy his image. Within this paradigm, there doesn't seem to exist the option of society acting spontaneously. But reality brings us that option and other surprises, because what is true is that in the underground, the elite includes those who submit to political power *and* those who criticize the president—which shows, among other things, that we can't approach the study of the elite as if it were an isolated factor.

Political jokes in general line up against political power, distilling what irritates society regarding a specific presidential tenure. In the case of Mexico, the main irritation is the concentration of presidential power, an irritation that is perceived as part of the Mexican's anti-authoritarian and anti-power sentiments. These sentiments focus on specific subjects; with Cárdenas, for example, they were his economic program, his social reforms (Teichman, 1988:32), and his agrarian politics. According to official history, he has been greatly credited for the benefits peasants received, but what has never been formally recognized is the great trouble caused by the handout of lands by Cárdenas. However, humor *does not* demonstrate it; in addition to the Nobel Prize joke mentioned earlier, see the following example:

> The famous maxim about Benito Juárez [*El respeto al derecho ajeno es la paz*—"Peace is respect for the other's rights"] interpreted by Lázaro Cárdenas has remained like this: "*Respeto por lo ajeno es la reforma agraria.* [Respect for what's not yours is the agrarian handout.]" (Coronado, 1984:143)

Political jokes that fall out of circulation because they were created to attack certain dated decisions may re-emerge from the collective memory when another president or his government commits the same excesses or errors.

Regarding another important form of humor—the cartoon—Pruneda (1958:12) notes:

> When the cartoon presents firmly our protests, it performs a social function of power and efficiency of nearly limitless action. Under that definition, the art in which we are involved has as its primary objective, in the peoples, which have suffered conquest and domination, which have lived oppressed or enslaved for centuries, such as ours, lash out against iniquity, without pity show the injustice, making fun of the defects of the mark of the limp of the tyrants and the surrender of the prevaricators.

Regarding this, García Cantú (1976:7–8) said, "The cartoon was a response toward servility, fear or degradation; the revenge of a defenseless people, unarmed and without judges. The cartoon was, and has been, in our country a place of refuge." Just as the joke can become a reality when the public tires of the regime.

During a good part of the nineteenth century, the cartoon in Mexico was a form of opposition, and the cartoonists ended up paying with their lives for their intrepid attack of the dictator Porfirio Díaz, as was the case with Jesús Martínez Carrión, who contracted typhus while in the jail of Belén in Mexico City. Nevertheless, the cartoon was also an instrument used by politicians who launched humoristic publications in which they settle accounts among themselves. This was the case during the confrontation between Bernardo Reyes and Ives Limantur, as well as between other individuals and groups, such as the *científicos* and Francisco I. Madero (Pruneda, 1958).

Other humoristic expressions, such as comic poetry,[3] were lost because they were written as graffiti in bathrooms or on walls and ended up erased without ever having been recorded. Nicknames also fell into oblivion when people faced new politicians with whom to struggle. Anagrams and acronyms also passed on to a better life since Calles and Obregón seem to no longer exist. There is no doubt that the intractable passage of time does what it does—among other things, it erases social expressions.

It hasn't done so with epigrams, however, which still appear daily in Mexican newspapers. Likewise, religious parodies still exist in Mexico—I have collected them since 1970, and even though they have surely existed in the past in other countries, I haven't found examples in the literature. Being extremely long, these parodies lose the comic effect of shorter humor pieces like the joke, and—while provoking notoriety in their protagonist, they hold risks, which was no small thing in a country dominated by caciques, militarists, and even a dictator, all aggravated by the moral and political weight of the church and the long association between power and the religious hierarchy.

It must be considered that with the modernization of forms of communication, humor has been modified regarding the speed with which it is disseminated, its symbolic language, and its social accessibility. Hypothetically, a portion of the population that normally didn't participate in humor, due to that population's lack of certain habits, might now access it; it may now be the case that jokes and cartoons are transmitted through the Internet and are usually disseminated by young people, though it is assumed that they don't read newspapers in which such cartoons are published. But let us move on from the notion that the Internet has been able to break many of the former chains of censorship in more modern times (see a thought regarding this means of communication in the light of the 2006 elections in the postscript).

In the nineteenth century, written media was predominant. Here, epigrams, posters, anagrams, and other forms taken by humorous commentary were abundant in print. This reflected that originally, the social target of the middle class and its "clientele" was basically made up of the literate population. It can't be denied that since many commentaries were expressed on walls, the illiterate also had access to them (in chapter 1, I have already debated regarding the notion of the revolutionary potential of cartoons)—but perhaps with a lesser impact than is commonly believed.

By the twentieth century, oral means of communication became more common—they circulated more and promised less. Electronic means of communication have taken the place of graphic ones. Radio and television penetrate every social level, subjecting their messages to a different game of political and ideological mediation, including a complex relationship with the government. In the case of television, the government renews concessions with a certain frequency, and in the case of both television and radio, it manages to create public contracts whose weight is fundamental for the economic viability of radio and television companies. The paradox is that, apparently, there is more liberty—that is, as we suggested, there is much more penetration throughout different social groups—yet in exchange, these forms of communication seem to be more controlled by the government than common modes of communication were in the nineteenth century.

Today, the majority of Mexicans read little—neither books nor newspapers. The level of *functional* illiteracy is still high in Mexico (many people who at one time learned to read and write have become functional illiterates), and the average level of education is low. The few dissident publications are still restricted to the educated portion of the population, and faced with the electronic era, they have very few opportunities of reaching the masses. The political consequence is that we have an unequal competence between electronic means, which are heavily controlled by the government and which are in the possession of only a few families who can negotiate political opinion and cover the news—or even the lack of it. Thus we have censored media, even when graphic, when communicating with marginalized groups; and even though these means are more open, they have a very limited substantial impact.[4] As opposed to the rest of society, political jokes have been innovators; they have rapidly escaped censorship and motivate more participation, though they haven't pushed the system toward democracy nor motivated or stimulated open or conventional political participation.

The joke is the most prolific and long-lived humoristic form because it possesses several advantages. First, it is easy to transmit; it is anonymous, and it functions as an instrument of malleable and adaptable political opinion. Second, it answers to natural Mexican fatalism; the Mexican is irreverent and laughs easily at all types of subjects. Third, Mexicans prefer using indirect forms of expression to struggle against authority and political power, a pattern that the government has contributed to. It is important that, after more than seventy years of the PRI government,[5] the Mexican hasn't lost his sense of humor! Perhaps we should give credit to the PRI as the catalyst for the Mexican to keep laughing—better yet, perhaps we should also recognize the PAN and the other political parties for helping keep the spirit of laughter alive.

Humor and Nationalism

It has become popular to think that globalization encourages nationalism to the point that nationalism might atomize a society. One region whose story might foster this idea is the Balkan Peninsula, though we must point out that those countries are fragmented probably because the totalitarian cement that bonded them was so fragile that they fell apart at the first opportunity. Mexico has seen itself attacked by economic forces, which don't fragment it but rather relatively weaken it; poverty was chosen as having comparative advantages over fragmentation. And if economic weakness attracted many businesses that used cheap manual labor, it also sped up the exit of the workforce—to the degree that in the 1990s, an estimated 800,000 people emigrated annually (this number went down to 400,000 in the 2000s). It might be suggested that nationalistic love ended, and people abandoned the motherland in search of opportunities that this system could not provide.

The analysis of Mexican political humor can lead us to doubt the strength of nationalism. Nationality, in its legal sense, can be considered to refer to one's birth in a certain country or the country of which one wants to become a citizen. But in its emotional or value-oriented dimension, it involves identification with national symbols, institutions, political hierarchy, and social and political norms and values.

The destruction of Mexico's indigenous population after the European conquest was followed by a turbulent period that made difficult the creation of a new nation. Some scholars think that the mestizo society generated the birth of the Mexican nation (Basave, 1992), which is actually undeniable. However, it is wise to look at the emotional factor that was created by the traumatic inheritance of the Spanish conquest. An example is the vision of the Spanish conquerors defeating the great Aztec civilization (seen critically, of course), which caused Mexicans to hate and fear that component in themselves, and for that reason to enclose themselves in a xenophobia that projects the hatred they have for themselves[6] combined with the sensation of defeat felt by the indigenous peoples. We find a hybrid that doesn't ingratiate itself to itself. It's a country full of resentments derived from poorly resolved political disputes, from a system of privileges, vulgar and insulting; of racial and class hatreds; a heavy-footed Mexicanism that leads to excessive screaming of *¡Viva México!* ("Long live Mexico!")—while the Mexican's fellow citizens are assaulted and stepped on. Over and above other curses, the greatest insult in Mexico is *pinche indio* ("dumbass Indian"), which reminds others that perhaps the indigenous person's defeat in the fifteenth century was his fault, just as was the prevalence of the Spaniard in the mixing of the races. Not even the revolutionary discourse of the twentieth century served to bring harmony to the Mexican society. The revolutionary regimes are perceived to be authoritarian and the mestizo culture to be an imposition: the Mexican who hates the past also begins to hate the present and the future.

National values reflect those of the dominant Spanish society. Consequently, Mexicans make fun of these principles by denying the legitimacy of the structure of power. In the 1986 World Cup inaugural ceremony, the president got a reception of screams and whistles, and the audience laughed at the national symbols; the flag is not an untouchable symbol[7] and has even become a target for ridicule:

> "Why do you say that your uncle is a tricolored old guy?"
> "Because his nose is red, his head is white and he has a green butt [meaning 'a dirty old man']."

Political jokes wear down the importance of heroism. We can see this when examining political humor regarding the Mexican-American War of 1847, when the American invading forces captured the Chapultepec castle in Mexico City, center of political power at that time. The castle was heroically defended until the end by a group of young cadets. The official record states that when defeat was imminent, the remaining six young cadets committed suicide. The cadets were so young that they are known as the *niños héroes* ("child heroes"). One of them, faced with the imminent loss of the castle to foreign hands, wrapped himself in the flag and jumped over the wall. Even though he gave up his life to protect the flag, political humor takes away the heroic context from this action.

> They say that the child hero, wrapped up in the flag at the Chapultepec castle, didn't throw himself down, but rather he was pushed.[8]

The merits of the Aztec warriors and the heroic defense of Tenochtitlán are also demolished:

> "Do you know what the meaning of Azteca is?"
> "That when the Spaniards arrived they said to them: *hazte cabrón, hazte cabrón* [move over, asshole]."

This joke affirms the superiority of the Spaniards and degrades the indigenous people. In fact, in Mexico, this manner of speaking denotes derogatory treatment.

Another anecdote refers to the great odyssey of the Aztecs that ended in the founding of Tenochtitlán in the valley of Anáhuac, capital of its kingdom and precursor of Mexico City. The omen that the Aztecs found at the end of their journey is printed on the national emblem: an eagle standing on a cactus devouring a serpent. Humor has given an explanation, saying that here is found the key to national values: the eagle is not devouring the serpent; rather it is biting it (*mordiendo*, "biting," is a play on words, with *morder* also meaning "to bribe") and it is jabbing it with its claw (in Spanish, also slang for pickpocketing).[9] The posture of the eagle on the national flag has changed over the years, and now it is standing in profile. Salgado (1986:32–33) explains that the position of the eagle has changed so that it faces forward because previously the eagle was squatting in order to defecate. This image has penetrated folklore to the degree that when one uses public bathrooms (which in general are very dirty), one squats over the toilet and defecates *de aguilita* ("eagle style").

More recently, the eagle emblem has been used to get even with the government in the case of ex-president Salinas:

> The Salinas family emblem has changed, it is an eagle devouring a maid [play on words—*sirvienta* meaning "maid," *serpiente* meaning "serpent"].

Here, reference is made to the assassination of the Salinas family maid, when Carlitos was a little boy (the subject is discussed further in chapter 4). With an interesting play on words, it is suggested that the ex-president had taken hold of the country to such a degree that the national emblem became that of his family. The other example involves Ernesto Zedillo and Vicente Fox:

> The national emblem was changed, now it is a seal. We're in water up to our necks and we still applaud.

This joke refers to the change that Fox made to the eagle on the flag, which, when trying to stylize the eagle, he cut part of it off, but even more it is an acknowledgement of the difficult situation in the country.

The national anthem has also suffered a humoristic assault. Frequently, the original opening lyrics (*Mexicanos al grito de guerra*, or "Mexicans to the call of war") are modified. I collected the following humorous versions that came out of schools in Mexico City, attended by upper-middle-class students:

> A group of third graders changed the lyrics to:
> "Mexicans to the call of *gorra* [play on words with *Guerra—war*, to *gorra*—literally 'hat' but in slang meaning 'Mexicans to the call of sponging of others at their expense']."
>
> A high school student decided to sing it in Latin:
> "Mexicanus al gritus de guerrus."
>
> Students in second grade sang the following version:
> "Mexicans, louses of war, stole my ham sandwich."
>
> A person from Oaxaca always says:
> "[*Mexicanos changuitos de Guerra*] Mexicans, monkeys of war."

Mexicans make fun of their heroes, degrading the image of those whom they emphasize historically, such as is shown in the following joke:

> Who was the first fireman in Mexico?
> *Bomberito* [play on words replacing his real name Benito, and meaning "Little Fireman"] Juárez.

Benito Juárez is one of the most prominent figures in Mexican history; he is revered because in the nineteenth century, he succeeded in separating church and state with the Laws of Reform. Notwithstanding, the official history has hidden the fact that he had such a proclivity for re-election that many say if he hadn't died of chest angina, he would still be president. During the Echeverría administration, the comedian Manuel El Loco Valdéz used this joke on television, and was punished by the station. His program was suspended, and according to rumor, he was made to pay a fine. When he returned to the air, he commented on his reprimand as follows:

"Who was *Bomberito* ['Little Fireman'] Juárez' helper?"
"Mrs. *Manguerita* [meaning 'Little Hose' (as in fireman's hose) and play on words with Margarita, which was Juárez' wife's name] Maza de Juárez."

When Mexican comedians want to tell political jokes they worry little about fines they may need to pay. It is said that during the 1960s, regarding the famous comedian "Palillo," the police would be waiting next to the stage at his performances to arrest him, while his audience—in a show of solidarity—would throw money to him to pay the fine he'd soon be given (Ramírez, 1987).

The knocking down of heroes involves sarcasm, such as in the joke regarding the child heroes, or such as in the conversation I heard while standing at the foot of Chapultepec Castle in February 1987, between two female middle school students. As they looked up, one of the girls said:

"The kid fell from all the way up there? He got really banged up!"
The other girl answered: "No wonder he killed himself."

These adolescents from Mexico City invalidate the patriotic symbol of the historic defense when they assume not only that the child-hero cadet, instead of jumping, simply fell accidentally, but also that he only died because he was so high up. This comment represents the tearing down of one of the most revered Mexican heroic acts.

The satiric author Marco Antonio Flota (1985) wrote a dictionary of political terms, in which, among others, he pokes fun at revolutionary leader Francisco I. Madero, who in 1910 lead a rebellion against dictator Porfirio Díaz. Madero's motto—which has been adopted as a fundamental principle of the Mexican political system—was, "Effective suffrage, not re-election." Flota presents it in the following manner in his definition of Madero:

Madero: Urinal in a *pulque* [alcoholic beverage derived from the fermentation of a cactus] bar called Effective Suffrage.

Mexicans make fun of the martyrology that seeks to teach about heroism. They also make fun of those who are summoned to give themselves over to a cause, as is shown in the following examples that refer to the last Aztec emperors:

Montezuma fell
Montezuma, from a table

> Montezuma broke
> Montezuma, his head (in Spanish this is a rhyme)

> The Spaniards were burning Cuauhtémoc's feet so that he would divulge the location of the gold, yet he would say nothing. Finally, when the torturer became desperate he told the interpreter to tell Cuauhtémoc that they were going to bring his whole family and that they were going to begin to torture them too. At that moment Cuauhtémoc gave up and revealed where the gold was, telling exactly through what step to enter the pyramid, exactly which pass to take, etc. The interpreter carefully memorized the details that Cuauhtémoc was revealing, and he said to the torturer:
>
> "The emperor says he doesn't care."[10]

It is very possible that this type of irreverence was due to the fact that Mexican history counts on a growing group of defeated heroes, whose personae accumulate with the retelling of their feats, which seems to have left deep scars in Mexican culture. The historic retellings begin with the last Aztec emperor, who was tortured into giving over all of the riches; then go on to the children heroes, who were the protagonists of a heroic suicide; and culminate in the death by betrayal of the victors of the Mexican Revolution: Venustiano Carranza, Francisco I. Madero, Emiliano Zapata, and Francisco Villa. The political joke is an instrument of self-denial that helps to free the frustration implied in having a history of not much to be proud of.

The following joke reveals how society confronts the historic trauma of the Madero term:

> When President Madero dies and goes to heaven, he asks St. Peter if Christ can receive him. St. Peter takes the message to Christ, who responds:
>
> "Sure, let Madero come through; like me, he promised a lot and didn't follow through on anything." (Lomas 1975:155)

Perhaps due to their country's traumatic history, Mexicans have adopted Juárez and Cárdenas as their two top heroes. These two died of natural causes, completing their political and historic cycles without being defeated by betrayal.

The Mexican is used to betrayal. He's seen a history plagued with betrayal, in which many of his heroes have perished. Thus, everyone fears and looks out to not be betrayed. Politicians believe that their phones are tapped and are very cautious when using this mode of communication. Álvarez (1992:153), referring to the telephone call he received letting him know who would be the presidential candidate in 1982, said, "My reply was very brief. That is the habit when you speak on the net and in general when you speak on the phone, because the famous 'birds on the wire' show up on the most unexpected lines." One maneuver favored by politicians, used to affect the careers of *other* politicians, consists of a series of dirty tricks, the so-called *chicanas*. For example, one person speaks badly about the boss to another person. Then, the first person goes to the boss and tells him what the second person said, making it appear as though the second person had started the conversation criticizing the boss. This maneuver is called "throwing thread to pull a strand." Certainly, this trick can mean the end of the betrayed person's political career, as well as the promotion of the person who betrayed him. In this instance, betrayal is thereby rewarded, showing that dishonesty can be fostered and can pay dividends. We may assume that the reason to have censored the movie *La sombra del caudillo* (*The Shadow of the Caudillo*, 1960) is that it presents the betrayal that took place within the military in the 1920s.

Mistrust is one principle that guides the Mexican's behavior and makes up his culture. One finds politicians (at least second and third tier) who, when told a joke about the current president, act as if it bothers them, and they may even make a gesture for the joke teller to keep quiet, as if there were microphones in the walls. In reality, these politicians worry about not knowing whether the joker's intentions are good ones. They reveal their fear by being part of the attack. The "Big Brother" culture of among Mexican politicians—the feeling of always being watched—reinforces their sense of importance, yet also their lack of freedom.

In Mexican political culture, the common mistrust turns into incredulity. Democracy requires credibility, and in its absence, it's doubtful that there exists the strength for social and political relations to act autonomously. There is always the suspicion of a hidden agenda, and the good faith that politicians so espouse reverts when it exists in such a highly demagogic context. The Mexican believes that there are hidden forces that make things happen, and that they are arranged according to secret plans.[11]

Politics is secret, underground—it appears to be part of an exclusive brotherhood and to act according to an incomprehensible design, though it may very well not be or do so. Juxtaposed with all of this is the method of greatest political participation in Mexico: humor.

Regarding the role of territory in the formation of a national identity, we find that the Mexican recognizes national territory as his point of reference—but only with difficulty. This can be seen in the frustrated attempts for territorial separation of the southern states of the republic[12] during the nineteenth century, whose final expression was seen in Chiapas in the eighties, when a separatist movement attempted to create the free and sovereign state of the Soconusco. Another reference in the same century is the little protest offered toward the annexation of half of the country to the United States, or the northern states' systematic resistance, to date, against the central part of the country. One reason perhaps is that Mexico City has practiced centralist policies that contradict the federal system and the Constitution—and even the federalist rhetoric that emerged in the nineteenth century. Mexicans have a deep-rooted identity with their hometown, the place where they were born[13] and where they have the right to return because of their blood. Hernández and Narro (1987:22) found that 57 percent of Mexicans surveyed identified first with their village or city, 18 percent identified with their state, and only 18 percent identified with Mexico as a nation.

In any case, these close ties to geographic roots can be useful. Politicians can be absent from their place of birth for nearly all their lives, but they're ready to sacrifice themselves in order to govern their home state. We can mention two interesting cases of politicians and their hometowns. Miguel de la Madrid was born in Colima but left at two years of age, never to return. Still, he always considered Colima his hometown, and this allowed him to show that he was sensitive to the provinces outside of the Mexican capital. Of course, some of his governmental programs specifically benefited his state, and we must ask if there was a hidden personal or family interest involved.

Carlos Salinas de Gortari was born and raised in Mexico City, but his parents are from Agualeguas, Nuevo León, a small town close to Monterrey. Since he considers this his hometown, he kicked off his presidential campaign in Agualeguas. He always kept a centrally located country home there, and he founded an annual race during the Easter Week holiday. This might have helped him stave off the arrogance and aggressiveness that Chilangos (those from Mexico City) are accused of, especially when there was so much animosity against them in several places throughout the country.

In recent years, an interesting phenomenon has evolved in Mexico City. Young people who were born in marginal areas have formed gangs (García-Robles, 1985). They paint their individual symbols on walls to establish and identify the boundaries of their territory.[14] The *chavo banda* or *cholo*, which is what these young people are known as, are not citizens of a geographical or political entity, but rather of their neighborhood, restricting their identities to even smaller "hometowns."

Nationality is a technical question and a voluntary process ensured by means of a legal ordinance, something one can also use to obtain a passport or a driver's license. But *nationalism* is something else, something requiring the ingredients of emotion, identity, loyalty, and belonging. Someone can be Mexican and be little interested in national questions, including those of politics. Moreover, his interests are affected—he looks to protect himself as best he can, but not necessarily to look out for the good of the country; if he is in a position of wealth, if necessary he will surely take his money out of the country, or perhaps he will steal or become corrupt.

Considering how pervasive this behavior is in Mexico, we might venture that there is no civic culture in the country.[15] There is in fact an underdeveloped social commitment, and little resolve to bring it together. It's still not clear if a national plan exists.[16] In an uncertain environment, social contracts are thus developed.[17] When social commitments are established and they're not carried out, there is no confidence; for this reason, these all-important transactions require certification by a notary public.

There is a marked tendency to see Mexico as a patrimonial culture. Power, posts, and authority are all to be used, but not to carry out social programs. When the Mexican takes his money out of the country, he cites his lack of trust for the government, which must give guarantees for everything. The politician becomes corrupt because first comes his personal security; this results in a notable disconnect between the individual and the collective.

For these reasons the government tries to generate national identity factors, even though it does so by decree, which can be counterproductive given Mexico's climate of rejection for authority and power. For example, there is the decree establishing that the national anthem must be sung daily on radio and television, or else the "national hour" must be transmitted for one hour per week on a national radio chain, when all the stations in the country are tied together—but, according to vox populi, the public turns off all its radios. It seems as though the government wants to impose compulsive nationalism and it does in fact effectively control this discourse within the schools. But society in general doesn't share respect for—nor does it foster—civic values thus promoted.

To evade serious and responsible social analysis regarding the lack of national sentiment, it's common to blame the Spanish conquest for Mexico's lack of patriotism. The conquest provoked a conflict of cultures in which Spanish values prevailed and certain social sectors were excluded. The recrimination is to such a degree that even today, more than five hundred years after the conquest, the Spaniards are ill spoken of and referred to as *gachupines*, a degrading term for Spanish settlers in America. Maybe because of this, the multiple nationalities that Mexico has received have brought little to the national culture. All that is Mexican seems to be closed to new contributions, and furthermore, the newly arrived absorb the worst part of Mexican culture: xenophobia. Mexicans hate foreigners, and foreigners look down on Mexicans—there is a mutual loathing shared between the two.[18]

Therefore, when humor ridicules the country and all that it holds sacred, it is because what is national doesn't exist; hence, there is nothing to defend. A historic model for which to be proud doesn't exist. In Bartra's words (1987:171), "Nationalism is the recapitulation of Mexican history, but the recollection is one of traumatic events that consequently lead Mexicans to not have much of a historical base for pride."

The political joke has a long reach; it doesn't only harm a nation's image, but also that of politicians. The joke denigrates and ridicules the national image, sending a strong message to politicians, who in the end are responsible for guarding the national interest and national growth. Consider the effect that the following jokes have on the image of Mexico:

> They say that if Mexico hadn't come into existence, surely Walt Disney would have invented it.

> They say that the question is that the country still has not been inaugurated, because tests are just now being done.[19]

> When God created the world, he got to Mexico and said: "Let's give it oceans."
>
> And he gave it oceans.
>
> "Let's give it metals."
>
> And God gave it gold and silver.
>
> "Let's give it energy power."
>
> And he gave it oil.
>
> "Let's give it lands."
>
> And he gave it fertile lands. And this is how he went on until his advisors said:

"Sir, look how you have imbalanced that country. You've given it a little of everything."

To which God responded: "OK, to balance it out let's fill it with Mexicans."

Mexico borders the United States to the north, Guatemala to the south, it's surrounded by water and filled with Mexicans, and it still manages to subsist.

When one hears jokes such as these, there's little doubt that we are faced with self-denigration and certain self-destructive tendencies. I have two hypotheses with respect to this. One would consider that the person telling the joke doesn't see himself as being part of the Mexico that's being attacked, leaving those responsible for having created the implied traumatic situation to absorb the blow. The one who tells the joke is among those who test the country for its good; he is not one who God put there to bring balance, and he isn't one of those against whom the country remains in opposition. Politicians are to blame for faults and irresponsibility. Seen through a wide lens, these considerations can support the argument that the Mexican has an inferiority complex, as some authors suggest (see chapter 2). Nevertheless, the second hypothesis considers that self-degrading jokes can also actually be a mechanism for the protection and even elevation of self-esteem. Díaz Guerrero (1961:59) says, "These Mexicans who laugh at themselves and enjoy it have disconnected from an abnormal compensatory need and have found a positive and valid aspect to develop self-esteem by means of a healthy sense of humor."

Self-degrading jokes may thus be a defense mechanism for the vulnerable individual who prefers to laugh at himself before others laugh at him, stripping them of their power to criticize. Obviously, not all Mexicans are guilty of corruption or incompetence, but we are still doubtful as to why they tell or laugh at themselves or at jokes about themselves:

It is said that the Martians sent a mission to earth. Upon their return they were asked what they saw.

"A Soviet satellite."

"How do you know it was Soviet?"

"Oh, because it had a picture of Lenin, a red flag with a sickle and hammer, and it said CCCP."

Then they were sent on a second mission and when they returned they were asked what they saw.

"Now we saw an American satellite."

"And how do you know it was American?"

"Oh, because it had a picture of Lincoln, a flag with stars and stripes, and it said USA."

Finally they were sent on a third mission and when they returned they were asked: "Now what did you see?"

"A Mexican satellite."

"And how did you recognize it?"

"Very easily, the paint was chipping and it was in ruins. It has some strange letters that said MORELOS and when we saw it from behind it said: WHAT ARE YOU LOOKING AT, YOU JERK?"

Obviously, Mexicans would rather be associated with satellites that look well maintained, and whose astronauts are efficient and intelligent.

The Mexican exonerates himself from making fun of the motherland, of its symbols and heroes, because he believes he is above all of that. In fact, he turns his dissatisfaction with it into aggression. One hears that due to mutual rejection, when outside the country, Mexicans feel nothing for one another, and that there's nothing worse than running into another Mexican when abroad. Inside the country, when someone gets upset about someone else's negative attitude, he tends to say, "That's why we are where we are." José Agustín (1968:149) rephrases it, alluding to the "appearance," which is so important in Mexico: "We are the way we seem to be." The philosopher de Güemes (Durón Ruiz, 1992:202) refines it even further in this way: "We are where we are because we are the way we are." Blaming any problem on the ethereal collective helps Mexicans strip themselves of their individual responsibilities, even though it may pertain to a critique to correct this.

There is no doubt that the Mexican seems to have lost the passion demanded by patriotism[20] and the motherland has been displaced in the order of priorities. The principle of "The motherland is first" seems to have been cast aside and left in the past; when it should in fact be above one's own life, today it is just one more witty saying.

There exists the erosion of civic values and symbols, the political consequences of which are reflected in the absence of a relative consensus,[21] which makes the government's job difficult to do. When this panorama is combined with the negative perception of power, one can only ask oneself how it is possible that the Mexican political system has achieved stability for several decades without any major revolts.

The Individual against Power

Humor reflects social opinion, as well as the nature of fears and taboos, especially regarding the mysterious and unknown. It is a mechanism that frees us from what troubles us. In the case of political humor, the troubling notion in question is the nature of power and the mystery of its use.

The individual believes that democracy means government of the people, but it has problems accepting this when it can't confront it because it doesn't understand mechanisms of power and its ominous excesses. The following Israeli joke serves to explain the feeling that many people have toward democracy:

> "What is democracy?"
> "A situation where people say what they want and the government does what it wants." (Kanar, 1974:80)

Here, we can recall the joke about the earthquake mentioned in chapter 2, in which the crux of the matter to the mayor is to satisfy the higher spheres of power, independent of what might happen to the people. In Mexico, the mystery regarding the exercise of power seems to consist in any official owing loyalty and submission to his superiors, because they can make or break political careers. This is even at the cost of disloyalty to the public, and even the Constitution, which at some point he swore to uphold. This mentality allows and provokes the general abuse of power, though humor basically records the abuse committed by the police.[22] See the following example:

> A group of policemen walk into the precinct and they pick out a little drunkard who has been detained. They take him where they have a barrel filled with excrement, and they ask him:
> "Where are the jewels?"
> The little drunkard says he doesn't know, and so they submerge him into the barrel. They take him out and ask him again, and again they get the same negative answer, and again they submerge him several times, until the little drunkard says:
> "Look, I don't see any jewels; it's better if you find another scuba diver."

By definition, authoritarian systems are maintained by an excessive use of force, which can in part be due to a hidden dominating apparatus after the luck of a secret brotherhood that hides the relationships of power. This mystery imposes complicity among its keepers and is translated into a distancing between those who retain power and the citizens. This situation in turn creates an unequal confrontation in which the individual can only use humor—not to defeat the powerful, nor to explain the mystery, but rather to ridicule the powerful. It is social revenge that perhaps won't go very far, but it allows the Mexican to express his antagonism toward the government—which, according to Iturriaga (1951:235), drives him to a marginal civic life, because "instead of associating with political parties, he prefers to create political opposition helped by the anonymity offered by bathroom walls."[23] This unusual platform serves itself to demonstrate its resentments and desires against the top oppressor or loathed enemy. The following graffiti referring to the PRI turned up on a bathroom wall:

[In Spanish this rhymes]

Vale una pura tiznada	Our official party
nuestro partido oficial	Matters a hell of a little
porque como este sitial	Because like this seat of honor
tiene un olor a manada.	It has the smell of the herd.

(Jiménez, 1960:119)

Iturriaga suggests that this rejection for the governing political party is historic. The Mexican rejects it for being an institution that doesn't promote his interests, and he rejects the PRI because it has been a visible means for domination.

The anti-party attitude can also be explained hypothetically: as the rejection of Euro-centrism. For the Mexican, who was colonized by Europeans at a very high cost, political parties are a product of their political evolution: they are another form of European cultural domination. If political participation requires political parties, it's possible for the Mexican to deny the modern symbol of colonial domination by turning his back on the party. He counts on two possibilities: to openly confront the system and suffer the consequences, or to search for a path that won't put him within sight of repressive forces as if he were an enemy of the system—this is the case with humor.

In this type of confrontation, humor represents the citizen's self-defense. In an open system, the citizen can create alternative institutions to vent political revenge, caused by his frustration. In closed systems, there is a greater motivation to choose humor, because it's an implacable method that politicians can't obstruct nor turn against society—that is, society can't be robbed of nor be degraded by its own protest instrument. Humor has destructive effects against politicians without risking the system. This is how, still within the democratic system, for the first time the people are the winners in the confrontation. Or, as the American ex-presidential candidate Mo Udall concluded (1988:12), "In a democracy, the people always have the last laugh."

With the joke, the attacked politician's image emerges the way society wants to see it, not the way he wants to be seen. He has been deprived of his successes, and society passes him in the game of perceptions because it laughs without giving him a chance to respond. By using the self-denigrating joke, the Mexican protects himself and at the same time takes away politicians' real achievements. This is unfortunate because, as useful as it is to show national failures, the demolishing attack of the joke also destroys the pride that should accompany the triumphs. Even before Mexico's first astronaut had taken off, Mexican society humiliated and made nothing out of him,[24] preventing anything constructive to come out of his achievement. See the following jokes:

> They say that when Rodolfo Neri Vela, the first Mexican astronaut, got out of the rocket ship, his hands were swollen. When they asked him what had happened he said:
>
> "Every time I wanted to touch something the gringos would give me a slap on the hand and would say don't touch."

~

> They sent a Mexican into space with a monkey. The instructions were that when a green light lit up it was an instruction for the monkey and when a red light lit up it was an instruction for the Mexican.
>
> The voyage begins and the first green light comes on. The monkey stands up and sees a sign saying: Do experiment number 1. The voyage continues and the anxious Mexican sees the green light on the panel go on again: Do experiment number 2. And like this the voyage continues with only green lights. When they are about to return to earth, finally a red light goes on, the Mexican looks at the panel instruction that says: Feed the monkey.

The person who tells a self-denigrating joke exposes an embarrassing situation he wishes to overcome. The one who listens to the joke uses his imagination to attribute and personify blame. Political jokes enable criticism, as they are inherently impersonal, which is convenient to avoid negative consequences; furthermore, their adaptability adds to their comic value. See the Argentine joke about the president, who is a son of a bitch, and the policemen, who affirm that they can't be fooled because they know whom the joke is about. When the name of the subject is absent, the joke teller waits for the listener to supply his favored politician, or assign whomever he wishes—it's about sharing criticism, whether it be that of an abstract political figure or that of any specific figure. In this way, the politician is attacked under a general category, as we can see in the following joke:

> A politician goes before the Tarahumara Indians and begins his long tiresome speech:
>
> "I'll give you schools . . ."
>
> And the residents respond:
>
> "*Basachic, basachic.*"
>
> "I'll bring you progress . . ."
>
> "*Basachic, basachic.*"
>
> Later he asks one of the locals who is accompanying him, "Where can I go to the bathroom?"
>
> "There, in between the trees, but don't step in the *basachic*." (Salgado, 1986b:158)[25]

By the same token, the political joke, as an instrument of transgression, attacks political values and symbols. For example:

> Pepito gets a homework assignment to write an essay about politics. He gets home and after asking his mother, sister, grandmother, etc. He then asks his father who responds:
>
> "Look, I don't know the meaning of politics, but I'm going to give you an example: I am power, your mother is justice, our housekeeper is the people, you are youth and your brother is the future."
>
> That night the little brother needs to go to the bathroom and he asks Pepito to help him. Pepito goes to call his mother and finds her asleep, he then goes to get the housekeeper and finds his father on top of her. The next day at breakfast he says:
>
> "Now I understand politics: JUSTICE IS ASLEEP, POWER IS ON TOP OF THE PEOPLE, YOUTH IS BAFFLED AND THE FUTURE IS IN DEEP SHIT."[26]

Jokes are a form of political passive resistance. They do the job of destroying political values and are focused against power and government, who are the guardians of those values. Failing to protect these values can be interpreted as a failure in the safekeeping of the national treasure. In this sense, humor can be compared to guerrilla warfare. Guerrilla groups look to prove that the government can't provide security. And jokes try to prove that the government can't defend political values, and therefore assure or defend political dignity.

The joke's attack on values isn't necessarily an attack on ideology. Ideological values represent a world concept and a life concept that together offer support for the social, economic, and political system. The State creates the conditions for the system to reproduce. Here, change of governments or even a change in values can occur. Within ideology, there can be changes in values without this necessarily creating a destabilizing effect that impedes the State from creating governments that will uphold them. This way, values and governments are temporary, and the State and ideology in general have a longer existence. Humor can attack the boundaries of certain values, but not the ideological buttress of the system. Therefore, political jokes can attack values and symbols imposed by the government without changing the ideology of the system. To destroy ideology or the State, more drastic political measures—such as a revolution—are required, and even a revolution might not annihilate all the symbol and value framework, because there are elements of the past that remain useful. On the other hand, the resistance toward political domination is not necessarily resistance toward ideological domination.

The breaking-down of heroes has nothing to do with ideology, but rather with the symbols and temporary powers or the joint expression of the needs of the political system. For this reason, when society attacks, it can "scrape" those joint needs without destroying the base upon which those same needs sit. In the case of Mexico, the attack attempts to strip politicians of their superhuman powers. It also seeks to knock down official heroic history, a history that was built by means of domination, which metaphorically works as a general censure—because if one attacks the symbolic result, one attacks those in charge of ensuring that those symbols are absorbed by society.

The joke criticizes the solemnity of political discourse and governmental values. The following is an example:

> At a protocol meeting in Buckingham Palace, England, the Queen who was suffering from post-dinner indigestion passed gas.
>
> Next, the Japanese ambassador said:
>
> "Ladies and gentlemen, I beg your forgiveness, but I am somewhat sick to my stomach."

> Shortly after that, the Queen passed another gas and so the Dutch ambassador said:
>
> "Ladies and gentlemen, please forgive me, but something that I ate didn't sit right."
>
> Then the Mexican ambassador who was surprised by each response, said:
>
> "Ladies and gentlemen, let me announce that from now on, all of the Queen's farts can be put on my country's tab." (Jiménez, 1960:32–33)

This joke was also adapted to President Fox and can be constantly readjusted to fit other personalities because it ridicules the protocol of political power. The potential destructive nature of humor is not to recognize a politician's oratorical skill, but rather to judge the credibility of his words. And it is just that, frequently, political discourse is clearly demagogic. Perhaps people are irritated because politicians are so zealous about dazzling the public. For example, in this case, a queen's gasses seem absolutely natural to her, as are our own. What is ridiculous is that a diplomat should try to excuse what doesn't need to be excused, and that the Mexican is so stupid as to think that he has to beat the others to the punch to vindicate the queen's gasses. Once the joke is told, the political discourse loses pomposity, validity and even its space for expression.

The previous joke refers to two traditionally embarrassing subjects: respect for intimacy (so important to contemporary Western civilization) and current mores with reference to modesty. In this way, the aspects pertinent to politics and the attack on politician's private affairs are joined, which is especially effective for ridicule.

When the joke focuses on the president, he is used as a primary symbol for power. Themes change according to each presidential term. They can have to do with a physical feature or a president's peculiar feature, whether public or private. Consider the following joke regarding Gustavo Díaz Ordaz, based on his ugliness:

> They say that when he was on a stop in *Tehuacán* [the name of a city and the name of a type of club soda] during his electoral campaign trail, he saw writing on a wall that read: TEHUACÁN WITH DÍAZ ORDAZ [meaning that the locals supported him]. He turned around and said:
>
> "That must taste like all hell [meaning the beverage mixed with Díaz Ordaz]."[27]

In a country where drinking helps solidify social relations and business negotiations, a bad drink has several negative attributes. The joke about

Díaz Ordaz's ugly looks might be analogous with bad taste and possibly a bad political decision.

Occasionally, jokes that criticize the president are used by politicians who, under different circumstances, wouldn't dare to do so. Before 1968, criticism of the president was considered taboo. During that year, the government showed its distaste—because protesting students offended the president in public—and claimed that students were undermining the principle of authority. Since then, the president has been criticized and even insulted in public, albeit through anonymous criticism such as the booing of a president in a stadium, where thousands and thousands of boos drown out individual ones. The previous prohibition seems to have passed on to another life, being as an inordinate number of jokes have sprung up since 1970. It is difficult to compare the number of jokes before and after 1970, which is the year I started my joke collection (due to the lack of other collections); popular wisdom recognizes that with Echeverría a multitude of political jokes emerged. It is difficult to calculate an exact number, since to this date (2006) I continue to collect Echeverría jokes.

Another reason for the profuse amount of jokes could be an inadequate democratic transition. Though the problem people have with presidents may derive from comparing democracy with the number of political parties or systematically clean elections, it could be that none of the presidents work for people who express their opinions, or that they truly represent the popular will. In fact, in the last three decades, no president has enjoyed an absolute majority. Therein, humor continues to be the instrument of last resort. It doesn't cease to amaze that the profusion of political humor in the theater hasn't been censored. We can assume that thanks to mass media, permissiveness is greater; this also occurs with books and, more recently, with newspaper political cartoons and caricatures.

Jokes don't require a formal argument—they synthesize pointed opinions without being apologetic[28]—nor do they encompass firm, long-winded discussions. The following joke synthesizes what Mexicans thought about the abilities of President Echeverría's cabinet, and what they thought about possible dissent and the lack of freedom:

> Echeverría goes to lunch with six of his ministers. They bring the check, which adds up to 28 pesos. So then he asks the minister of finance how much each should pay. The minister calculates it this way:
>
> "We have 28 divided by 7, where 8 divided by 7 is 1 with a remainder of 1:

  1
7/28
 -7
  1

"We bring down the 2 and we have: 21. Then we have 21 divided by seven is the same as three:

 13
7/28
 -7
 21
-21
  0

"We each need to pay 13 pesos, Mr. President!"

Echeverría carefully gazes at the check, and being doubtful he asks the secretary of the presidency to check it over. The secretary thinks: If the minister of finance already did the calculation, and I come up with a different answer, surely he'll be upset, but the president asked me to do it so I'll see how it turns out:

"Let's see, the Minister of Finance said that it would be 13 pesos per person, so let me confirm it: 3 times 7 = 21, and 1 times 7 = 7, therefore: 21 + 7 = 28.

3 × 7 = 21
1 × 7 = 7
21 + 7 = 28

"It's correct, Mr. President; it is 13 pesos per person."

Not convinced, Echeverría keeps gazing at the check and says:

"I'm going to check it myself. Let's see, we're 7, right? So then let's add seven times thirteen.

13
13
13
13
13
13
13."

And he starts to add the threes in descending order: 3, 6, 9, 12, 15, 18, 21, and so on, then he begins to count the ones in ascending order from 21: 22, 23, 24, 25, 26, 27, 28.

"It's right," Echeverría says, "it's thirteen pesos per person, pay up."

This joke is a mathematical game masterfully adapted to politics, and its logical incongruence encompasses several aspects: the expectation that the president, the highest-ranking person, will not look to divvy up the check, but rather handle it himself; the fact that the finance minister, he who manages national finances, should commit such a basic arithmetical error; the fact that the secretary, who at that time was responsible for public investments, should be made to inspect the check—yet who beforehand worries so much about avoiding the conflict that could result from contradicting a fellow cabinet minister that he revises it according to the mistake and ratifies it; and finally, that the president—the superman, the one who knows it all—should commit another mistake and make his ministers pay the check. Meanwhile, the person who hears the joke knows that the one who will collect the money is the one who will pocket the difference, who in this case is the president, which once more goes to show that corruption in fact is topped off at the head. The joke refers to Echeverría's incompetence, his corruptions, his submissive ministers, and the inefficiency of the presidential cabinet. It's interesting to note that this criticism emerged when a period of economic stability of forty years came to an end, followed by instability that fell mainly within the scope of responsibility of the president of the republic (Whitehead, 1980) and the government.[29]

Under similar circumstances, the individual can't compete with power, and that is why with the joke, he goes underground and gets even with a universe that he neither understands nor controls—though theory and demagoguery may state the opposite—but that he feels he can sabotage and bombard.

Humor and Participation

Mexico has experienced a process of political modernization, with new institutions that facilitate individual political participation and promote respect for achievements. Nevertheless, this process doesn't correspond with the magnitude of economic modernization and social-economic changes.[30] The idea of political modernization is associated with that of participation, and this with electoral rights, and from there, we may have arrived at the point at which some analysts conclude that people do not participate when there is a very elevated electoral abstention, which is true to a certain point. In Mexico, the rate of abstention has increased, registering at 59 percent in 1970 and 81 percent in 1979 (Schmidt, 1988).[31]

In 1988, this number exceeded 66 percent (Schmidt, 1990b). It's interesting that abstention has increased drastically after the "democratic opening" of the '70s and the "political reform" of the '80s. This increase in abstention occurred even when the number of political parties increased, offering more options across the entire ideological spectrum, but in this case, that didn't necessarily translate to a greater number of votes.

The greater voting abstention of 1988 is surprising because in that election, seven political parties were competing, and there was the impression that the formation of an electoral block in the National Democratic Front offered a true alternative to the PRI.[32] Surprisingly, the abstention rate was greater than in 1982. Many explanations can be offered, although we must consider that the rate of abstention is generally inflated because many people register without the intention of ever voting. That situation became worse since the voter's credential was instituted, because it has turned into drawing for an identity card—the people who get the card don't necessarily use it for voting purposes. The percentage of abstention probably increases because (1) people reject political parties as well as the channels of participation; 2) voters have no new options—the National Democratic Front gathered old forces that were able to come together, but that were hypothetically unable to attract new voters; (3) the Mexican citizen doesn't believe that his vote has any influence and therefore that his electoral participation makes no difference;[33] (4) electoral politics are irrelevant to a great number of Mexicans; and (5) politicians lack credibility.

We can assume that all of this derives from the fact that the Mexican feels that he has no influence over the system or the government, which is shown by Almond and Verba in their 1963 study regarding political culture. In a Delphi study I undertook with Joge Gil in 1983, following Almond and Verba, we asked: If an individual suffers a traffic accident with someone of influence who is at fault, what are his chances of winning the case before a judge? The subjects in our study thought they had very little chance of influencing the result of the mishap. Our resulting numbers were even lower than Almond and Verba's; nevertheless, I want to emphasize that while the American scholars analyzed a random sample, we concentrated on a sample of 108 members of the Mexican elite—which included workers, laborers, peasants, scholars, politicians, public officials of different levels, and entrepreneurial leaders. The majority of the group felt that they would lose. The conclusion is that Mexicans think that they'll always run into someone more influential, and that fairness is irrelevant because it depends on power or money; in other words, Mexico is a culture of inequality, of privilege and injustice.

Electoral habits reverted in 1994, when there was greater voter turnout, partly due to the psychological impact of the war in Chiapas and the climate of fear it caused, as well as the assassination of the PRI presidential candidate Luis Donaldo Colosio. Finally, toward the year 2000, the PRI lost the presidential election because many young people and women voted. But after that year, results revealed that high voter abstention persisted, and the PRI was gaining ground—that is, that authoritarian culture has not disappeared, and society seems to be willing to return to the past. Here, we could apply a phrase uttered by a Peruvian woman during the presidential election in that country in 2006: "We are better off with a known thief than to have to get to know a new thief."

Regarding the economy, a long period of stability and growth (known by economists as "the Mexican miracle") ended at the beginning of the 1970s. A long crisis ensued—and does not seem to have an ending. The country doesn't grow, and on the contrary, it registers a fall in indicators of human capital and with relation to other countries. This situation has brought about turbulence and strong social reaction such as an expected generalized explosion of violence that hasn't arrived, though there have been explosions of varying reach in some post-election processes throughout the entire country, and instances in which society has taken justice into its own hands. At the end of the 1980s and the beginning of the 1990s, there were rumors about guerrilla warfare in the south (Correa, 1993:1821); on January 1, 1994, the indigenous rebellion exploded in Chiapas and toward the year 2000, the government recognized the existence of a group of one hundred guerrillas. Guerrilla warfare is a form of political action, but different Mexican social classes are still far from confronting the system in the way that humor does; instead, we see rebellion and irritation. This constituted a background of ample political violence and allowed speculation as to whether the cycle of revolutions of each century will repeat itself (1810, 1910, 2010?). In our study, we found an explosion of political jokes that, according to the progress of the crisis, became more and more caustic. Mexican society has chosen them to send a very strong message to politicians without yet being prone to general violence, and apparently the revolutionary cycle has stopped.

Traditionally, Mexicans saw each changeover of government as a renovation—even a mythical millennium—since the new administration offered a clean and promising new beginning. However, recent jokes show that this type of hope has reached its limit. Previously, when a new presidential term began, the president enjoyed a grace period of about a year, during which people observed very carefully the mistakes he was making, his style of government, and even his private life in order to later sharpen the darts. Furthermore, jokes usually involved the current president's predecessor, such as in the following case:

> They call López Portillo the tractor . . . because he comes to substitute the mule.

The same joke was made about Echeverría in relation to Díaz Ordaz.

However, in 1988, for Carlos Salinas de Gortari, there was no truce—even though his case was unique, given his high position as secretary. As soon as he was inaugurated, he became the victim of several jokes (Schmidt, 1995a) that focused on his physical appearance and on the politics of cutting public spending, as well as on a rumor that when he was a child he had killed his housekeeper (González Meza and López Koehl, 1987). Salinas was boldly attacked because, in addition to the traditional PRI imposition, he represented the nearly stubborn decision of a poorly looked-upon president who, according to popular image, did not attain the heights that the country's circumstances demanded of their leader. The individual in Mexico has few instruments to tell politicians that he is opposed to the status quo without being considered a rebel or an aggressor against the political system. Any type of dissidence confronts repression and is the butt of epithets such as "not institutional" or "conflictive." In any Mexican institution, to be classified as not institutional implies disloyalty, a categorization for which the person will fall into disgrace. If he is a politician, his career will run the risk of being derailed, or at least of stopping short.

Here, I will offer an example of printed media being used as an instrument of communication, but having little effect because it is co-opted and controlled in addition to having little reach in the country due to a lack of readership (Schmidt, 2003). The government persecuted the only magazine that covered the guerrillas in the 1970s until the police destroyed the magazine's offices in 1976. At that time, there was little protest on the part of intellectuals, who, just a few months previously, had raised their voice against the departure of the director of the newspaper *Excelsior*, provoked by governmental intervention. The commonly scant defense of liberties is perhaps one of the causes that allows the government to pressure and to repress, and possibly because of this, Mexico is close to first place in the world in the persecution and assassination of journalists.

The instrument of protest for entrepreneurs is taking their money out of the country or simply not investing it at all. There are estimates about the existence of between $80–120 billion outside of the country belonging to

Mexicans. This represents more than the entire central Mexican government's foreign debt in the early 2000s. In contrast, to protest, the laborer can go on strike and the peasant can invade lands, but in the end, the citizen who doesn't manifest himself in a specific area (such as a laborer, student, or peasant) can abstain from voting or go on the offensive by means of political humor. Each one of these forms of expression receives a response from the State. The regime can control the press; it can limit the escape of capital by means of legal controls or by manipulating the rates of exchange or the interest rate; it can repress strikes and the invasion of land, and by means of statistical manipulation and electoral fraud, it can mask electoral abstention. Nevertheless, the impact of political jokes must be absorbed by the political system because they are impossible to avoid.

Paradoxically, while the political system tries to enlarge the formal aspects of democracy, society turns to informal participation, creating for itself a gap between the government's expectations and the wishes of society. In the area of politics, open participation helps establish consensus and legitimacy, while informal participation, such as political humor, erodes. Within the context of underground participation, society seems to have a greater chance of winning because it can criticize, attack, and sabotage without being pressured. The government is defenseless in this situation, and without means of responding. In the underground world, political culture reverts; the powerful lack informal political power and the dominated get even, though it may just be through laughter.

The Mexican government continues to be responsible for social tranquility, as it is for the advance and progress of society. To achieve these objectives, it undoubtedly requires a consensus and legitimacy, while humor, as an autonomous manifestation of society, daily threatens to destroy these political values. Even when it is difficult to gather scientific evidence about the weight of political humor, we must consider it as a detector of public opinion, which allows us to become familiar with different points of view within society, its vision regarding social and historic occurrences. These expressions show us the direction in which the society's vengeful pounding is moving—which, in the case of Mexico, is toward the president. This is the subject to which we will dedicate the next two chapters.

CHAPTER FOUR

Political Jokes against Mexican Presidents

Once upon a time Carlos Salinas and Cecilia Occeli were celebrating their silver wedding anniversary and their sixtieth birthdays. During the celebration they had a visit from a fairy godmother, who said: "As a prize for having a model marriage for twenty-five years, I give you each one wish." "I want to take a trip around the world with my dear husband!" Cecilia requested. The Fairy waved the magic wand and . . . Abracadabra! The tickets appeared in the hands of the woman. Then it was Carlitos' [diminutive for Carlos] Orejas [Spanish for ears—nicknamed so because of his big protruding ears] de Gortari; he thought for a moment and said: "Very well, this moment is very romantic but an opportunity like this comes along once in a lifetime. For this reason . . . forgive me my love, but . . . my wish is to have a woman 30 years younger than me, someone like Adela Noriega. . . ." Cecilia was shocked, but a wish is a wish. The fairy waved her magic wand and . . . Abracadabra! Carlitos Orejas ["Big ears"] de Gortari became a ninety year old!!!

The moral of the story: Salinas is an ass, but fairy godmothers . . . are female!

Introduction

Political jokes concentrate on symbols of power, and in Mexico, the most powerful symbol is the president: he finds himself on top of the pyramid of power, symbolizing and personifying the secrets and mysteries of power, and commonly known as omnipotent. Conspiracies are born from power circles around him, and it is he who dispenses favors and political and economic rewards to such a degree that in the Mexican political vernacular, he cuts the cake, he makes or breaks careers—that is to say, he is *the one*.

It's common that when a new government or administration begins, politicians find out who got what position or what was said to whom. We're in a system in which the chief or president, who in this case is the supreme leader, grants the positions. This is the patrimonial stamp of the Mexican political system.[1] A place or position exists to be filled, since from it springs a system of complicities serving, among other things, to finance political activities and support the political apparatus. In this way, said patrimony reaches much further than politics, into a wide gamut of activities. Every person who is able to use the country in a patrimonial manner will do so. This reinforces the lack of civic conscience, because the nation is used without social commitment, and those who do it are more interested in getting themselves a godfather or a protector than in ensuring social, civil, and political rights.

As a result of the high degree of centralization in Mexico, public business not only takes place in the shadow of the president—it emanates from him. It shouldn't surprise us, therefore, that he should be the primary symbol of abuse and excess of power. This image is passed on to his collaborators because they are expected to behave like their boss, who is their role model. If the president is corrupt, we can deduce that they will follow in his footsteps. The following riddle exemplifies this:

> It is a play.
> First act: Miguel Alemán appears with his collaborators.
> Second Act: Miguel Alemán appears with his friends.
> Third Act: Miguel Alemán appears with his family.
> What is title of the play?
> *Ali Baba and the Forty Thieves*.

In my research into political perception as reflected in humor, I have found that humor has emphasized the traumatic historical events of Mexico, as well as the power of the head of state. Jokes specifically have helped perpetuate and record the negative impact that traumatic historical events have had on Mexican culture.

Throughout Mexican history, the concentration of power has been one of the main characteristics of political domination. During the twentieth century, political power was concentrated in the president, turning him into a symbol of oppression—and resulting in an abundance of presidential jokes.

There is evidence of the great social rejection of the strong presidencies that emerged in the nineteenth century, culminating with the dictatorship of Porfirio Díaz, whose model continued through the revolutionary and PRI governments of the twentieth century. The consolidation of the presidency was accompanied by the concentration of power and its abuse over and above repeating the perverse features of a system rhetorically labeled democratic, yet whose structure is based on authoritarianism. Mexican scholars classify the national leadership as "authoritarian or paternalistic while keeping its personnel in its grasp under conditions of dependency and inferiority, without the least appreciation for its capacity or contributions" (Rodríguez Estrada and Ramírez-Buendía, 1992:89).

In this chapter, we will travel through the history of Mexico to research the means of political humor, in its wide range of manifestations, by the reflection of political leadership.

Colonial Times

Research of political humor in Mexican history suggests that there's a direct correlation between jokes and traumatic historical events. An inventory of jokes shows that they reflect a response to serious subjects and emerge in times of crisis; the first of these times was the Spanish conquest, which was motivated by the search for gold (Díaz del Castillo, 1985). According to Le Clézio (1992:43), the symbols of the conquest were the iron bars and chains of the slaves. The avarice of the Spanish leaders was so great that they even deceived their own soldiers, stealing the soldiers' cut of the booty. Cortés kept one-fifth of the gold discovered, as did the king, leaving the soldiers each with one hundred pesos of a total of six hundred thousand pesos in gold. Chronicles relate the unfairness of the system, which obviously provoked protests. Gallo (1987:20) gives us a poem written by an anonymous soldier on a wall in Tenochtitlán:

Cortés, quemaste los pies	Cortés, you burnt the feet of
a Guatemoc por el oro,	Guautemoc for gold,
y aqueste es el día que añoro	And the day I long for
que a este súbdito	That to this subject
le des	You shall give
una brizna del tesoro	A drop of the treasure
aunque lo escondas después.	Even if you hide it later.

Jokes about the conquest appeared several centuries later, seeming to answer a need to overcome the trauma of having seen the great indigenous civilizations trampled and destroyed. Consider the following examples:

> Hernán Cortés says to Montezuma:
>
> "We came to conquer America."
>
> "It doesn't matter, says Montezuma, "I'm for Guadalajara." (Salgado, 1986b:150)

This joke uses as a catharsis the soccer rivalry between the two teams (America and Guadalajara) and is known as the grand classic of Mexican football. Apparently, through humor, the trauma of the Spanish conquest is eased. Along the same lines is found the joke cited in chapter 3 that refers to the origin of the name "Aztec," and the following joke is isomorphic to the previous one, since it plays on the name of the 1960s Jalisco team:

> The Spaniards were torturing Cuauhtémoc, burning his feet to make him reveal the location of the Aztec treasures. When they ask him where the gold is, desperate, he answers:
>
> "Playing against Guadalajara [he makes reference to an old soccer team named Oro (gold)]."

Psychologists use several schemes to get their patients to manage their frustrations or traumas, and one of these revolves around humor. Football (soccer, in America) rivalries seems to reduce the trauma of having been conquered. Let's recall, in chapter 3, the joke about the interpreter who sacrificed Cuauhtémoc's family in order to keep the gold for himself. That joke illustrates the betrayal that eclipses many valiant acts in Mexican history.

Jokes about the conquest attack the corrupt Spanish leadership and diminish the hero status of the Aztec leadership, though they concentrate more on doing the latter. This perhaps shows the resentment that Mexicans hold toward the failure of the indigenous peoples—the multiple mistakes they made, their rivalries, and their belief that the Spaniards were gods, which without a doubt allowed the conquest and sped up the destruction of the Indian nations.

We might say that historic conditions of the indigenous civilization (namely, the disagreement that existed between towns dominated by the Aztecs and the myths regarding the arrival of the Spaniards), along with the superiority of Spanish weaponry, contributed to the success of the conquest, but since Mexicans need to blame someone, who better than the Spaniards and the Aztec emperor?

The Years of Independence

The nineteenth century, the century that the nation of Mexico was built, recorded great political instability, wars, and foreign intervention. The actors of the War of Independence had many nicknames: Don Miguel Hidalgo y Costilla (the heroic priest who declared Mexico's independence) was nicknamed "El Zorro" (The Fox). Three insurgent priests were dubbed "El Caballo Flaco" (The Skinny Horse), "Chinguirito" (Cheap Rum), and "Zapatitos" (Little Shoes). The royalist priest, José Francisco Álvarez, was called "El Padre Chicharronero" (The Crackling Priest), Vicente Gómez was "El Castrador" (The Castrator), and Magdaleno Medina was known as "El Cojo" (The Lame One)—who managed to scare away some Spaniards from Rancho del Muerto with sticks and stones.

With the exception of the defeat of the French in the Battle of the Fifth of May (Cinco de Mayo), there seems to be nothing else for Mexicans to be proud of throughout Mexican history. The Mexican invasion by the United States provoked the loss of half of its territory and has deeply affected the Mexican psyche. It's possible that the great hatred Mexicans have for foreigners was forged during the course of three hundred years of colonization, along with the traumatic experience with the United States, because the war of the cakes[2] didn't produce resentment against the French, such as Mexicans have toward Americans. If colonization yanked away Mexicans' identity, the Americans yanked their territory—and without beating around the bush, political humor placed the blame:

> Unofficial history tells us that the war between Mexico and the United States, in which our motherland lost more than half of its territory, at a given moment (that is, when the Mexican troops were making life very difficult for the gringos, with Antonio López de Santa Anna at the lead) was difficult for both armies, so they each decided to send a message of surrender to the enemy. When the messengers crossed paths, each one with his respective surrender, the gringo soldier asked first:
>
> "Hey you, Mexicanous, where you go?"
>
> And the Mexican said, "I am carrying notice of surrender of our troops."

> And the gringo said, "Oh, so you come over here with us."
> If the Mexican had been an expert in screwing up, he would have spoken like the little Chinese guy: "You tell first," who knew how things were; that Mexican has not been forgiven his stupidity, but at this juncture what does it serve to recall all of that. (Salgado, 1986:120–121)

The uniqueness of this joke is that it exonerates Santa Anna of any wrongdoing (for the loss of territory and the great national defeat) and is attributed to a simple messenger classified as an ass, Aguilar Camin (1991:46). The joke paints Santa Anna as a "no account talent, loved, hated, controversial, undisputed, who dazzled the Mexicans and made them lose half of their national territory." Santa Anna is considered the archetypal traitor of the motherland. He commanded the armed forces,[3] but if the defeat was painful, people still considered his greater crime to be the sale of national territory. And making these offenses worse, he had his leg—which he lost in the war—buried with honors, as you would a head of state. The following anonymous epitaph appeared on his leg's grave:

Es Santa sin ser mujer	She's a saint without being a woman
Es rey sin cetro real	He is king without a royal scepter
es hombre, mas no cabal	He is a man but not sane
y sultán al parecer.	And appears to be a sultan.
Parte en el sepulcro esta	Part of him is in the grave
y parte dándonos guerra	And part is making trouble for us
Así, será esto de la tierra	That is how this will be about the land
o que demonios será?	Or what the hell will it be?
(Homero, 1974:34–36)	

A song said:

Santa Anna se fue al infierno	Santa Anna went to hell
Ardiendo como tecata	Burning like a fruit skin
Y los diablos le dijeron	And the devils told him
A ti te falta una pata	You're missing a leg

But as if the situation were not bad enough with three centuries of colonialism and a traumatic nineteenth century, Mexicans still had to bear the dictatorship of Porfirio Díaz. His more than thirty years of political domination established the base for economic development, but it also strengthened the position of foreign interest in Mexico (Ceceña, 1970), which incited and reinforced Mexican xenophobia. To top it all off, the emergence of democracy was halted, which motivated the appearance of political humorists.

At that time, there emerged a great number of cartoons and humoristic publications, even though the governing elite subsidized many, so that individuals could get even with political groups. Once again, the president was the central target of humor. This humor emphasized the attributes of the dictator but also attacked the members of the cabinet and governors, paying special attention to those who had presidential ambitions. Because of his repressive politics, Porfirio Díaz was nicknamed "Porfirioxtli," which comes from combining his name with the name of Huitzilopochtli, an Aztec blood deity (Trujillo Barriga, 1990:58, citing *El hijo del Ahuizote*). Political jokes also ridiculed Díaz's weakness, calling him "El Llorón de Icamole" (The Cry Baby from Icamole), because he cried after losing the battle of Icamole. It is assumed that a soldier, and especially if he is a political leader, shouldn't cry, since that puts him at a level with mortals and brings him down from Olympus.

Díaz's private life was also the object of humoristic attack. One of the subjects was his getting married by means of a power of attorney:

> Porfirio Díaz was married by power and divorced because of a lack of it.

With respect to his very prolonged administration, the following joke emerged:

> When a head of state would get to heaven, God stood up to welcome him. Only when Porfirio Díaz arrived, the creator didn't get up. Saint Peter said to him:
>
> "Eternal father, he's the president of the Republic of Mexico; why didn't you get up?"
>
> "If I had gotten up, he would have sat in my throne." (Lomas, 1975:154)[4]

Jokes about heads of state who go before God are very popular. Maybe, through them, society reminds its leaders that there is always someone above them, even if that someone is God. It's not clear if these jokes were told during Díaz's dictatorship; nevertheless, it's important to note the subject matter by which the presidential image was tarnished, as well as the symbol society uses to exorcize the traumatic legacy of dictatorship.

The Revolutionary Regimes (1917–1934)

The Mexican Revolution is without a doubt the political event of the twentieth century. From its beginning, the historic legitimacy of the revolutionary government was established, creating a unifying political credo (Padgett, 1976) as well as the institutions that allowed the building of consensus (Newell and Rubio, 1984). Notwithstanding the resulting political wealth, later events, and the actions of governments that argued over the revolutionary legacy, the leadership became a socioeconomic and cultural trauma for a large sector of society. Loyal to the image of concentrated power, jokes focused on revolutionary leadership, occasionally being kind and occasionally being cruel, depending on historic circumstances. This tendency is especially clear in the cartoons of Francisco I. Madero (González Ramírez, 1974), which little by little, and steadily, belittled him. The kind jokes show optimism:

> When Madero arrived triumphantly in Mexico City, there was a parade in which he was going along in a car with his wife. A vulgar person asked, "Who is that woman?"
>
> They answer, "It's the famous Victoria [in Spanish, the word *victoria* means 'victory']."

Here, there is a play on words—between the name of Madero's wife, Victoria, and the word "victory"—to emphasize the triumph of the revolution, but when the political winds begin to change direction, so does society's perception. Madero's nicknames change, and, alluding to his short stature, they call him "El Enano del Tapanco" (The Midget of the Shed). Sheds are usually used to put away things that are no longer of use. Could it be that President Madero was perceived as a politician who had fallen into disuse? They also called him "El Chaparrito," "Shorty," and "El Presidente Pinguica," the last referring to a Mexican diuretic plant that grows profusely. The jokes then became even more degrading:

> Madero hands a document he had written to an Indian friend of his to get his opinion, and the friend responds:

"Very good, *Panchito* [nickname for Francisco], but *coger* is written with a g for *Güey* [as if to say *screw* is written with an *s* for 'Sam,' the word *coger* in slang means 'to screw' and the word *güey* means 'jackass']."

The president is seen as ignorant to the degree that an Indian (Indians being considered illiterate, given their social and economic conditions) corrects his Spanish, and the joke is insulting in describing this interaction.

The revolution involved most of Mexican society, and while many suffered and others prospered, a minority were actually winners.[5] Some were proud, or maybe they were just fishing to gain social recognition, but humor quickly removed their joy, as shown in the following joke:

In a talk between musicians, one pianist says to the rest:
"My grandfather accompanied Pancho Villa."
And another answered:
"At the piano?" (Salgado, 1986b:90)

Revolutionary leaders were left disarmed with offensive jokes. In the same way that Madero's joke paints him as ignorant, we have the same joke about Villa:[6]

Pancho Villa was inspecting the riches with his treasurer and he reads:
"Pancho, 3.00 pesos; Juan, 4.00 pesos; Vicente, 2.50 pesos; Pedro, 1.50 pesos . . . Total, 25.00 pesos."
Troubled, he tells the treasurer:
"And who is this son of a bitch named Total who is making so much?"

Within the tendency to knock down heroes, we have the following poem about Villa, which, by the way, attacks women, perhaps because of his reputation for being a ladies' man (Villa, 1999). This is an important subject, though this is not the place to analyze the misogyny within the joke:

Como centauro se admira	As a centaur he is admired
todavía a Pancho Villa	Still Pancho Villa
pero arriba de la silla	But on the chair
por una hembra suspira.	For a woman he sighs
Muy romántico delira	Very romantic he is delirious
sus lágrimas son chubascos	His tears are downpours
piensa caballo y mujer	He thinks horse and woman

por igual deben tener	Should both have
la ligereza de cascos.	The agility of fleshy layers.
(Coronado, 1984:137)	

The play on words here refers to a horse's speed and the lightness of a woman.

In the period from the end of the revolution to the institutionalization of political power in 1934, political humor increasingly concentrated on moral and physical characteristics of the head of state. Venustiano Carranza, the first constitutional leader of the revolution, was nicknamed "Barbastenango," as seen in the following poem:

Si vas a Tlaxcaltenango	If you go to Tlaxcaltenango
procura ponerte chango	Make sure you are careful
porque allí a Barbastenango	Because that's where Barbastenango
le sacaron el mondongo.	Had the shit beat out of him.

It was in Tlaxcaltenango that Carranza was assassinated while sleeping. That is why his beard is combined with the ridicule of the betrayal that put an end to his life.

There is a good number of jokes about the excess and abuses of the revolutionary forces and their leaders, including references to the rape of women and theft. The verb *carrancear* means "to steal."

Álvaro Obregón was responsible, together with others known as the Sonora group, for bringing the revolution to an end. He had a strong presidency to the degree that he felt tempted to stay in power and modify the Constitution to have himself reelected. His nickname was "El Manco de Celaya," for his loss of an arm in the battle of Celaya. Given his reputation as corrupt, he was also called "El Quince Uñas" (Fifteen Nails) because to dig in a nail, in Spanish, also means "to steal." The president only had fifteen nails, of course, because he was missing an arm, for which society benefited—*what would have happened if he had had twenty?* Regarding the same subject, his anagram read *VENGO A ROBARLO* ("I come to steal from you"). The following jokes about the same subject are in abundance:

> An employee of an important carmaker went to offer Obregón a late model car.
>
> "The president says he cannot receive such an expensive gift and that he should name the price and he will pay for it."
>
> The carmaker employee, who had orders to give the gift no matter what, said to general Obregón:

"Very well, Mr. President, give me one peso."

With this unexpected response Obregón said:

"Just one peso? How cheap! Here, take two pesos and bring me another car as well." (Salgado, 1986a:34)[7]

A Mexican says to a gringo:

"Did you see the monument to Álvaro Obregón?

"Oh yes," the gringo says.

"The best Mexican president."

"What do you say?"

"Yes, the most honest president that we have had in Mexico."

"Why?"

"Because he only had one hand [to steal with]." (Ramírez, 1987:45)

There is an anecdote where Obregón himself told a joke about his own corruption:

> When Obregón lost his arm in the battle of Celaya, they were trying to find it, but couldn't, until he thought of a different way. He threw a gold coin in the air and the arm jumped up to catch it.

Obregón's reputation as corrupt was reinforced when, according to what is said, he invented the "50,000 peso cannon shoots," an idea referring to his belief that this was the amount that would buy loyalty from military leaders. That phrase could have appeared when Carranza rewarded colonel Jesús Guajardo 50,000 pesos and promoted him to general for the assassination of Zapata (Rius, 1992:174–177). Arnulfo Gómez makes clear that the phrase, though attributed to the one-armed Álvaro Obregón, was a phrase from his grandfather General Arnulfo R. Gómez, who sent a personal message: "The armless one thinks that there isn't a general who will withstand the 50,000 peso bribe." The following poem is a comic version of the Obregón corruption subject:

Cuando Obregón se enteró	When Obregón found out
que el diablo no lo quería	That the devil didn't want him
muy serio reflexionó	He reflected very seriously
de qué medios se valdría.	By what means he would get along.
Obregón, inteligente	Intelligent Obregón
siempre tuvo sus chispazos	Always had bright ideas

le vinieron a la mente	came to his mind
sus famosos cañonazos.	His famous cannon shots
Conferenció con Luzbel	He talked to Luzbel
para hacerle convenir	To make him agree
estar en todo con él	To be in on it with him
mediante los cincuenta mil.	Through the fifty thousand.

Plutarco Elías Calles, member of the Sonora group, heir to Obregón, and self-promoted top chief, established a nearly absolute dominion over Mexican politics for more than a decade. During this period, and as a result of Obregón's assassination, he instituted the Partido Nacional Revolucionario (PNR or National Revolutionary Party), which was a predecessor to the present-day PRI. His nickname was "El Turco" (The Turk), an allusion to his Lebanese origins and stemming from the fact that, to Mexicans, all Arabs are Turks. His ambition for power was his most relevant characteristic, for which Plutarco Elías Calles's anagram became: *EL TURCO PESCA LA SILLA* ("THE TURK FISHES FOR THE CHAIR"). Furthermore, jokes that allude to the fact that Calles's house was in front of Chapultepec castle (in those days, the presidential residence), which was called the corner of the woods, and people used to say:

El presidente vive aquí, pero el que manda vive enfrente.
The president lives here, but the boss lives across the street.

I have heard attempts to revive this joke, but it's almost impossible that an ex-president should move in front of Los Pinos (the current presidential residence) because on one side there is an amusement park and the part that's not surrounded by the Chapultepec woods is made up of a lower-middle-class neighborhood, a status that no Mexican ex-president can descend to. Political jokes express a certain fear of Calles's supreme power, seen in the following two jokes:

There were two frogs talking in Chapultepec castle. One croaked:
"I don't like Serrano."
And the other one says:
"It's better than Calles."

The play on words means "Es mejor que Calles"—literally, "He is better than Calles," but the real meaning is, "It is better to keep your mouth shut."

In those days, it was indeed prudent to keep one's mouth shut. The following joke insists on this:

> Things are going so badly for us with Morones! [labor leader]. But in any case, he's better than Calles. [Again, the reference is to keep your mouth shut—*en cualquier caso es major que Calles*].

It seems that Calles was no stranger to corruption, and it could be that he may have looked for Obregón's bribes; therefore, the following phrase was attributed to him:

> There is no congressman nor senator who can resist the caress of the treasury general.

And his acronym also refers to corruption:

> What does CROM mean? *COMO ROBA ORO MORONES* [HOW MORONES STEALS GOLD].
>
> And what does MORC mean? *MAS ORO ROBA CALLES* [CALLES STEALS MORE GOLD].

Luis N. Morones was the secretary general of the CROM (Confederación Regional de Obreros Mexicanos, or Regional Confederacy of Mexican Workers) and increased his power during the presidency of Calles, when he was designated secretary of Labor. MORC (*MAS ORO ROBA CALLES*) is the acronym of CROM (*COMO ROBA ORO MORONES*).

Calles' influence went beyond his term until the period known as El Maximato, because he was the top chief and he dominated politics entirely. The three presidents who succeeded him: Emilio Portes Gil, Pascual Ortiz Rubio, and Abelardo Rodríguez, went on to be known as *pelele I, II,* and *III* (puppet I, II, III), respectively. Additionally, Rodríguez was nicknamed "El Nopalito" (The Cactus), because of its dark and slimy qualities. Cacti release a liquid that is like saliva and people who drool are normally considered idiots. Cactus darkens when it is cooked and Rodríguez was dark-skinned.

Of Pasqual Ortiz Rubio, who was an engineer by profession, it was said that he was a problem for Einstein because:

He was relatively an engineer, and relatively a president. (Gallo, 1987:250)

The Institutionalization of Political Power (1934–1970)

The culmination of the institutional process was turbulent and apparently required the expulsion of Calles from the country. The election of Lázaro

Cárdenas, a man very close to the Sonora group, was key in this process, because he did remove Calles from power, and the country instituted political movements that led to sociopolitical institutions that would allow the handling of social conflict within governmental auspices. Among other things, he reduced the role of the military (Camp, 1992), strengthened the governing party, and initiated the construction of the Mexican corporate system. Nevertheless, the system for presidential succession did not change, and he held on to the concentration of power.

From the beginning of peaceful presidential successions, within the post-revolutionary institutional framework,[8] the process of designation of the presidential candidate for the governing party, who has invariably won the elections, has been a mystery. Everything seems to indicate that his designation was yet one more power emanating from the president. To expose this mystery, we go to the following, previously mentioned anecdote:

> Calles invites Cárdenas to his office and says:
>
> "You have come to our attention to potentially become the president of the Republic by virtue of your revolutionary stock [*cepa*]."
>
> Cárdenas, with an imperturbable expression, answers:
>
> "Pardon my ignorance, my general, what is *cepa*?"
>
> Don Plutarco, surprised by the question and stroking his hair, answered:
>
> "Well, *cepa* is . . ."
>
> "Who the hell knows? *Sepa la tiznada!* [This is a play on words of *cepa* and *sepa*.] The important thing is that you will be the next president of Mexico." (Gallo, 1987:251–52)

Cárdenas was nicknamed "El Trompudo" (Big-Snouted), and the jokes treat him in an ambiguous way. At times, they elevate him:

> "How is Cárdenas like a brassiere?"
>
> "He squeezes the uplifted and uplifts the fallen."

The joke does not use the brassiere with a negative connotation, but rather praises Cárdenas's actions against the enemies of the system (the uplifted) and favors of the poor (the fallen).

On other occasions, the jokes show a sharp criticism of Cárdenas's politics. The criticism emphasizes the troubled agrarian politics, which apparently were disliked by members of the elite. *Agraristas*, or pro-agrarians (those in favor of divvying up and handing out the land) were called *agarristas*, meaning "land grabbers"—a play on like-sounding words. The traditional song "Cuatro milpas" ("Four Corn Patches") was distorted in the following manner:

> Four corn patches are all I have left, of the little ranch I had.

After a labor conflict, as a great act of nationalism, Cárdenas expropriated the oil companies. He sped up land division, driving the discourse toward revolutionary justice for the ravaged. He created La Compañía Nacional de Subsistencias Populares (CONASUPO) to intervene in the marketing of agricultural products and finalized the expropriation of the railroad (symbolizing an end to the Porfirio Díaz legacy of having given this mode of transportation over to foreigners).

If these decisions were well accepted and supported by the political elite and the left, there is evidence that there were some members of the elite who were not happy. According to Knight (1994:83):

> Rumors of coup d'etat and revolts were frequent during 1935–1936; after a brief respite they came back after the nationalization (expropriation) of oil in March of 1938; and received great stimulus due to the Cedillo revolt (May 1938) and the presidential election of 1940.

The following verse serves to synthesize president Cárdenas's image:

Vivito y coleando está	Alive and well he is
sin que lo arredre la suerte	Without scaring luck away
porque inmortal él será	Because immortal he will be
al expropiar a la muerte.	As he expropriates death.

But, as we have suggested, the political joke helps us to learn "unofficial" history, and from what we can see, not all of Cárdenas's image was honey and gold. Let's look at the following jokes, which have been adapted to fit several presidents:

> Lázaro Cárdenas was given the Nobel Prize in mathematics because: he divided the land, multiplied the troubles, and subtracted in the capital.

> There was a world contest of elephants. In comes a Hindu person who says that he has an elephant who can carry fifteen tons. Then an African

> person says that his elephant can throw down half of a jungle with one pull. The Mexican comes along and says: we have a president who, with his trunk, knocks everything down [referring to Cárdenas's big mouth].

Presidents of the Mexican Miracle (1940–1970)

The period of 1940–1970 is considered a favorable economic and political time in Mexico. With the exception of some dramatic events, such as the violent prohibition of strikes, the assassination of peasant leaders, and the repression of social movements, these years are known as the Mexican miracle. During this time there was constant economic growth, low inflation, and political stability to the degree that the PRI looked good, and politicians in the world studied it as a successful political paradigm. Therefore, benevolent political jokes emerged:

> "So you're a marriageable young lady?"
> "Yes, mister policeman."
> "And what exactly are you doing here at the PRI headquarters?"
> "My mother sent me. She told me that I had to find a good party and here I am."

Political humor wasn't very abrasive. Manuel Ávila Camacho's nickname was "El Buche," with reference to his great double chin and the jokes about corruption that were told about his brother:

> When president Manuel Ávila Camacho named his brother, Maximino Ávila Camacho, as secretary of communications, he designated a person with a reputation for honesty to a position where money had to be managed. After a few months, this person bought himself a house, and to thank his boss for the opportunity given him, he invited him over to dinner at his house. Ávila Camacho rejected the invitation, but his collaborator insisted so much that he finally went.
>
> He got to the house, which turned out to be a great mansion full of very costly works and objects of art. The collaborator greeted him and thanked him for having come. Later, in conversation, Ávila Camacho asked him:
>
> "Tell me, was this house expensive?"
>
> "Well, no sir. The owner was very anxious and sold it to me for two hundred thousand pesos."

"And the repairs and the furniture?"

"Well, you see, I didn't fix anything and the furniture I bought on sale, so the final cost of the house came out to be three hundred thousand pesos."

Then Ávila Camacho said:

"Look how lucky you are, you just made one hundred thousand pesos. I'm going to buy it from you for four hundred thousand pesos. Bring the papers to the office in the morning because a notary public will be waiting there."

This joke is an allusion to the cynicism of corruption, but, in the end, corruption is a cynical approximation regarding public works. As we saw under patrimonialism, the chief has the definitive right to take advantage of economic opportunities, and Ávila Camacho was the chief. What is unusual is that the jokes of the time emphasized the corruption of the brother because it was said that the president was a weak man. Humor reveals the mystery:

> Ávila Camacho had to be satisfied with a plate of tongue for breakfast, because the eggs [slang meaning "testicles"] belonged to Maximino. (Mejía Prieto, 1992:96)

In Mexican culture, abuse has become so deeply rooted that this explains the great tolerance for corruption, so it's no surprise that the following popular saying has became wedged in the psyche: "Thief who steals from thief has 100 years of pardon." Luis Vega Monroy wrote the following epigram about this saying, regarding a policeman who stole from the judges of a precinct and embezzled the safety box:

Usted lector ¿qué le haría	You, reader, what would you do
sin penas y sin temores	Without troubles or fears
a ese señor policía	To that policeman
que hizo tamaños horrores?	Who committed such great horrors?
¿De la horca lo colgaba?	Would you hang him by the neck?
¿Lo ponía en el paredón?	Would you put him before the firing squad?
¡No sea injusto! Yo le daba	Don't be unfair! I would give him
sus cien años de perdón.	His one hundred years of pardon.

For many years, Miguel Alemán was a controversial figure to historians and political scientists. His rise to power breaks with the series of generals who governed. It is possible that being the son of a general helped him to the throne. He represents the time when young professionals gained power as if a new idea had sprung up for the role of the State as promoter of economic development. Everything pertaining to the big policies of the revolutionary regime was forced into reverse, while he kept up a progressive discourse. Alemán reformed the PRI by putting the word "institutional" in the name and amended the relegation of members of the military. Though his policies were anti-labor, during his presidency he was designated by the Federation of Mexican Laborers (Confederación de Trabajadores de México, or CTM) the "Pet of the Revolution." Throughout his tenure, tourism was strongly promoted, including the development of Acapulco, a project for which he was rumored to have benefited, bestowing on him a reputation of corruption:[9]

> Garizurieta says to his friend Héctor Pérez Martínez, secretary of the interior during the Alemán years:
>
> "I've read your book regarding the piracy in Campeche, and I think that it should be extended with research encompassing all of the other pirate incursions into the Gulf Coast of Mexico."
>
> Pérez Martínez responds:
>
> "César, I confess that I do examine the subject closely, but my research has been halted because I haven't been able to bring to light who the Dutch Pirate was who plundered Veracruz."
>
> "Mr. Héctor, you are mistaken. It was a pirate and he plundered Veracruz; he wasn't a Dutchman but rather Alemán [German]."

As previously mentioned, the boss is the role model, and in the popular perception, it was thought that the members of the cabinet were as corrupt as their boss—at least the following joke reflects this:

> Alemán comes out to give the traditional *grito*—outcry on independence day, and Rogerio de la Selva whispers in his ear:
>
> "Sir, the band is missing."
>
> Alemán says:
>
> "What do you mean? Ortiz Mena, Ramos Millán, and others are right here."
>
> "No sir, I mean the presidential band [he is referring to the presidential sash, while Alemán is referring to his gang]."

After leaving the presidency and until his death in the 1980s, Alemán became and remained president of the National Tourism Council, where he promoted his personal financial interests. For these merits, Tomás Perrín named him the Downfall of National Tourism. Without a doubt, he was the first president to earn the reputation for corruption; see the following joke:

> Where is Ali Baba from? From Turkey.
> And the forty thieves? From Veracruz.

Because members of the military resisted leaving their positions of power, and even though they clashed with Miguel Alemán's youth (he had been the youngest president of Mexico and had apparently attempted to be re-elected), they were able to put in place a man who grew up in on both slopes: as paymaster of the military and as an attorney. Nevertheless, jokes were made about Adolfo Ruíz Cortines, making fun of his old age. His nickname was with reference to his initials (ARC), which truly stand for Antigua Reliquia Colonial but jokingly stand for "antique colonial relic," and the jokes focused on the same subject:

> During his presidential campaign Ruíz Cortines found himself in Guadalajara, when he decided to go for a walk with some of his colleagues. All of a sudden he asks one of them:
>
> "Well, what jokes have you heard out there?"
>
> "Well, the usual, about the fact that you're old, you're aged, that you can't do it anymore."
>
> Ruíz Cortines responds:
>
> "Well, do they want me to rule or as a stud?"

~

> The inside of Ruíz Cortines' pocket was torn. He put his hand in and said:
>
> "Raisins, raisins, but I didn't buy raisins."

In the previous joke, there are several incongruities: one, being a powerful and corrupt president, Ruíz Cortines shouldn't be going around with torn pockets; and two, being in a society that is measured by the model of the macho, to have small testicles (raisins) represents low sexual prowess, and consequently, having a lack of courage, audacity and power—unacceptable characteristics for a president. Expanding on this subject, the following joke was made about him:

> "What are the three most useless things about Mexico?"

"The useless life of Pito Pérez,[10] the fucked up life of Pita Amor,[11] and the useless *pito* [penis] of Ruíz Cortines. [*Pito* literally means 'whistle' or 'penis.']" (Trueba Lara, 1993)

Jokes about age were also made about his wife. They played with her name, changing it from María Izaguirre de Ruíz Cortines to María Izarrugas (referring to *arrugas* [wrinkles]) de Ruíz Cortines, and this seems to have been a novelty because she held a certain unusual notoriety among the previous first ladies:

Someone says to Ruíz Cortines: "Mr. President, tell your wife to lift up her drooping stockings."

He responds: "Man, those aren't her stockings, those are her wrinkles."

Ruíz Cortines was famous for his love of the game of dominoes and for wearing bow ties. Playing with these habits Flota (1985) included this definition in his dictionary:

Adolfmino. Rule for the use of a white bow tie with little black polka dots upon opening a game when he doesn't get a *mula de seises* [the double sixes].

Flota's reference is to the ease with which the president cheats, because being so powerful, he must open the game; if he doesn't have the double sixes, he will always be able to use his bow tie. This suggests something about corruption because, with Ruíz Cortines having based his government on a campaign of punishment of the Alemán corruption, the society paid more attention to the alleged reputation of his wife as the owner of brothels. The following joke is very explicit:

Durante el campeonato mundial de fútbol, un ayudante le dice a la señora Ruíz Cortines:

"Señora, perdimos con Gales."

Ella responde:

"No se preocupen ahorita le hablo a Adolfo y nos lo devuelven de inmediato."

During the soccer world cup an assistant says to Mrs. Ruíz Cortines:

"Madam, we lost against Gales."

She responds:

"Don't worry, I'll call Adolfo right now and they will give it back immediately."

The confusion stems from "*con Gales*"—Gales being the Spanish word for the country Wales on the British island—and the word "*congales*," which means brothels. The narrator could have said, "We lost against Gales," but the humor would have been lost. This joke reflects the ingenious Mexican ability to play with language and transmit meaningful messages, which, by the way, reaffirm the version that the first lady had a prostitution business and the corollary that by presidential decree, the law is overlooked.

Adolfo López Mateos succeeded Ruíz Cortines as president and began to extend Mexico's international presence, traveling intensely. This became the motive for a series of jokes and his nickname "López Paseos" (López Travels), as if instead of representing the country, which was gaining notoriety in the world at that time, he was simply traveling at his leisure. Other jokes, like the following one, considered him stupid:

López Mateos was talking to Francisco Franco and he asked him:

"*Caudillo*, how have you been able to govern with such success?"

Franco answered:

"I always hire aides that are more ignorant than me. I'm going to give you an example. Call in one of my aides and tell him to go to my house and see if General Franco is there."

The aid goes quickly and a little while later comes back, out of breath, and says: "No, my general."

Franco says to López Mateos: "You see how dumb my aide is?"

And López Mateos answers: "He sure is. In his place, I would have called on the telephone."

This joke has come back, but with a different twist, as we will see, with respect to Salinas and Fox. In this case, it attacks from several angles. On the one hand, it's illogical for López Mateos to question Franco, being that Mexico had no relations with Spain from the time Franco was in power and Mexico supported the Spanish Republican government in exile, which was in fact seated in Mexico. On the other hand, it is comical that the president should ask such an illogical question as he does above, and much less so when he could count on an army of aides that he could have sent.

Another object of comic ridicule was López Mateos's wardrobe, for the suits he wore he earned him the nickname "El Mangotas" (Mr. Huge Sleeves).

His administration wasn't well received due to its ambiguous posture. On the one hand, he repressed popular protests and jailed their leaders. Also, when he arrested David Alfaro Siqueiros, he earned the nickname "El Mazmorras" (The Dungeon). On the other hand, he declared himself the defender of the constitutional left, opposing support for the U.S. embargo on Cuba, which engendered great adversity. It is altogether possible that with that action, he earned yet another one of his nicknames: "Largos y Malos" (Long and Bad), referring to the L&M brand cigarettes that were trendy at that time, whose initials matched those of López Mateos. Marco Antonio Flota summarizes López Mateos' tenure in the following way:

> *Agdolfo* [his real name being Adolfo—without the *g*): Popular mandate initiating the trend of *viajes y viejas*—trips and women.

Golfos are high-living individuals, and this president went down in history as a womanizer and man who busied himself with life's pleasures while the National Treasury footed the bill, without the country reaping any benefit. There has been much speculation regarding his illness. It is maintained that he suffered from migraines or from a debilitating aneurism. It is thought that the government was in reality run by his minister of the interior, Gustavo Díaz Ordaz. The following epigram by Francisco Liguori summarizes the transition of power:

> The travels are over
> Oh Paladin of Peace!
> You are leaving now López Mateos
> López Mateos you are leaving now
> And you're leaving—*haciendo feos*—with a frown
> Well you made Díaz Ordaz [who was considered ugly—*feo*].
> (Gallo 1987:260)[12]

Gustavo Díaz Ordaz was the last president considered part of the Mexican Miracle, according to Crouch (2004:19):

> The decade of the 1960s brought to fruition a new, more self-confident generation, that culminated in a phenomenon known as October of '68.

Between students, laborers and other groups, new demands for participation and involvement in work and public life were born.

This government was insensitive to these changes, and instead of trying to understand what was happening with the protesting social sectors, it confronted them with a tough and implacable hand. There was repression in response to a strike of physicians, and student conflicts in 1966 and 1968. Mejía Prieto (1992:143–144) mentions two jokes about the belligerent nature of the president:

> Díaz Ordaz was a boxer of a president, because he started out his tenure with a *madrazo* [*punch* is a play on words because Madrazo was also the name of the PRI candidate who was "knocked out"].
>
> ~
>
> He was entirely a knockout artist; he threw a *madrazo* [blow], and knocked out Uruchurtu.

Uruchurtu was the head of the Federal District Department. Madrazo died in an airplane accident and Uruchurtu was forced to resign. All these events were irrelevant—for what did it matter if monetary values were stable, inflation was low, and there was economic growth? The government had crushed the children of the middle class, and its image for posterity remained one of brutality and the assailing of political and democratic rights. Political humor ridiculed Díaz Ordaz's physical features, nicknaming him "El Feo" (The Ugly), and "El Pozole," (*pozole* being a Mexican soup made with a pig snout and pig ears—such as people said were Díaz Ordaz's ugly features).

> In reference to Hitchcock's movie Psycho (*Psicosis*), it was said:
>
> "Do you know what movie is going to be ordered shown, by presidential decree, in all of the movie theaters in Mexico?"
>
> "No, which?"
>
> "*Hocicosis* [the word *hocico* means 'snout,' therefore meaning 'snoutitis,' and *Hocicosis* carries the cord *Psicosis* within it]." (Mejía Prieto, 1992:142)

Velasco Piña (2005:82) describes Díaz Ordaz in the following manner: "In addition to being ugly, Díaz Ordaz had brusque and authoritarian mannerisms which made people restrained and fearful in his presence." It's not unusual, then, that one of Díaz Ordaz's most common nicknames was "El Chango" (The Monkey), which is a clear allusion to the feminine sexual organ in common Mexican jargon. On June 23, 1966, it just so "occurred" that in the newspaper *Diario de Mexico* there was an interchange in the captions of two photographs that appeared side by side. In one, a group of gasoline station owners were paying tribute to the president, so there appeared a photo of Díaz Ordaz behind the podium. In the other photo there were two gorillas in a cage. At the bottom of the photo in which the president was being honored, the caption read:

> The zoo is enriched. This photo shows the new specimen acquired by the authority for the entertainment of Mexico City residents. The goal is to make the Mexico City Zoo one of the most complete zoos, in which the greatest variety of creatures is exhibited, representing the complete fauna in its varied expressions. Such as reflected in the present case, the goal is that the bringing together of creatures will result in a growth in the number of creatures exhibited. These monkeys were placed in their respective cages yesterday.

The caption at the foot of the photo with the gorillas read:

> Convention of Gasoline Station Owners. At the beginning of the 4th Annual National Convention of Gasoline Retailers, the leader of the CNOP—PRI organization to which they all belong—Doctor Renaldo Guzmán Orozco—leads in a conceptual message. In the photo he is shown speaking. Presiding at the podium are: Carlos Rafael Franyutti, president of the Union, Jorge Espinoza de los Reyes, vice-president of Pemex and Fernando Díaz Durán, secretary general of CEN (the national committee) of the PRI. (Ochoa, 1990:20)

Needless to say, the chief editor of the newspaper was "convinced" to resign. The jokes also focused on Díaz Ordaz's physical ugliness:

> One time, they told Díaz Ordaz that the people from Puebla were two faced, to which he answered:
>
> "It's not true because if they were, I would have already put on the other face."

> Díaz Ordaz was sitting next to Governor López Arias on a visit to the Port of Veracruz. The sky was very cloudy when all of a sudden the governor whispered into the president's ear:
>
> "How ugly these days are [here we have a play on words because the word for *days* is *días*, which is also the last name of the president], aren't they, Mr. President?"
>
> Díaz Ordaz answered:
>
> "That's how it is, Mr. Governor, but don't you believe that the Lópezes [the governor's last name] are any better looking."

There was a rumor that the actress Irma Serrano, whose nickname was "the Tigress," was Díaz Ordaz's lover, and she took care to assure that this rumor was true, while at the same time slandering members of Díaz Ordaz's cabinet, especially Luis Echeverría (Serrano and Robledo, 1978). Flota (1985) uses this version to include the following definition in his dictionary:

> *Camafeo* [one word made up of two; *cama* and *feo*. Root of the fortune of the famous Tigress during the 1964–1970 presidential term, *cama* (bed) and *feo* (ugly)].

On the subject of the events of 1968, which can be considered the most traumatic of the presidential term, there is an anecdote that if not absolutely directed at the president, shows society's desire to get even with those responsible:

> A reporter was pressuring Carlos Madrazo to divulge his possible participation as the brains behind the student movement. The politician from Tabasco smiled at the naïve question and answered:
>
> I am of the *madrazos* [this is his last name, but the word also means "punches" such as the blows that took place during the student riots] of Tabasco not of Tlatelolco [the square of Mexico City where many students were killed on October 2, 1968].

Bureaucratic Presidents, 1970–1994

The Mexican Miracle came to an end with Luis Echeverría (Schmidt, 1991b). After 1970, there began an economic recession and a crisis (which, according to some, still hasn't ended) in which inflation rose. Political peace was something of the past: independent movements arose among laborers, peasants, and segments of the middle class who looked to distance themselves from the State and from pro-government organizations. Guerrilla groups sprang up along the length and width of the country, showing that the social peace, of which the PRI and the government had been so proud, had now come to an end. The guerillas committed certain extraordinary acts, such as the kidnapping of the president's father-in-law. Society blamed the president for the dominating situation, and jokes expressed this in the following way:

> One day, upon reflection, Díaz Ordaz arrived at the conclusion that the people of the nation had been unfair to him. They had made fun of his ugly looks, and they exaggeratedly blamed him for 68, and so he planned a great revenge on Mexico and designated Luis Echeverría as his successor.

Since the government of Díaz Ordaz, the presidential image lost its luster, and stopped being venerated, becoming more vulnerable to society's attacks. Echeverría was thought to be a verbose, messianic egomaniac (Velasco Piña, 2005:91). Perhaps his lowest popular point came when he was hit on the head with a stone when visiting the National Autonomous University of México (UNAM) campus in 1975. The jokesters hit the jackpot:

> At that time, it was said that the trendiest drink in the bars around the university was *presidente con sangrita*. [This is a play on words—*presidente* means president, but it's also the name of a brandy, and *sangrita* literally means a little blood, but it is also the name of the spicy mix used to drink with tequila.]

Echeverría had to confront a very unusual situation. He won the presidency at the cost of being stigmatized by the repression of 1968, since he was Díaz Ordaz's minister of the interior, and as such was responsible for internal security. The magazine *Revelación* (1990, number 120) supports this argument, based on a declaration by Rafael Hernández Ochoa, ex-governor of Veracruz, stating that Echeverría planned the massacre at Tlatelolco, using it as a springboard to the presidency. Velasco Piña supports this version, which maintains that the shootout at Tlatelolco was started by government agents. For his part, in an attempt to clear Marcelino Garcia Barragán's reputation, Scherer (Scherer and Monsiváis, 1999), national defense secretary at the time, maintains that the presidential guard[13] was to blame. In terms of public opinion, Echeverría was to blame for the lack of prosperity, and for the fact that the crisis long predicted by the left had finally arrived. Society used political humor to respond to this traumatic situation, and the president was disarmed by the humoristic attack. Velasco Piña adds (2005:92):

> Only a few weeks had passed since his coming to power, and already the entire country was making jokes in which he appeared as the most perfect idiot in a variety of anecdotes, real or invented in which the president committed the silliest acts [. . .] the people ended up attributing Echeverría's personality as possessing a perverse malignancy.

The situation arose, among the wave of rumors unleashed during the presidential term, that he who would tell jokes about Echeverría would be incarcerated, which discouraged anyone from telling such jokes. The jokes focused on the supposed stupidity (*pendejismo*) of the president:

> Echeverría was going down the stairs of the presidential mansion *Los Pinos* dressed in a tuxedo. When he was asked where he was going, he answered:
>
> "I'm going to the graduation of my eyeglasses [in Spanish, 'graduation of eyeglasses' means an eyeglass prescription, so we have a play on words with academic graduation]."

What's illogical here is simply the president's lack of intelligence, which makes him think that eyeglasses undergo a formal graduation. And in the same vein:

> A Mexican gets to heaven and they show him some watches that mark the stupid things presidents do. He sees that of López Mateos, Alemán, etc., which are progressing at a moderate pace. He then asks about Echeverría's and they tell him:
>
> "We're using it as a fan in the game room."

The following joke made a comeback in 2005, adapted to fit Vicente Fox, making fun of his great ignorance:

> Echeverría receives an automatic transmission station wagon as a gift, but the next day he complains that the car doesn't work, and when they ask him what's wrong, he says:

"I was on the highway and had it in *D* for *despacio* [slow]; when a car passed me, I tried to catch up to it, so I put the car on *R* for *rapidisimo* [very fast] and the car broke down."

~

Echeverría was with María Esther (his wife) in the desert and a black man was fanning them, but not to Echeverría's satisfaction, so he said to him:

"Get away, I'm going to show you how it's done."

When they switch places the man gets in the mood and makes love to María Esther, and when Echeverría hears the sounds of satisfaction, he says to him:

"You see how it's done you idiot [pendejo]?"

The jokes about Echeverría also focused on the rumor that his wife "wore the pants" in the family, a very important aspect in a country with a still largely chauvinistic mentality:

They call Los Pinos the haunted house because in it there is a woman with balls and a headless man.

As we saw earlier there had been jokes about the wife of Ruíz Cortinez, that now turned to María Esther Zuno de Echeverría, who became the butt of ridicule for her great interest in folklore, to the point that in the presidential residence she would wear typical native dress and serve typical native fruit juices. Flota (1985) includes her in his dictionary with the following entry:

Estheril [play on words between her first name Esther and the word *sterile*]. Failed six-year attempt to make the country folkloric.

The jokes about corruption did not cease, though most of them were based on the accusation that Echeverría had properties in Cancún, which was the reason behind the government's push toward tourist development in the area. That accusation possibly alludes to Echeverría's intention to emulate what Miguel Alemán did in Acapulco:

Echeverría gets to heaven and St. Peter says to him:

"What would you like, my son?"

"La Paz [meaning "peace" but also the capital city of Baja California Sur]."

"What, Cancún was not enough for you?"

"Which is Echeverría's dog?"
"Can Cun." [*Can* means "dog."]

The humoristic verses became virulent and aggressive, insulting Echeverría and his wife, as seen in the sonnet *Adios Chivarrías*. Religious parodies acquired the same tone, as seen in *Oración al piadoso Señor Echeverría* and in *El credo*.

Credo
Según San Político
Creo en el PRI todopoderoso,
Creador de candidatos en la tierra
de Echeverría su único hijo
Señor nuestro que fue elegido por
obra y gracia del espíritu cuento;
nació de la Secretaria de Gobernación
y apareció bajo el poder de Díaz Ordaz;
fue maquillado, retratado y amplificado;
demostró ser el BUENO y, al tercer día
resucitó entre los tapados.
¡Subió a Los Pinos y está sentado a la
derecha del PRI todopoderoso
desde ahí hace combatir
y exterminar a los benefactores del pueblo!
¡Creemos en su Espíritu Santo . . .
en la Santa Constitución,
la amplificación de los empleos,
el perdón de los impuestos,
la reducción de los precios
y la vida tranquila del mundo futuro.
Amén . . . digo!

Credo
By Saint politician
I believe in the PRI almighty,
Creator of candidates on earth
of Echeverría his only son
He was conceived by the

> power of the Holy Story;
> Born in the ministry of the interior
> appeared under the Díaz Ordaz power;
> with make up, was photographed and amplified;
> proved to be the GOOD ONE,
> On the third day he rose again from the veiled.
> He ascended into Los Pinos
> and is seated at the right hand of the almighty PRI
> From where he fights and exterminates
> All the people's benefactors!
> We believe in his Holy Spirit . . .
> the holy Constitution,
> expansion of jobs,
> the forgiveness of taxes,
> Price reduction
> and the life everlasting of the future world.
> Amen

The pun on the "Amen" is on "putting together" in Spanish. *A méndigo* here means "oh, dude."

When López Portillo took over the presidency, he was received with a combination of relief and hope. The country was getting rid of a hyper-active president who had shown the economic elite some troublesome leanings to the left. After the devaluation of the peso in 1976, when the peso began to float, it was said that:

> A different type of change [*tipo de cambio* means "exchange rate"] wasn't necessary, but rather the change of a certain type [the person at the helm, the president].

In this way, he was made to seem like a serene person who would have the ability to revive national solidarity. The jokes started out benevolently:

> They call López Portillo "The Tampax" because he is in the best place at the wrong time.

This is an isomorphic joke to the one about the president who is nicknamed "The Tractor" because he has come to replace the ass.

The relief that many felt at the end of the Echeverría nightmare was invested in a new president who was seen as an educated professional, a reasonable and measured man with the desire to restore harmony among Mexicans. His nickname, "Jolopo," was simply a combination of the first two letters of his first and last names connected by one extra syllable, but the tone in which it was vocalized began to harden as the years went by.

The economic crisis forced the government to negotiate with the International Monetary Fund (IMF), allowing foreign intervention within the country and therefore aggravating national pride. Propelled by economic circumstances, once again Mexican xenophobia surfaced as visions of the conquest and foreign invasion were revived in the collective imagination.

The discovery of new oil reserves in the country (Díaz Serrano, 1989) seemed to give López Portillo a certain reprieve. Thanks to the oil, the government cancelled its agreement with the IMF and began a period of prosperity, though short lived. The president turned into the most optimistic person in the country. He began an ambitious program of oil exploration and exploitation and petrochemical production through which he assured the country that it would have to learn to "administer abundance." The private business affairs of Echeverría had amassed him a great fortune, yet the fortune of López Portillo grew even faster. The dollar was very cheap, and national capital kept escaping from the country, as much that of businessmen as that of politicians, showing once again that the elite abuse the nation. Businessmen justified their actions by saying that there was no confidence in the country, though it was they who were creating the conditions for low confidence. The jokes began to turn on the president:

> What does JLP [the president's initials] mean?
> *Jamás Lo Pensamos.* [We never thought it.]

Politically, the situation seemed to have returned to normal. The guerrilla problem had been solved, independent organizations had been combated and had nearly disappeared, and new political parties emerged, moving social conflict from the streets to the Congress, in what seemed to be democratic progress. It didn't matter that López Portillo hadn't had a political rival, because he had officially received a copious vote and the country was calm once again.

But corruption was once again seen, accompanied by a refined nepotism. The president's sisters occupied important positions in public administration, and when the president named his son as undersecretary, he cynically said that he was his "favorite nepotism." It wasn't surprising, then, that humor was on the attack against the public's perception of having been tricked. The following joke appeared on the pages of a newspaper in Mexico City:

> This is López Portillo's bank account number:
> 0TI9 13 0IT3M Z0N 3939
> Seen reflected in the mirror it reads:
> PEPE NOS METIÓ EL PITO. ["Pepe dicked us."]

Once again the president was responsible for the difficult situation that the country was facing, and the people continued to keep in mind Echeverría's management. The charming and charismatic president stopped being so. Instead, one joke characterized him thus:

> López Portillo is called "Chamomile Tea" because he sits well with everybody, but he's of no use.

Perhaps the informal suspicions and accusations of corruption weren't sufficient, but the publicity of his alleged amorous relationship with an official who was elevated to the position of secretary of state infuriated a people whose hopes had been raised for a president who would be a model of moral behavior:

> López Portillo was awarded with the international leather-tanning award because he turned a *cuero* into a *cartera*. [A *cuero* is a piece of hide and can also mean "a sexy, good looking woman" and a *cartera* is a wallet or purse, and also a presidential cabinet position.]

The jokes tackled the president's family life and left a bitter taste of decadence and depravity. They allude to his relationship with Rosa Luz Alegría (the secretary of tourism), and they also comment on his wife Carmen, criticizing her vulgar personality:

> López Portillo was in bed when all of a sudden there was an electric power outage. He called his military attaché in and when he arrived he said to him:
>
> "Where's the light [*luz*—meaning 'light'—and also the name of the secretary of tourism]?"
>
> "Next to you, Mr. President."
>
> "Don't be a pendejo, where is *la corriente* [meaning 'the electrical power' and also 'the vulgar one']?"
>
> "Oh, she's in Europe touring with the symphonic orchestra."

It was rumored that López Portillo's marriage was in disarray, and even though his wife was a patron of the arts, she frequently traveled with the symphony orchestra (and even with a piano that she stubbornly insisted on having installed in her room at the Waldorf Astoria in New York). But humor was unforgiving and made fun of the deteriorating marriage of the first family, combining criticism of the president's love affair with accusations of corruption:

> "What song did Rosa Luz Alegría sing to López Portillo?"
> "I will be your lover, you bandit, you bandit."[14]

The image of the first lady was also damaged, considering that she had mannerisms and tastes that were inappropriate for her position, as would be the case with Ernesto Zedillo's wife further down the road. There were rumors that she, just like her husband, engaged in dissolute behavior, for which reason the image of the whole family was that of moral dissipation:

> On the first of December there is going to be a blackout in Los Pinos, because both the *Luz* and the *Corriente* are leaving.

López Portillo didn't finish out his presidential term "administrating abundance"; poor management of the economy and the lack of unity and commitment of business leaders aggravated the crisis—and this, among other things, sped up inflation and the peso's devaluation.[15] In 1982, the mistaken policy of public debt and exorbitant interest rates led Mexico to suspend all payments. The peso was devalued after the president made one of his most dramatic commitments to protect it. Some years after the end of his term, the thought of him and his incompetence still sent bullets straight to the heart. Due to the earthquake in September 1985 and the arrival of dogs to help out in the rescue, Jeronimo published a cartoon in the *Heraldo* (October 6, 1985) in which a young man asks a young woman:

> "What's the difference between a Mexican dog and a foreign one?"
> She answers: "I don't know—what is it?"
> "The Mexican one left us in ruins."

For Mexicans, the parity of the peso represents the success or failure of the government.[16] López Portillo reaffirmed this when he said he would defend the peso "like a dog," but since his image was already gravely damaged, the only thing he accomplished with that declaration was to feed the national humor frenzy. He was immediately nicknamed "The Dog," and the group of homes he was building in the Mexico City suburbs, a questionable gift from Carlos Hank González, became known as La Colina del Perro—"Dog's Hill." The following implacable joke killed him off:

> When he inaugurated his equestrian statue in Monterrey, Nuevo Leon, people said that he had inaugurated the statue of the animals, one riding on top of the other.

There are reports of someone barking at him in Madrid after he left the presidency, and at that moment the most caustic jokes against him were invented:

> López Portillo is going along in a tuxedo [*frac*] on his way to meet with Ronald Reagan. Reagan says to him:
>
> "¡*Que fracaso!* What a failure, Mr. President." [*Que fracaso* can also mean "what a great tux!"]
>
> "Yes, it's *de sastre national* [which can mean 'made by a local tailor,' or 'a national disaster']."

The following joke makes fun of the great notoriety of the presidential family. It combines their excesses with the appropriation of public funds for personal use:

> At the close of his presidential term López Portillo said to his mother:
>
> "Mother, what would you like as a gift? I have a few days left as president, but I'll give you whatever you want."
>
> His mother answers:
>
> "No, son, you've already given me so much, thank you."
>
> But when López Portillo insists, his mother says:
>
> "Cut your leg off."
>
> "But why, mother?"
>
> "Because I prefer that they say 'good-bye, dumb lame one,' than they say 'good-bye, you son of a bitch.'"

Just as with López Mateos, society threw all of his frivolity, his corruption, and his fickleness as president in his face. This is well expressed in the following joke:

> The colors that destroyed Mexico were:
>
> Green (the color of the dollar)

Black (for Durazo, the corrupt Mexico City's chief of police)
Bright pink (for Rosa Luz—his lover and also *rosa* means "pink").

Another one of López Portillo's interests, which was taken as an affront by society, was Spain. Conscious of his Spanish origins, he visited the town where his family was from, in a return to his roots. This reopened the old Mexican trauma about the conquest, because he was not mestizo; he was a governing descendant of the Spaniards who openly wielded his Creole background. Furthermore, several Spanish descendants entered the cabinet and were nicknamed "Los Churumbeles" (Spanish gypsy dialect meaning "boys" or "children"). Mexican society, which is xenophobic to begin with, felt that the president was more interested in his genealogy than in the reality of national events. This joke emerged with that resentment:

Close to the end of his term as president, López Portillo went to the barbershop and asked the barber:

"Hey, I don't know how I should cut it [*pelarme* means 'to cut hair' or 'to flee']."

"Well, why don't you do it like Porfirio Díaz?"

"How did Porfirio Díaz do it?"

"Via Veracruz and by boat."

The joke plays with a double irony. On the one hand, López Portillo was almost bald, so it was ridiculous for him to go to the barbershop. On the other hand, *pelarse* means "to escape" and "to cut one's own hair," which suggests that the best way for him to end his term was to escape from the country, following the most despised dictator Díaz's steps.

As with Echeverría, the jokes were sanguine. López Portillo's family became the object of ridicule, and their tone was insulting. The poem "Disillusion" is harsh. The religious parodies seem to be tweaked adaptations of the old Echeverría jokes.

En el sexenio pasado	In the last six years
Un loco nos gobernó	we were governed by a mad man
Dejándonos bien fregados	leaving us a wreck
Y a todos nos rechingó	and all completely screwed
Hoy otro loco en Los Pinos	Now another fool in Los Pinos
Como perrito amistoso	Like a friendly puppy
Gobierna con desatino	governs with nonsense
Con su sistema mañoso	with his sneaky system
López Portillo ha creído	López Portillo has believed

Ser sabio y omnipotente	to be wise and omnipotent
Y es un pendejo engreído	and he is a conceited stupid
Un peligroso demente	dangerous demented
Arruinó la economía	he ruined our economy
Con planes descabellados	with crazy plans
Dejándonos arruinados	leaving us ruined
Nos devaluó la moneda	he devalued our currency
Encareció la pitanza	increased the price of food
Por poco nos deja	he almost left us
Nos dejó vacía la panza	he left us with our stomachs empty
Hipotecó la nación	he mortgaged the nation
Recurriendo al extranjero	Going to the foreigner
Con préstamos a montón	with loans by the tons
A Doña Carmen Romano	Donia Carmen Romano
La pinta un hábil pincel	is painted by a skillful brush
¿es modelo de Tamayo	is she a model for Tamayo?
O madrota de burdel?	or the madame of a brothel?
Y la hermana Margarita	and the sister Margarita
Con su cara de pambazo	with her sandwich face
Presume de muy bonita	Thinks she's so pretty
Y es ridículo payaso	but she's a ridiculous clown
Su hijo José Ramón	his son José Ramón
Con barbas como el cubano	with a beard like the Cuban
De los bancos usurero	To the banks a shark loaner
Comunista de salón	commie loudmouth
Rojillo guadalupano	red Guadalupan

When Miguel de la Madrid began his presidential term, Mexicans received him with great incredulity. The economic situation was very fragile. López Portillo's government had incurred great debt and politics had deteriorated, both of which perhaps lead to the great collapse of the peso. This joke took its revenge:

López Portillo received several Nobel Prizes:
He won the one in physics for making the peso float only to sink it later.
He won the one in chemistry for turning the peso into crap.
He won the one in biology for turning man into a dog.

If López Portillo took on the heavy cost of the devaluation to leave a more favorable playing field for his successor, it seems the damage had been done:

José López Porpillo [*Porpillo* means "for being a thief"] exited and in came Miguel de la Madrid Hurtando [meaning "embezzling," and a play on words with his name, *Hurtado*, which also means "stolen"].

In addition, changes in the power structure were already being felt. De la Madrid was the third president to ascend through bureaucratic channels, which not only weakened the political framework but also raised doubts as to his political abilities. To rise to the top power position, the PRI candidate no longer had to have had a long political career, nor did he have to retain the popular vote in an election, as he would have before 1970. Bureaucrat presidents seemed to have arrived at the presidency by being disciplined and not by having learnt to pull the strings of power that take a politician to the peak of the pyramid. In addition to all of this, de la Madrid assumed the presidency amidst a controversy between politicians and technocrats,[17] and he himself was seen as an unsuccessful technocrat. The following joke is one that was re-adapted from one about López Portillo, and it is indicative of society's opinion of de la Madrid:

> They call de la Madrid "The Tailor" because he takes measurements all the time. [*Tomando medidas* means "to take measurements" and also "to take measures."]

The following isomorphic joke alludes to his administration:

> This is the presidential term of the tailor because he takes measures [measurements], he makes cuts and cuts some more just like a *tailor*.

Several jokes allude to his alleged cowardice, his boldlessness, and timidity. People considered him a weak, childish, chicken-hearted president with little personality. This feeling was reaffirmed after his timid response to the 1985 earthquake:

> "Why does de la Madrid have small *huevos* [literally meaning 'eggs' but in slang meaning 'testicles']."
>
> "Because they are Paloma's [*paloma* means 'pigeon,' but it was also the name of the president's wife—in essence, the president had small testicles, the size of a pigeon's]."

Let's remember that Mexicans equate the size of one's testicles to the amount of power, and when they refer to a coward they say he has no *huevos* (testicles) or is castrated. In this case the following joke gives the idea that de la Madrid is considered faint-hearted:

> They call de la Madrid the one hundred-peso milk shake because the two hundred-peso shake has eggs added [*eggs*, in this case, means "testicles"].

In addition to his weakness, the fact that de la Madrid was named by López Portillo made people immediately associate him with the latter's corruption. Logic dictates that the president names a successor who will watch his back after he leaves his post. Since, according to popular opinion, López Portillo was extremely corrupt, it was assumed that there would be a continuity of corruption. See the previous joke that plays with both ex-presidents' last names, and the following one, which is one of the first jokes of its type:

> What belongs to de la Madrid belongs to the people and what is embezzled [hurtado] belongs to Miguel.

The president insisted that he was going to renew public morale to attack corruption head on, but even at the inception of his electoral campaign, a painted wall in Mexico City summarized this opinion:

> MMH [the president's initials] = *muerte, miseria, hambre* [death, misery, hunger].

The jokes were conclusive:

> De la Madrid's administration wasn't that of moral renewal but rather it was the administration of the renewal of the oaf [*morral*].

His reactions after the 1985 earthquake reinforced his weak image. See the following jokes:

> Who is the only woman in Mexico with three animal names?
>
> Paloma Cordero of de la Madrid [this was the president's wife's name; *paloma* means "pigeon"; her last name *Cordero* means "lamb," and the use here of *de la Madrid* implies that he was an animal].

The joke mentions two peaceful animals; therefore, de la Madrid is defined by extension a peaceful animal with the courage of a pigeon. In comparison with the fist lady who preceded her, Mrs. de la Madrid decided to assume a very low profile, for which reason the jokes that were made had to do with her husband's insipid qualities. There is this one that compares her to López Portillo's wife:

> They call Paloma Cordero "Resistol" [an all-purpose glue] because she replaced *Kola Loca* [a type of crazy glue, but in slang it can also mean "a loose woman"—alluding to López Portillo's wife's habits].

The jokes about the president became sharper, as did his nicknames. At the beginning they called him Mike; then he became "Mickey Mouse"; and even later, when his political public debt policy consisted in continued payment of the debt and refusing a moratorium, his nickname became "El Abonero" (which means "a street vendor who sells on installments"). By 1987, he was called "El Tibio y el Morelos," which referred to the first Mexican satellite, because he is supposedly in orbit or out of reach.[18]

In fact, many jokes suggest that de la Madrid was not in control of what was happening in his administration:

> "What do de la Madrid and Tarzan have in common?"
> "Both are surrounded by animals."
> "But they do listen to Tarzan."

> De la Madrid is going to go to Israel and Egypt so that they *medio orienten* him. [*Medio oriente* means "Middle East," and can also mean "to partially instruct somebody."]

The same subject will reappear and will be applied to Salinas after he supported the Persian Gulf War (see the respective joke at the end of this chapter), as well as to Fox. The following joke refers to the presidential succession of 1987:

> There are three possible presidential candidates: Alfredo del Mazo, Manuel Bartlett, and Miguel de la Madrid.

As if de la Madrid hadn't governed and his private secretary Emilio Gamboa had. The following joke came out in the same vein:

> Emilio Gamboa is not run to be a presidential candidate because reelection isn't allowed.

Gamboa had great power. Within political inner circles, it's maintained that he was responsible for blocking presidential access to Porfirio Muñoz Ledo and Cuauhtémoc Cárdenas, in order to eventually name Salinas as the candidate. This created the biggest rupture within the history of the PRI. Somehow, these stories turn the president into an idiot. See the following examples, the first of which reminds us of an isomorphic joke about Echeverría:

> Miguel de la Madrid was named director of the governmental publishing house Fondo de Cultura Económica because down deep he's not such an ass. [The word for *fund* is *fondo*, which can also mean "bottom deep."]

> There is an American, a Mexican, and a Russian.
>
> The American says, "Listen, in our country, a farmer in Kansas was walking along when he was run over by a train that cut off his two legs; we fitted him with bionic legs, and now he is a champion in the one hundred meter race."
>
> The Russian says, "Listen, in my country, a laborer was working in the iron and steel industry where he lost his two arms in an accident, but we fitted him with robotic arms, and now he is a weight lifting champion."
>
> The Mexican says, "Man, that's nothing, over in my country, we found a man without a brain, we put an avocado pit in its place, and now he's president of the republic."

This joke makes a comeback with Vicente Fox, but with him it's about a man without a head and replace it with an excrement-filled coconut.

> "Why does de la Madrid's brain measure four centimeters in width?"
>
> "Because it's swollen."[19]

> They say that Miguel de la Madrid was breastfed; that's why they call him the sucker.

The isomorphic joke says the following:

The mothers of Reagan, Gorbachev, and de la Madrid find themselves together, and Reagan's mother says, "I fed Ronnie buffalo milk only; that's why he has such vigor and strength."

Gorbachev's mother says, "I fed Misha bear's milk; that's why he has such strength and courage."

De la Madrid's mother says, "I fed Mickey Phillip's Milk of Magnesia; that's why he makes a crap here, he makes a crap there . . . [he makes crap out of situations]."

De la Madrid and Silva Herzog went to filling the tank up at a gasoline station when they realized they have no money. They told the manager who they were but he asked them to prove it or he would call the police. Silva Herzog said to him, "Inflation is going to come to a halt."

The manager answered, "Now, anyone would say that."

Then Silva said to de la Madrid, "Miguel, please say something."

"I can only think of dumb ass things to say."

The manager answered, "Now I believe who you are; you can go."

Since then, this joke has been played on presidents, and even on Andrés Manuel López Obrador when he was a candidate in 2005.

Jokes that compare de la Madrid with his two predecessors show a societal revenge and synthesize the painful and inexplicable history of many Mexicans, who while having a country with abundant natural resources, see very little hope of getting out from under.

De la Madrid, López Portillo, and Echeverría were riding on a train when it suddenly broke down. Echeverría said, "Keep calm, gentlemen, let's form a committee to study the problem, and with its recommendations, we'll form a trusteeship and we'll solve it."

López Portillo says, "No, listen, we'll ask for a foreign loan, we'll lay a new rail line, we'll buy another train, and we'll party with what's left."

De la Madrid says, "No, listen, better yet, let's sit down, balance each other on the sides, we'll say choo choo choo and we'll pretend it's moving."[20]

The old political ideological balance of the PRI ended by the close of de la Madrid's administration, leading to the biggest divide ever within the governing party. One of the reasons for this could have been the forcing of another bureaucrat into the presidency, or it could have been that the group in charge of power was so closed that it excluded groups that had been important in the recent history of the country. What is true is that Carlos Salinas de Gortari's nomination was accompanied by a split in the party with the resignation of Cuauhtémoc Cárdenas, the son of the revered Lázaro Cárdenas, as well as that of Porfirio Muñoz Ledo, ex-president of the PRI; both were defenders of a progressive current.

Salinas was attacked without mercy because his nomination was considered a capricious imposition of an unpopular president. If he was incapable of resolving the nation's problems, his appointee was much less so.

The de la Madrid–Salinas duet represented political economic failure, and Salinas appeared as the skilled craftsman, given his prominent role on the government's economic team. The economy was destabilized, and toward 1988, inflation was at 150 percent and there was a serious economic recession. The root of the problem came during the ruinous Echeverría economic policy, yet the public blamed the present administration and the jokes got even with them:

> When Salinas was unveiled, Mexicans were happy because they had the baldy [dick] inside.

Already as secretary, Salinas became the unusual victim of jokes, perhaps because he was a strong and very visible secretary who every year went for an optimistic discourse, declaring that they had nearly hit bottom and therefore the crisis was nearly over and recovery was just around the corner. With time, scholars began to joke that Salinas didn't know the meaning of "crisis," or "bottom." Just as Echeverría was associated with the repression of '68, Salinas was associated with the economic crisis of the de la Madrid administration. He was the director of the political economy, and then he became the secretary for programming and budgets; as such, he was in charge of designing and implementing economic measures. This was reflected in the humor.

Salinas was nicknamed "Salinas Recortari" (Salinas the Cutter) which alluded to a program of administrative budget cuts he designed.

In contrast with previous administrations that enjoyed a grace period, Salinas received no respite. Not even as a candidate did the jokes give him a break. Whether it was because of de la Madrid's irrelevance, or through his own protagonist acts, Salinas was the target of the jokes, while being assigned the paternity of politics. The subject of the economy appeared in jokes during his campaign:

During the next administration, there are going to be several state-owned companies, especially a scissors company so that Salinas can cut to his liking.

Apparently, society—as well as politicians—resented Salinas's tremendous power, and this was reflected in the nicknames he was given. Some of them emphasized his physical characteristics, combined with his political power. They called him "the Atomic Ant" due to his bald head. His large ears were ridiculed when he was nicknamed "Super Rat." After the presidential nomination, he turned into "the Head of the Mickey Mouse Club," since his predecessor had been nicknamed "Mickey Mouse." With relation to his physical appearance and suggesting a certain silliness, he was nicknamed "Topogigio," who was a trendy television character (a mole) at the time.

On the other hand, religious parodies continued to be adaptations of those that were made up regarding the three previous presidents. The aggressive jokes are characteristic of his administration. The paradox was that he seemed to be a president with one of the highest approval ratings in the twentieth century. Perhaps we find ourselves confronted with the difference between formal research that reflects a certain state of mind, and spontaneous and free political opinions reflected in the joke that can't be stopped nor changed by governmental propaganda.

An early wave of jokes enveloped Salinas. Society was getting even with the outgoing president and his successor at the same time, and assumed that there was an error from the beginning. They didn't give him the opportunity to prove his skills; he was never given the benefit of the doubt. To make matters worse for society, Salinas encompassed several factors that were rejected. Continuing a tendency that was begun by Echeverría, he turned into the fourth president who came to power by means of bureaucracy (he was the fourth consecutive president from Mexico City)[21] and he was the third technocrat:

Good news and bad news.
The good news: Salinas has AIDS.
The bad news: he screwed all the Mexicans.

A Mario Benedetti poem was adapted to Salinas when he was secretary—which in and of itself is unusual, but even more so because Salinas was already seen as insensitive and a stranger to the needs of society. See excerpts of the poem:

¿De qué se ríe?
En una exacta
foto del diario
señor ministro del
 imposible
Tienen sus hijos
ojos de mando
pero otros tienen
mirada triste.
Ustedes duros
con nuestra gente.

What are you laughing at?
In an identical
picture from the newspaper
Mr. Secretary of Impossible Affairs
 of the State
Your offspring
have the power in their eyes
but others carry
a long face.
You are hard
on our people.

The jokes about him began early, since as secretary he was exposed to the public opinion's critique. Presidents are overexposed to society's judgment; they take up all eight columns of the newspaper on a daily basis, while the ministers keep a modest profile. Even when there are stern journalistic controls, presidents are very vulnerable in comparison to their ministers, who stay relatively safe, with the exception of being endangered by the shootouts amongst themselves. Salinas was already a target of jokes before assuming the presidency; therefore, he had no grace period.

The Salinas election was not an open political competition. It seemed to be one more in a long series of impositions, many of which were accomplished through fraud. The National Democratic Front (FDN), created by Cárdenas, Muñoz Ledo, and other forces, claimed to have won the election and built a post-electoral campaign arguing that Salinas was an illegitimate president. When the Partido de la Revolución Democrática (PRD) was formed, the accusation of illegitimacy turned into the main focus of who was opposed to Salinas. Humor was on the opposing side in the following way:

> Salinas, Bush, and the Pope were in an airplane traveling when the airplane started to fail. The pilot came out and said, "Gentlemen, this is a high security airplane, but something has gone wrong. Unfortunately we have only one parachute, so you will have to decide who will use it."
>
> Bush said, "There is no doubt that the parachute must be for the leader of the free world."
>
> The Pope said, "No, the parachute must be used to save the leader of Catholicism, the most important religion."
>
> Salinas said, "Listen, we're living modern politicians, so let's take a vote."

The three agreed and after some minutes, Salinas was seen jumping in the parachute, while Bush asked the Pope:

"OK, so how did he manage to get forty-five votes if we are only three?"

While Salinas was busy modernizing the Mexican economy and reforming the political system, humor insisted on presidential corruption:

Snow White, the Beast, and Ali Baba were in a forest:

"I'm the most beautiful," says Snow White.

"I'm the ugliest," says the Beast.

"I'm the greatest thief," says Ali Baba.

"Let's prove it," say the three of them and they go see a wise hermit.

Snow White goes in and comes out very happy:

"I'm the most beautiful in the world!"

The Beast goes in and comes out happy:

"I'm the ugliest one in the world!"

Ali Baba goes in and comes out screaming and with the face of an ogre:

"Who the hell is Carlos Salinas?"

The attempt to modernize the political system included three electoral reforms in less than six years (Camou, 1993), even though none of them managed to eliminate the shadow of electoral fraud, under which Salinas was elected in 1988[22] and maintained its illegitimacy. In an unusual declaration, Miguel de la Madrid confirmed in 2005 the version that Salinas had lost the election, which only served to record this as a historical novelty, not to change the events that took place in the country and those to which Mexican society reacted.

The government's political maneuver to unveil Salinas turned into a farce. Six potential candidates were nominated by the PRI to present their platforms, even though in reality five of them were simple figures that adorned Salinas's nomination, when he had in reality already been elected. The nomination, therefore, did not have anything democratic about it. People were hoping without wishing that Salinas would win, and their worst hopes were granted, disillusioning a great number of Mexicans. It's not only the fact that Mexicans generally cheer for the underdog—it's that on that occasion, they confronted a public frustration and wanted to avoid it, but as we have seen, the Mexican has few possibilities of influencing the political system, and adjusts the score by laughing. Humor summarized the appearance of nominees in the following manner:

There was a second appearance of the nominees, who were asked that they should say a word with hyper. Bartlett said:

"Hyperactive."

"Very good," they answered, "see his mental agility."

It was Salinas's turn and he said:

"Hyperinflation."

"Excellent, see how he is in touch with the subjects in his area."

It was Ramón Aguirre's turn and he said:

"Pharmacy."

"Hey, what do you mean, 'pharmacy'?"

"Yes, pharmacy and perfume store [*farmacia y per fumeria* was the typical name for a drugstore that used to sell prescription drugs and toiletries (perfume)]."

An unusual number of Salinas jokes began to circulate. Many referred to his physical appearance:

"How are they going to make rum and coke drinks in the next presidential term?"

"You take a glass; you put ice in it, Coca Cola, and a pinch of *presidente* [the name of a type of brandy in Mexico, also meaning 'president']."

Surely, it seems that to have a pinch of a president would excite many Mexicans. Continuing with the jokes:

They call Salinas the chemist because he has nothing physical.

~

Snow White only has six dwarfs because Dopey is a PRI candidate.

A short time later the joke was corrected this way:

Snow White is happy because Dopey is president.

Combining the idea of the physical with the dopeyness, we have the following:

The CTM supports Salinas because C is for *Calvo* [bald], *T* is for *Tonto* [dopey], and *M* is for *Mediocre* [mediocre].

With reference to his baldness:

> Salinas was chosen because he doesn't have one hair of stupidity.

The size of his ears inspired the following:

> They are going to forbid dancing "Zorba the Greek," because Salinas steps on his own ears.

The subject of silliness haunts Salinas well into his term, reviving an isomorphic joke that was earlier told regarding López Mateos, which was later adapted to Fox:

> Salinas goes to see Bush and Bush says to him, "Look, I'm going to show you how intelligent my aides are."
>
> He calls for Shultz and says to him, "Shultz, who is the son of your parents who is not your brother?"
>
> Shultz thinks for a moment and answers, "Well, me, Mr. President."
>
> "Very good, Shultz," says Bush.
>
> Salinas returns to Mexico, calls Camacho and says, "Manuel, who is the son of your parents and is not your brother?"
>
> Camacho answers, "May I ask for some time to analyze the problem with my advisors, and I will give you the answer shortly?"
>
> Several weeks later Salinas calls Camacho, "Do you have the answer for me, Manuel?"
>
> "No, Mr. President, give me another couple of weeks, please."
>
> Two weeks go by and, exasperated, Salinas calls for Camacho, and when he arrives, he says to him, "A lot of time has gone by; give me the answer."
>
> "Well, the truth is, I don't know, Mr. President."
>
> Salinas answers, "Well, it's Shultz, you dumb ass."[23]

~

> Salinas was about to leave on a trip for the United States, and he asked what caliber was the bullet of the Colorado Canyon [in Spanish, *canyon* can mean "a cannon"].

During the presidential campaign, a book was published (González, Meza, and López Koehl, 1987) that revisits the tragedy in which Carlos Salinas assassinated his housekeeper when he was just four years old. A repressive wave was unleashed against those involved in publishing the book, among them one of the authors who lives as a refugee in the United States. The editor landed in jail for tax evasion, and the person who financed the book landed in prison for fabricated crimes. But humor dealt with the subject in the following manner:

> The next presidential term there will be a permanent sign on the presidential mansion saying housekeeper wanted.

~

> "Why did Salinas kill his housekeeper?"
> "Because she went for the PAN [meaning "bread," but also the name of the opposing political party]."

Salinas can claim many political victories. With very little opposition, he renegotiated the foreign debt and privatized public enterprises, including some banks, which had been nationalized by López Portillo in 1982. His economic program satisfied the private sector and foreign neoliberals because he kept thinning out the public sector and progressed toward an open economy and economic deregulation. In contrast with the sharpness of poverty, he created the program Solidaridad (Solidarity), which not only served to fight poverty[24] but also served as the political structure supporting his candidate, and in the extreme case, to be able to replace the PRI. In 1993, Salinas signed the North American Free Trade Agreement with the United States and Canada. And finally, turning electoral trends around, the PRI easily won the congressional elections in 1991. All of this began to create a positive presidential image that was also reflected, albeit briefly, in the humor. Insisting on his physical appearance, the following joke was passed around in the U.S. embassy in Mexico:

> Salinas weighs forty pounds: eight pounds in ears and thirty-two in balls.

The joke insists on the concept that a macho man has big balls (testicles) and when facing the United States these were required, since many convictions and predominant Mexican groups had to be confronted to get the free trade agreement signed. Humor also responded in the following manner:

> Salinas notified the Mexicans very proudly that the free trade agreement with the United States and Canada had been approved and he said:
> "Now we have twenty-four hours to vacate the country."

It could be that the positive image may have been created by Salinas's public relations team, which disseminated rumors and positive anecdotes about Salinas, even though it was always insisted upon that he was very macho. One of the anecdotes said that Salinas had a team of secretaries in Los Pinos that satisfied his sexual appetite. He would simply cross the doorway into his office, he would choose one, he would have sexual relations with her in his private area, and he would send her back to work. These anecdotes yearned to neutralize the image of a short, balding, big-eared president who would get custom-made shoes with elevated heels in the United States in order to create the image of being a powerful and therefore successful politician. Nevertheless, the weight of the discontent was greater, and the jokes kept on doing their sandpapering job. For examples, see the following regarding the existing unfair political economy:

> They call Salinas Hood Robin because he takes away from the poor and gives to the rich.

It is no secret that since 1990, many Mexicans complain about the recession. One of the signs of its seriousness is told through humor in the following joke:

> This is the presidential term of consumerism. [In Spanish consumerism, *consumismo*, when separated into three words, *con*, *su*, *mismo*, can mean "with your same . . ."] With your same car, with your same house, with your same wife.

With regard to the idolatry of the market as the magic force that would save all of the imbalances, humor reacted this way:

> Mexico lives by the laws of supply and demand. It sells with supplies and charges with lawsuits [*demanda* means both "demand" and "lawsuit"].

A modification of a joke made about de la Madrid, regarding his inability to govern adding to the dependence on the United States, produced this joke:

> Salinas gets home one day and says to his wife, "Cecilia, pack up, I'm going to be the ambassador to the Middle East."
>
> "What? After all the trouble it took to redecorate Los Pinos?"
>
> "Yes, I spoke already to Bush and it's all arranged."
>
> "Look, Carlos, I'm going to talk to Barbara to confirm this."

> After a while, she comes back and says to him, "Look, Carlos, you're mistaken. Barbara says that Bush is going to send an ambassador to half-orient you [Middle East is translated as *Medio Oriente*, which can also mean 'to half-orient somebody']."

Salinas and Bush exploited their personal friendship, which, without a doubt, helped redirect some bi-national matters, among which was the approval of the North American Free Trade Agreement (NAFTA). Salinas and his ideological colleagues were satisfied to the degree that they made a toast when the U.S. Congress approved the treaty, but many other Mexicans held on to their doubts and suspicions regarding this alliance,[25] which among other things resulted in a posture of tolerance and support for Bush and U.S. intervention:

> Salinas sent two destroyers to the Persian Gulf: the Echeverría and the López Portillo.

The above joke shows social disapproval for the break with traditional policy of Mexican neutrality, and, by the way, expresses the common disdain for ex-presidents. That way, it kills two birds with one stone: it criticizes Salinas, who should have stayed neutral, and also puts down the ex-presidents who are remembered for their ruinous administrations. It wasn't in vain that Flota wrote a theatrical play called *The Tragic Dozen*, which parodies the events of the tragic ten days in the Ciudadela in Mexico City during the 1910 revolution.

The jokes suggest that Salinas lost credibility. Any traumatic event was his responsibility. The joke regarding the unfortunate assassination of Cardinal Posadas in Guadalajara ties Salinas's conflict with Cárdenas. Similar jokes were adapted to Zedillo.

> The police arrive and say to Salinas: "It's done, boss, we've killed the Cardinal."
>
> And he answers, "You are such dumb asses. I told you that you should kill Cárdenas!"

There is an isomorphic joke that blames him for Colosio's assassination (see chapter 5).

Jokes and rumors about presidential corruption circulated profusely. The first wave refers to the sale of nationalized businesses. Based in the old tradition of *name borrowing*, the jokes suggest that the true beneficiary of the Mexican telephone company (Telmex) was Salinas and not Carlos Slim:

> "How do you say 'Carlos Salinas' in Arabic?"
> "Carlos Slim."

The joke cuts to the accusation that the privatization program benefited the friends of Salinas, who kept all the better businesses. Names like Carlos Cabal Peniche, who from night to morning was made a multimillionaire in dollars and had to flee the country as a fugitive, and Carlos Slim, who after controlling the Mexican telephone company, with less than 15 percent of the stock, enjoyed a monopoly, and with the return of taxes has received more than what he invested. This has allowed him to become, in just a few years, one of the richest men in the world.[26] The jokes imply that the accusations are accurate:

> "How do you say Telephones of Mexico (Telmex)?"
> "Carlos 'n' Charlie's."

Playing with the name of the restaurant chain Carlos 'n' Charlie's, the joke assumes that the business of Telmex is a partnership between Salinas and Slim. The social imagination has no limits when it comes to Salinas's wealth. The fact that they found that his brother Raúl owned dozens of properties and more than 100 million dollars in Switzerland alone leads to the question: Just how much does Carlos Salinas own? This joke resolves it:

> One day they asked Salinas why he was selling the country and he answered:
> "Selling? You're crazy, I'm buying."

> Santa Anna sold the country and Salinas is buying it.

> They call Salinas the *cactus* because each day they find he has more properties.

To be compared with Santa Anna is the worst insult that a politician can receive, since he is the traitor par excellence. But the above joke also alludes to a rumored Salinas family relation involved in drug trafficking. After a legal complication with Swiss authorities because Raúl Salinas tried to return a large sum of money, the joke attempted to resolve several mysteries:

> The 84 million dollars that Raúl was going to return from Switzerland were to pay for the gifts in Almoloya. He had to buy Aburto's gift.

The joke refers to the December tradition in which people buy gifts and suggests that the Salinas family is not completely innocent in the assassination of the supposed heir. Aburto was sentenced as the killer.

The end of the Salinas administration was a horror story. He did everything possible to go down in history as if he had ended his presidential term with monetary tranquility and stability (without devaluating the peso). He only accomplished the latter, and he left it as a catastrophic inheritance to Zedillo, who couldn't manage an economy held up by pins (Pedro Aspe, Salinas's minister of finance, dixit). Salinas was so optimistic that he attempted to reelect himself; subsequently, with discretion, he looked to win the Nobel Peace Prize and then he boldly went for the position of secretary general of the World Trade Organization (WTO). But the country was falling apart.

During the Salinas administration, Mexico lived on a wave of political assassinations. More than five hundred members of the Partido de la Revolución Democrática (PRD) were assassinated, as were the presidential candidate of the PRI, Luis Donaldo Colosio, and the general secretary of the same party, José Francisco Ruiz Massieu—Salinas's ex-brother-in-law. In the first place, the jokes blame Carlos and in the second, jokes say the law put his brother Raúl behind bars.[27] Jokes have taken their toll. Regarding the attempt at re-election:

> Salinas got mad at his barber because he didn't want to give him a permanent.

Regarding Colosio's assassination, humor blamed, without a doubt:

> "Who killed Colosio?"
> "He is bald [in Spanish, *bald* is *pelón*, which can also mean 'it is difficult to know']."

~

> Salinas is very generous. He treats [*dispara*, which means "to treat" but also means "to shoot"] all of his friends.

When Cardinal Posadas was killed, he gets to heaven and Saint Peter says to him:

"But what are you doing here? You weren't programmed until a few years from now."

The Cardinal responds, "*La grilla Mexicana*. The Mexican squirrel."

"How?" asks Saint Peter.

And he writes in his journal: "The Mexican squirrel."

Colosio gets to heaven and goes through the same thing:

"What are you doing here?" says Saint Peter.

Colosio respond, "*La grilla Mexicana*. The Mexican squirrel."

Saint Peter is surprised but writes: "The Mexican Squirrel."

Ruiz Massieu arrives and everything is repeated once more and Saint Peter writes "The Mexican Squirrel."

God arrives to do an audit and asks what all of those answers are. Saint Peter responds that that is what they responded, and God sends for a dictionary and says:

"Squirrel. Small, big-eared animal that lives in the pines."

This joke is complicated to translate. All killed people answer "*La grilla Mexicana*"; *grilla* means "politics," but it can sound like *la ardilla*, which means "squirrel."

Finally, NAFTA was to start on January 1, 1994, fulfilling many expectations and confronting many criticisms; coincidentally, on that same day, a group of Chiapas Indians gave a vociferous shout of protest for their long oppression and repression. The jokes were conclusive:

There was a locksmith convention to see who could fix *Chapas* [play on words with Chiapas, the place, and *chapas*, meaning "locks"].

Salinas knew way before about Chiapas, that's why he killed his housekeeper.

And regarding Salinas's corruption, a very ingenious combination of patriotic colors was used with the figure of the only Brazilian president and perhaps the first in Latin America impeached on the charge of corruption:

Salinas is tricolored because he is three times worse than Collor de Melo.

The Mexican flag is tricolored, the emblem of the PRI is coincidentally also tricolored, and any team that represents Mexico has a tricolored uniform. The symbolism in this case cruelly destroys the image of a man who tried to go down in history as the great modernizer of Mexico and ended up being compared to a traitor, as corrupt and as an assassin. It was a tragic end for a politician educated to take power. When he left his post, Salinas dedicated himself to traveling incognito. For a long time, his whereabouts were unknown, and he turned into the reason for mocking any well-to-do Mexican. Maybe it is indicative that Raúl Salinas's mother-in-law declared, regarding the detention of her daughter in Switzerland when she was trying to withdraw 84 million dollars from a Swiss account that Raúl had under a false name: "About the Salinas, I can't speak, that's their thing; we are Castañón Rios Zertuche, a decent family" (Martínez, 1995:29). It nearly recalls the old Mexican discourse when well-to-do people were spoken of.

Salinas is one of the powerful actors in the country. Ex-presidents are weak, they lose control of the framework they created to giving continuity to their work. Contrary to the saying that any president creates a political current that identifies with him, I suggest here—and this must be elaborated upon—that just in the twentieth century, three presidents created great political groups that merit adding the suffix "-ism" to their last names: Cárdenas, Echeverría, and Salinas. These three left an indelible mark on the political system and established networks and political groups that outlasted their power throughout the decades. For their part, jokes, even though they don't attempt to debate or argue this perception, have without a doubt helped to seal the luck of these presidents, going further than formal scholarly or political discussions and summarizing what their role has been historically—and therein lies their power: to make society's opinion explicit.

Humor summarizes Salinas's image without beating around the bush, focusing on his great political and economic appetite and giving a rotund explanation for the 1994 presidential successions:

> Salinas was walking around on the beach when he found a magic lamp. He rubbed it and a genie appeared.
>
> "I will give you three wishes," said the genie, "what is the first?"
>
> "I would like to have a bank."
>
> "[*Confia*, the name of a bank, also means 'trust.'] Trust my friend, trust," answered the genie.

"I would like an airline."

"Ai Ta Esa [TAESA, the name of an airline, also means 'there is that one'']," answered the genie.

"And if it's not too much to ask," demands the president, "I want to keep governing for six more years."

Thèn the genie says, "*Conzedillo!*" [This is a play on words with *concedido*, which means "granted" and *con Zedillo*, the presidential successor.]

CHAPTER FIVE

Zedillo, Fox, and Calderón

Alternate Political Parties in Power under a Neoliberal Model

One day, a woman in a restaurant suddenly began shouting:

"Help! My son is choking! He swallowed a coin and can't breathe!"

Some man gets up from his table, grabs the kid by the testicles [balls—to the intellectual], and gives them a tremendous squeeze. The kid immediately spits up the coin. The man goes back to his table and sits down as if nothing has happened. The boy's thankful mother gets close to him and says:

"A thousand thanks, sir, what an effective method! Are you a doctor, or do you work for the Red Cross?"

"No," the man answered, "I am a tax auditor."

Introduction

With the passage of time, political jokes have consistently become more pointed and sharp, with each new presidential term and each new president, as they seem to satisfy Mexican society's demands less and less.

Ernesto Zedillo has few physical features that the joke can exploit. He is young, good looking, so modest in his dress that he can bore one to tears, and when he smiles he naturally produces sympathy. Those who know him say that, in short, he is fascinating; the problem is that *in short* is an irrelevant concept to a society that only sees him on television or across barricades with his sharp, monotonous crybaby singsong, and who in his statements proves to be arrogant and intolerant. One politician regally summarized the presidential image, when during a lunch meeting he said, "He even speaks better now."

The Zedillo joke explosion truly is unique. It's possible that just in the first fourteen months of his administration, more jokes were made about him than were made about other presidents during their entire terms. The jokes focus on three areas: the economic crisis, his silliness, and his chicken-heartedness. Many of the jokes have been taken from the past, being mere adaptations, but many others are specific to him, especially those that play with his last name. One added ingredient is that they have been circulated with unusual speed and have penetrated new areas. Even people who in the past thought little or not at all about humor began to tell Zedillo jokes. This could have the advantage of re-politicizing Mexican society, and what better method than through humor?

For everybody and even for him,[1] it is well known and obvious that he attained the presidency by accident. Diego Fernández demolished him with one great truth in the historic first televised debate: "You are the outcome of two tragedies: Colosio's assassination and presidential appointment." Presidential appointments that were a blessing and not a tragedy were beginning to look like part of a distant past. The problem was that the long Mexican political stability began to be stained with blood, bad economic decisions that generated poverty, and instability—and the political system showed fissures that daily grew larger.

In front of this type of perception, humor couldn't be benevolent, and not even courteous. If the end-of-grace periods began with Salinas, by attacking Zedillo immediately, the process continued: his mistakes as a member of the presidential cabinet earned him humoristic jabs. As minister of public education, he struggled to survive the scandal in which the Salinas intellectuals sunk him, because of the history textbook volume in which, with good reason, he placed responsibility for the 1968 killings on the army; humor brought the polemic to a close in a cutting manner:

> "In what way is Zedillo like Madonna?"
> "Neither one knows how to write children's books."

The long and drawn-out economic crisis, and the enormous failure to resolve it on the part of neoliberals, technocrats, bureaucrats, or whatever you might call them, caused growing resentment. Among the jokes involving the economic crisis, we found the following:

> The new national emblem has a seal [the animal] on it, because we're in water up to our necks and we keep on clapping.

~

Nineteen ninety-five is the year of José Luis Cuevas [a popular painter] because *pinta de la patada* [this is an expression with a double meaning: literally it means "he paints badly," but it also means "the outlook is bad (for the year)"].

"In what way is the minimum wage like menstruation?"
"It comes every twenty-eight days, lasts for five, and if it doesn't come, start worrying."

There was a sense of discouragement in the country; the crisis couldn't be stopped, and it contrasted greatly with the government's false optimistic discourse. It was treated as though it were a temporary social economic load that nevertheless didn't affect all of society. Humor resolved the question in this way:

There are two solutions to the crisis: one is technical and the other one miraculous.

The technical one involves going to the basilica and asking the virgin to perform a miracle.

The miraculous one involves firing the PRI and starting all over again.

Only six people have suffered in the crisis: me, you, him, us, they, and them.

The nomination of Luis Donaldo Colosio brought a sigh, or a hope for change, it seems, because having the same political orientation as Salinas, at least he had been tested within the political disputes; he showed that he could and he wanted to speak to members of the opposition, and it was hoped that he would have more of a sensibility to the great needs that had worsened the economic model. His assassination created a feeling that political control of the country had collapsed, that insurmountable fissures had been created within the governing elite, and that the rules for political cohabitation had been broken. A climate of confrontation and intolerance could be felt in the air, and popular wisdom looked toward the president of the republic, blaming him for the greatest tragedy in the history of the PRI:

They say to Salinas:
"Sir, they gave Colosio two shots."
He answers, "What, is it already seven thirty?"

The truth of truths mattered little, and perhaps will never be known. In contrast to the government's story, that a lone assassin had been responsible, humor created a societal truth that was enough to get even, for another national trauma. With the recent history of betrayal, there was nothing to suggest that this assassination was yet one more in a long series, and everybody suspected the president. PRI members complained that after having been wronged by being blamed for the assassination, they still had to prove their innocence, but society was unforgiving:

> They'll eventually find Colosio's brain, which was misplaced during the autopsy; the one they won't find is Zedillo's.

Because humor is so overwhelming, Zedillo arrives at the candidacy with the need to convince the public that he holds the merits for a mission of that magnitude, and that he is not there due to circumstances, nor as a mere replacement:

> Zedillo is *pedillo* [rhyming play on words meaning "Zedillo is a fart"] because he came out by accident.

In addition, he also has to confront the social rejection of the old PRI brotherhood, as much as it may be the body that knows best how to pull the power strings and manipulate the most relevant social and political groups. It is a group so powerful that it is able to move the vote in favor of its hegemonic party, going up against dissident powers dangerous to national stability and tranquility (for example, Cárdenas and the Zapata National Liberation Army). Nevertheless, society keeps resisting and resenting that democracy that appeared to be a great lie. It realized that it was all about one more presidential imposition, and that given the circumstances, it was impossible to celebrate the Zedillo candidacy in the traditional manner as if nothing had happened. Zedillo couldn't stop being seen simply as Salinas's governing puppet, and the jokes were exploding with the subject. For example, he was identified with a known ventriloquist named Carlos, who had two puppets named "Neto" (a nickname for Ernesto) and Titino, laying the groundwork for this joke:

> They call Zedillo Neto because he speaks like Titino and he is manipulated by Carlos.

Continuing with comic comparisons, and making reference to Charles M. Schulz's character Charlie Brown, humor dictates that:

They call Zedillo Snoopy because he's Charlie's dog.

As if being somebody's dog weren't degrading enough, leaving no doubt that Zedillo owed his designation to Salinas, we have the following joke:

They call Zedillo the sperm because he came from a *jalada del pelón* [literally meaning "a maneuver from the bald one"—a reference to Salinas—but also in slang meaning "a pull of the penis"].

In the midst of the presidential campaign, it was in this way that they made fun of his great political dependency, since his candidacy was handled from the center of absolute power, the presidential residence:

They call Zedillo the birdie because he doesn't leave Los Pinos.

If perhaps it had been thought that with the passage of time political jokes couldn't get sharper, such an assumption has been disproved since the term of Luis Echeverría, and there are several reasons for this.

There existed a strong contradiction between governmental economic stability discourse, and the sonorous collapse of well-being. Not only was the buying power diminished for the average salary, as was the economic viability for small- and medium-sized businesses; the social and economic gap was widening between a highly competitive minority sector and the bigger one, which saw its economic opportunity fade more and more. All of this was accelerated with the bank rescue (Fobaproa), which turned out to be the largest embezzlement in contemporary Mexican history; it didn't only affect the dispossessed, but also the middle class in general, as you cannot bet on future economic growth with an impoverished society.

It could be that the concentration of power in the Federal District was irritating. Zedillo was the fifth straight president to have been born or to have grown up in the capital. Though he claimed to have spent many of his childhood years in Mexicali—and he even adopted that city as his hometown—his culture was that of the Mexico City resident or *chilango*, as they are known in Mexico, and this gave an aura of exclusion toward the rest of the country.

It was irritating that career or professional politicians be replaced by bureaucrats who had no institutional commitment in the old Mexican Revolutionary sense and whose greatest asset was the willingness to obey their boss. The neoliberals wear out the PRI myth, and the social commitment toward a political cause ends up enlarging the gap between society and the party. We should keep in mind our explanation in the previous chapter, where the neoliberals lost the 1988 election, which implied that the party in power was becoming less and less attractive. Colosio's death caused a mini-revolt within the PRI in order to promote another politician and take away power from the technocrats. It seemed that the "traditional" PRI supporters would have said that the neoliberals used their opportunity in naming Colosio and that the president had confronted the signs of internal opposition head-on when he declared to PRI supporters that they should get it straight; Colosio was the candidate and there would be no change of horses midstream. There were those however, who felt that this group shouldn't have a second chance. Nevertheless, Salinas was able to designate two successors, and maybe this led to the candidate's death sentence because the dissidents took drastic action; humor established it in the following way:

> Salinas made three unveilings. In November when he designated Colosio, when he declared that they should get it straight, and when he designated the uncovering of his skull.

From here, comes another joke that shows discontent because the nomination seemed to be an affront:

> All PRI supporters became gay because they got a Zedillo shoved up their *Colosio* [play on words between the candidate's name and *cola* (ass) that can be understood to mean "up their ass"].

The neoliberal bureaucrats get to power and fall in love with him. They arrive at the government offices with great scholarly degrees, but with a great deal of disdain toward the social classes that put the government in their hands, without any democratic calling, of course, because authoritarianism is the instrument most used to take power. Salinas's case is perhaps the most dramatic; having studied the peasants, he created measures that ended up killing all of their hopes for a better standard of living. He changed the policies that had kept them tied to the government for seventy years, but at the same time he took away what little influence they had to begin with. It seemed that the intellectual had been allowed to die—the very germ sample he had put under the microscope to make his observations.

The Salinas strategy considered it necessary to create a political instrument that could eventually be used to kill off the PRI. This was the national solidarity program that was necessary in order to elect Zedillo. With him, paternalism was not only reaffirmed while giving resources to the destitute but also during the elections it acted as the placebo that once again confused the poor into voting for a candidate "for the good of their family." This demagogic slogan offered hope for improvement even though political economics assured that those who benefited from the program would continue to drown in the most disgraceful misery. If by 1994 it became clear that the economic model wasn't working, the choice of Zedillo showed obstinacy without parallel. The political elite insisted in applying a model that generated great suffering and that proposed to drive out an alarming number of members of the population. Nevertheless, maybe the president thought that by mentioning, in his political résumé, that he had come from a poor family, and that he'd had to shine shoes to survive, it would compensate for the situation. This type of folksy label is very good yet risky for a political campaign, because it becomes the focus of the economic policy package, and more so when government policies are reluctant to check the effectiveness and viability of the economic model that is leading the country to the edge of the precipice. The only thing missing was for someone to say, "Let's take one step forward."And this seemed to be the election. Humor summarized the popular sentiment:

> "What's needed for an explosion in Mexico?"
> "*Un Zedillo* [the rhyming word *cerillo* means 'a match']."

Neither humor nor social protest were able to convince the government that the model required reconsideration. As criticism grew louder, Zedillo became entangled in a battle with his adversaries, demanding proposals of them. When these were presented to him, he said that had they been his students, he would have failed them. And while the president entangled himself within this type of sterile discussion, the crisis would not let up, and the measures of the neoliberals became a kind of curse for the majority of Mexicans. Still, for the administration, the country was simply going through an annoying situation; it was just a matter of time for the benefits of their plan to work. In search of the troublesome obstacle, they blamed the impoverished anti-patriots to the degree that one undersecretary of this body of politicians (well educated, in fine dress, and full of fine food) declared that the neoliberal model was correct, even though they only had fifty million left. Was he perhaps referring to the forty-eight million that the government recognized as poor, and the other two million uncomfortable pals?

Society takes the pounding of government intolerance but gets even by deflating the presidential image. If jokes began to get cruel with Echeverría, with López Portillo they became biting, with de la Madrid they became sharp, with Salinas they became devastating, and with Zedillo they simply became suffocating. In Salinas's case, even after he left his government post, the jokes stubbornly persisted:

> Mexican ex-president Carlos Salinas and his chauffeur were traveling along a highway when they suddenly ran over a pig, killing it instantly. Salinas told the driver to go to the ranch and explain to the owner what had happened. An hour later he sees his driver staggering with a cigarette in one hand and a bottle in the other, and his clothes disheveled.
>
> "What happened?" asked the ex-president to the driver, who answered:
>
> "Well, the rancher gave me the wine, his wife gave me the cigarette, and his beautiful daughter made passionate love to me."
>
> "My God, what did you say to them?"
>
> "I said I'm Carlos Salinas's driver and I've just killed the pig!"

Zedillo enjoyed no respite and was doomed to be seen as an agent for Salinas. Not even the confrontation they had that resulted in Salinas's exit from the country, nor the incarceration of his brother Raúl, helped to erase public opinion of his much-criticized appointment and complicity, like the concealment of past presidential "crimes":

> They call Zedillo "El Condón" (The Condom) because he covers the *pelón* ["the bald one"—or slang for penis—meaning that Zedillo covers up and protects Salinas, who is bald].

Outside of his scholarly merits, which no one denies, nobody seems to find anything in Zedillo to be proud of. He doesn't seem to get any recognition from the public, and even what he may have done right seems to have come out wrong. One of the most notorious of these examples was the arrest of the drug dealer Juan García Abrego, head of the Gulf Cartel, which instead of giving Zedillo a reprieve, unleashed a tempest. At that time it was said that the government's performance had greatly depended on the United States, which was reaffirmed when Bill Clinton approved a financial-aid package to rescue Mexican finances and American banks:

> Zedillo shortened his last name, he took away the double *L* and now his name is Zedio [*se dio*—meaning "he gave up"].

Zedillo was in his office. His personal secretary says to him that there are two people outside wanting to meet with him. One is the Pope and the other is Clinton:

"Who will you see, Mr. President?"

"Do they have an appointment?"

"No, sir."

"So then I'll see the Pope."

"May I ask why, sir?"

"Because only God can help us, and as for the Pope, with him I only have to kiss his hand."

~

Zedillo and Salinas arrive at the White House and Clinton greets them:

"Welcome to the White House, *tocayos* [a word used when two people share the same first name, like namesake]."

And all night he kept saying *tocayos* until Salinas said:

"Hey, why are you calling us *tocayos* if my name is Carlos and his name is Ernesto?"

"Because my name is Bill and you're a *Vil* [word that sounds like Bill and means 'common'] thief and he's a *Vil* idiot."

Throughout the country, there seemed to linger an air of presidential lynching. For a society used to a strong president, Zedillo turns out to be extremely weak (the subject will also appear with Fox), and humor resolves the matter with the allusion to testicles:

They call Zedillo the three-minute guy because his eggs [testicles] are soft boiled.

The jokes also allude to the president's erratic behavior with an isomorphic joke made about de la Madrid:

They call Zedillo the Dutchman because he's either messing up here or he's messing up there. [*Holandés, o la anda cagando aquí o la anda cagando allá*: put together as *olanda*, meaning "Holanda, or Holand."]

~

They're going to put an eye on Zedillo's ass so that he can see where he's messing up.

~

> They call Zedillo the Pigeon because every two steps he messes up [takes a crap].

There are demands for a stronger president, even from those who demanded an end to the presidency, and it can be said that for the first time, under the dominion of the PRI, there are expectations that the president will step down.

> They call Zedillo Easter Week [or another variant of the joke: they call the Government Easter Week], because he doesn't know if it falls in March or in April.

This joke will return shortly, with Zedillo's successor. The Salinas time bomb blew up in Zedillo's hands and made López Portillo's phrase regarding the presidential failure and the peso's devaluation more true than ever. See an old joke that strongly comes back to life:

> "Why doesn't Zedillo's wife want to sleep with him?"
> "Because he turns her *pezones* [play on words with the monetary value the peso and the literal meaning, 'nipples'] into *tostones* [a coin worth fifty cents, therefore meaning that even her nipples have become devaluated]."

Salinas's finance minister, Pedro Aspe, declared that the economy was being held together by safety pins. It seems that Zedillo's official let go of the pins in such a stupid manner that it gave way to December's mistake, the mistake that led to the devaluation of the peso, within just one month from the beginning of his presidential term. For this reason, the least that could be expected was that the curse of failure would accompany him throughout his administration. There are several versions of descriptions of what took place during the months of transition between presidents. One is that Salinas refused to devalue the peso because he didn't want to finish out his term with that blot, which would have affected his chances of being the general secretary for the World Trade Organization (WTO). The other (and these descriptions are not mutually exclusive) is that Jaime Serra Puche, Zedillo's finance minister, consulted with bankers regarding the limit to which he should move the peso's flotation band, with which he was announcing the devaluation. From the secretary's office came the order for the purchase of dollars, throwing off the market and speeding up the collapse of the peso. This version continues to maintain that before the shift in American dollars, the Americans tried to find out what was happening, and Serra Puche refused to heed their call for an explanation, so in retaliation they ended up demolishing the peso. The presidential image became undeniably tarnished, and national economic viability was affected. In the meantime, Salinas's colleague, the finance minister, had to bite the dust, representing a loss of one of his most trusted advisors, which is reflected in the following joke:

> They call Jaime Serra Puche *Doctor Cetes* [government bonds] because he expired after twenty-eight days.

Politicians have to show their abilities and must prove themselves to the public. This is what Max Weber describes as charisma, which is obtained, among other ways, through political duels, in which many good men have ended up being unable to establish a charismatic leadership:

> The difference between an economist from the UNAM and one from the Instituto Politécnico Nacional [Poli, for short] is that the one from the UNAM destroyed the country in six years and the one from the Poli did it in three weeks.

Salinas was a graduate of the Universidad Nacional Autónoma de México (UNAM), and Zedillo of the Instituto Politécnico Nacional (IPN, or Poli); a couple of decades before, this would have made for a crucial rivalry, but toward the end of the twentieth century any rivalry had disappeared, and even the presidential nomination had turned into a corporate question that diminished the political advantages that being "nominated" had. One reason for this is that while being named CEO, and not the head of state, he had to overcome the loss of prestige at not having been elected by the society he was to govern. A spectacular act on his part, such as the incarceration of Salinas's brother, could have saved Zedillo, but his incompetence in handling the ruinous situation in which Salinas left the country played against him. If we add the tragic events that stained his nomination and his accidental acquisition of power, it's logical that his political and governmental abilities should be disqualified:

> They call Zedillo the Christmas tree decoration because he adorns Los Pinos.

Smoking is no longer allowed in Los Pinos because there's only one Zedillo [play on words with *cerillo*, meaning "match"] and it has no head.

During Ernesto Zedillo's administration, the country was in a pessimistic and fatalistic state; we've already seen that humor played with the option that the government should collapse, and to round things out, jokes expressed the lack of options:

Zedillo, Diego Fernández, and Cuauhtémoc Cárdenas [three presidential candidates] were in an airplane that was losing altitude, and they had to reduce the weight to save themselves. Zedillo weighed fifty kilograms; Diego, sixty-five; and Cárdenas, eighty.

"Who survived?"

"Mexico, all three perished."

~

Question. Answer it with sincerity since it's measuring your morality. It deals with an imaginary situation, but you have to decide what you would do. The situation is the following:

You are in the state of Chiapas on October 16, 1999, in the midst of the terrible moments of chaos that took place due to catastrophic floods. You're a journalistic photographer who works for CNN, and you are anxiously taking the most impacting photographs from within the debacle. All of a sudden you see Zedillo in his uniform, driving a Jeep, struggling desperately to not be swept away by the current, the mud, or the rocks. The torrential water has just swept his companion away, and you have two options. You have the opportunity to rescue him or to take the Pulitzer Prize-winning photograph, which would travel the world showing the death of the president.

The question is: Would you develop the film in color or in black-and-white?

It had been unprecedented to make fun of the Mexican president within the United States:

"Why won't Zedillo ever get hemorrhoids?"

"Because he is the perfect asshole."

This joke went around the United States embassy in Mexico:

They call Zedillo: *He can't believe he got the job.*

This joke is isomorphic with another joke that asks what the intitials JLP stand for: *jamás lo pensamos* ("we never would've thought").

That is, nobody could believe that somebody who was seen as such an incompetent person could be president. Innocent jokes that simply play with the president's name surface, reflecting the public's perspective of the president:

> In Mexico they no longer use lighters, but rather only Zedillos [*cerillos*].
> And the only one that was left had no head, what a disgrace! To be completely unprotected and ending up without fire, a return to cave times.

Others insisted on the possibility that a crime of state had taken place. It had even been thought that since Zedillo had benefited directly, he couldn't have been completely innocent:

> "Why didn't they cremate Colosio?"
> "Because there was only one Zedillo [*cerillo*] left."

Other jokes from the past repeat themselves, but the ingredient of the assassination of the candidate is added in:

> They call Zedillo the Kotex because he's in the best place at the worst moment and he is there as a result of a bloody incident.

It is interesting that a joke arose around a version of a supposed homosexual conspiracy in Mexico. This has, in fact, been picked up by a novelist (Loret de Mola, 2001).[2] In a country where chauvinistic culture predominates (Paz, 1986), jokes regarding homosexuality reflect a rejection of the image of politicians who supposedly must be very "macho." When the homosexual joke is applied to politics (Schmidt, 2005), it doesn't only attack politics; it also concretely attacks the politician's position, whose reputation will forever be diminished by this form of societal revenge. This type of joke allows a glimpse at homophobia, unusual in a country accustomed to having men touch each other physically and verbally—and it is also misogynistic, so that only the true "machos" are spared. An irrefutable truth is uncovered. While the political joke leaves no room for debate whatsoever, the homosexual political joke allows for no possible confirmation, or denial, and the damage is unequivocal. Once again, as with the political joke, society triumphs and democracy quietly observes as authoritarianism is overcome.

> Just after Zedillo takes power he runs into the former rector of UNAM, the national university, Jorge Carpizo, and he says:
>
> "OK, now tell me the real truth [*dime la neta*]." [*Neto* is short for people named Ernesto, which is Zedillo's first name.]
>
> Carpizo answers:
>
> "Only if you call me Jorja." [His name is Jorge, but if the *e* is replaced with an *a*, making it Jorja, it is the feminine version of his name. He was rumored to be gay, so the joke assumes both are gay.]

This is a very witty play on words because it takes delight in playing with Neto, which is short for Ernesto, and in the case of a homosexual would be Neta (*neta* meaning "the truth" in slang).

On his visit to Paris, Zedillo—due to the austere conditions back home—was going to spend the night in the embassy, where Carpizo was ambassador and where they warned Zedillo to be very careful and close his door at night because "the Pink Panther" had a commonly known tendency to be very playful.

Jokes about Zedillo's stupidity and silliness began very early on, and never left him:

> They call Zedillo the baby panda, because it took him forty days to open his eyes.

> They call Zedillo the cactus *por baboso* [the word *baboso* means "stupid dribbling fool," and it also means "slimy"—when cactus is prepared to eat we see that it is filled with slime].

This joke is isomorphic with an Abelardo Rodríguez joke. The longevity of public memory can be surprising when the public wants to get even with its government officials.

> They call Zedillo the flea infested dog because he only moves at the smack of a newspaper.

> Zedillo went to the ISSSTE [social security institute for public employees] to get six years of disability.

This joke seemed to have passed on to a better life, but it was obviously reanimated.

> "What does Zedillo have in common with the Politecnico Institute [the school is broken up by departments]?"
> "He has no faculties."

An alternative answer is:

> They are both asses [*burros*].

The mascot for the National Polytechnic Institute is the *burro* (donkey), so this joke plays with the school's mascot and Zedillo's quality of being a donkey—that is, it pokes fun at his ignorance.

> "What do a pregnant prostitute, a drunk barman, and Zedillo have in common?"
> "That none of the three did their job properly."

An old joke seen in chapter 1 is revived:

> The three most coveted organs in Mexico are:
> Zedillo's brain.
> José Madariaga's [the president of the Bankers' Association] heart.
> Chuayfett's testicles [he was Zedillo's secretary of the interior, who was a rumored homosexual who was part of the gay conspiracy].
> They've all barely been used.

Regarding Zedillo's timidity, we have the following examples, which of course have to do with the size of testicles, as discussed in chapters 3 and 4:

> The call Zedillo the hundred-peso milkshake because the two hundred milkshake includes *huevos* [eggs, or testicles].

An isomorphic version is:

> They call Zedillo the fifty-peso milkshake because the hundred-peso milkshake includes milk.

This joke alludes to semen; someone with a low amount has the problem of not being "macho" enough.

"In what way is Zedillo like Bimbo Bread [Mexican version of Wonder Bread]?"
"In that he's square, he's mushy, and he has no eggs."

Moving on to the subject of politicians who resolve their political disputes with weapons, we will introduce the emergence of the following joke—an isomorphic version of the one about Salinas in which he orders the murder of Cárdenas:

Zedillo gets a phone call from Selena's murderer and says to him:
"I've murdered Selena, sir."
He responds:
"You are such an ass. I said Salinas!"

Neither the president's wife nor his children survive the jokes:

Salinas murdered his housekeeper and Zedillo married her.

~

There are three Volkswagens in Zedillo's house: one *Volfo* (his son's), a Jetta (his wife's) and a Sedan (because that's for any ass to drive).

Allow me to share an anecdote regarding this last joke. After presenting a book at a university in Mexico City, a group of us presenters went out for a drink. After a while, one of those in the group asked me, "Are you the one who talks about the jokes?" When I answered "yes," he told me that his printing house published the magazine *La Crisis*, in which an article of mine was published regarding Zedillo jokes, including this joke. His company then got audited by the federal government—the type of audit that liquidates political enemies. The auditor told him that she had been sent by order of the first lady, and that she had instructions to *chingarselo* ("fuck him over"). The audit lasted two years, and in the end, the government found irregularities that added up to five thousand pesos (less than five hundred dollars). The second part of the story is that when President Zedillo read this joke, he ordered the magazine to be closed down. The closure was avoided by his personal secretary due to the fact that his director was the influential columnist Carlos Ramírez. I'm under the impression that there were no political or economic consequences for me, given the fact that many politicians assumed that, with my last name being Schmidt, I was not Mexican. Since the article was published while I was working at the University of Texas in El Paso, I found myself out of reach from the repressive and fiscally vengeful regime. This was not the case with the owner of the printing house, who was the weakest link. I always ended my articles in the daily paper *El Universal* with a political joke, and the only one who occasionally protested this openly was the spokesman for the finance minister, José Angel Gurría. He was so upset by the jokes that he did not acknowledge me at an academic conference at the University of Texas in Austin.

The approaching end of the century caused great anxiety and discouragement among Mexicans; the government seemed to move backward, while wanting to successfully confront the challenges of the twenty-first century. The end-of-the-world myth and the arrival of the catastrophic year 2000 were an assault on Mexico and Mexicans; the country was in disarray, and the political leadership was not at the level of being able to handle these types of circumstances. We find old and new jokes reflecting that Mexicans were more pessimistic and had fewer options than ever.

"How is Pedro Domecq [the winery that makes a brandy called *Presidente* (president)] and the PRI alike?"
"In that, as time goes by, the *presidente* comes out worse and worse."

~

"In what way are Zedillo and Tarzan alike and different?"
"In that both of them are surrounded by animals, but they do listen to Tarzan."

~

"Who is the sexiest man in the world?"
"Zedillo, because every time it gets harder and harder."

Finally, jokes that put the president's intelligence under a magnifying glass were inevitable. Some were recycled from the past, and others were new:

They call Zedillo the highway because he has so many stupid exits (outs) that drive the Mexicans crazy.

~

Zedillo goes to the bank to cash a check and when they ask him for his identification, he answers in a huff:

"Hey, I'm the president of Mexico."

"It doesn't matter, those are the rules," answers the employee, "but if you can prove to me that you are Ernesto Zedillo . . ."

"Well, I can only think of stupid things."

The cashier answers, "How do you want it, tens or twenties?"

And this joke appears with one modification:

"In what way are the White House and Los Pinos alike?"

"The White House has Bill Clinton and Los Pinos has a *Vil Pendejo* [play on words with *Vil*, which means 'common fool,' and Bill]."

If we wanted to summarize the opinion about the condition and mood of the country about what awaited Zedillo during his six-year term, we can do so with the following joke:

"Why do they call Salinas 'The Alchemist'?"

"Because he made the rich poor, he made fools out of the poor, and he made an even bigger fool as president."

Zedillo wanted to go down in history as the great democrat, as the man who made the great democratic leap possible by bringing power to the PAN; nevertheless, he was accused of doing everything possible to destroy the PRI (Velasco Piña, 2005). He won a place in history as the president who rewarded transnational companies, especially those from the United States. And when he left the presidency, he accepted a job in the United States with the same companies that had benefited by his administration. The truth is that not even the defeat of the PRI could change the image that political humor had created for him, because this form of social expression has staying power, and its influence over political events, no matter how drastic, is undeniable, such as the end of the PRI's dominance.

Mr. Zedillo was walking down the street one day, when he heard a voice say, "Death to the president." Disconcerted, he looks around and sees a parrot in a window, so he decides to knock on the door. As she opens the door, disgusted, the president says to the owner that he was going to go by tomorrow and that the parrot shouldn't repeat what he had said.

Worried, the woman goes to her priest and exchanges her parrot for his and takes it home.

The next day Zedillo walks by and notices that the parrot says nothing, and he angrily says to the parrot:

"Aren't you going to say that the president should die?"
The parrot answered:
"May God hear you my son, may God hear you!"

Ernesto Zedillo went to visit a fourth grade class in an elementary school. He arrived at a moment when they were discussing words and their meanings. The teacher asked the president if he would like to participate in the discussion regarding the meaning of the word *tragedy*. A little boy stood up and said:

"If a friend of mine is playing on the street and he gets run over by a car, that is a tragedy."

"No," said Zedillo, "that would be an accident."

A little girl raised her hand and said:

"If a school bus falls off a cliff and all of the occupants on board die, that would be a tragedy."

"I'm afraid not," maintained the president, "we could call that a great loss."

The classroom grew silent. No other student expressed a desire to give an answer. Zedillo encouraged them to go on, saying:

"Isn't there anybody who can give me an example of a tragedy?"

Finally, at the back of the classroom, a little boy raised his hand and in a tenuous voice said:

"If the president and his cabinet are riding on an airplane and a missile blows it to smithereens, that would be a tragedy."

"Fantastic," said Zedillo, "that's very good. And could you tell me why that would be a tragedy?"

"Yes," said the boy, "because in the first place that wouldn't have been an accident, and secondly, it wouldn't have been a great loss."

Ernesto Zedillo is hanging out with three beautiful women at a discotheque: a redhead, a blonde and a brunette. Sitting down next to them he asks the redhead:

"I'm the president, how much would you charge to spend the night with me?"

The redhead answers, "For you, Mr. President, it will be two thousand pesos."

Then he asks the blonde the same question, and she answers:

"For you, it will be one thousand pesos."

When he looks over at the brunette and asks her the same question, she answers:

"Mr. President, if you can lift my skirt up as high as the tax rate, and lower my panties as low as the minimum wage, take out that thing of yours and get it as hard as life itself, maintain it as high as inflation, and you can fuck me as sweetly gently as you have fucked the people, for you, Mr. President, IT'S FREE."

The problems with Cuba began to be fodder for jokes, maybe because the common Mexican stood in solidarity with the Caribbean island, and it bothered him that the government should throw away a relationship with which it would have been symbolically important to confront the United States:

Zedillo goes to Cuba and at the meeting with Castro, Fidel says to him:

"What would you like to drink, Mr. President?"

Zedillo answers, "A Cuba Libre [name of a cocktail made of rum and coke but literally meaning 'free Cuba']."

Fidel doesn't like the choice, and when Zedillo asks, "And you, Commander, what are you going to drink?"

Fidel answers, "A Presidente Derecho [the name of a brandy, which means 'straight,' but with the double meaning of 'honest president']."

Regarding Vicente Fox, someone wrote the following:

To gain our vote
You made yourself funny
To fulfill your promises
You play dumb.
(Bumper sticker on a car in Mexico City, October 25, 2004)

With—yet not *because of*—the new millennium, out went the PRI authoritarian presidential regime. The defeat of the PRI began an important polemic about Mexican democratic transition, and the great hope for breaking the chains that prostrated the country. But the replacement was a great disappointment, and humor was not ambivalent. See the following joke that emerged very early on in Fox's presidential term:

Very early on the morning of January 1, 2007 the telephone rings at 7 at the presidential mansion: ring, ring, ring. They answer:

"Official residence of Los Pinos, how may I help you?"

"May I speak to Mr. Vicente Fox or with Mrs. Martha Sahagún?"

"We're sorry, those people don't live here anymore. But are you the same person who's been calling us for the last thirty-one days, at seven in the morning on the dot and asks the same question? We already told you since the third time you called that the Mexican public sent them to hell. Are you stubborn, deaf or dumb or what's the matter with you? Why have you been calling all these days, when we've already explained to the limit that the Mexican public has sent that couple to hell? For this reason, I repeat, that said people no longer live here, they've gone to hell; do you understand me?"

"Yes, I understand, but you don't know what joy it gives me to hear it."

The idea that youth was not interested in politics vanished with the birth of the Internet. Not only did the youth prove their lack of apathy by voting for Fox, but having found a form of communication to their liking, they didn't hesitate to let their opinion be known. A good number of messages with political jokes sent by students circulated on the Web, which confirms that jokes circulate among the elite. In Mexico, by 2002, there were only 2.5 million Internet users, and many of them were in schools and businesses. From my students, I've received many collections of political jokes whose threads can be traced across several universities.

The Internet has facilitated the transmission of graphic interpretations and has popularized the ability to chat, which is a form of real-time communication across the Web, and there's never a lack of witty individuals who mix both mediums.

Vicente Fox came to power under a mixed set of circumstances, the understanding of which seems to be above comprehension. The PRI system was in a deep state of disrepair and was passing through a credibility crisis; highlighted among the serious conflicts within the PRI was the confrontation between the president and different PRI groups who believed that he had usurped a role that didn't belong to him. Yet they submitted themselves to his mandate as a result of an anachronistic concept of discipline. It was thought that Zedillo felt that his political legacy should be to pass down the presidency to the PAN, which is a popular version within the PRI used to explain the debacle it suffered in the year 2000. Nevertheless, there are always those who say that it was a condition laid out by the United States in order to save the Mexican economy, with a loan of twenty billion dollars to correct the December mistake.[3] In many senses, the year 2000 was a mythic one: it was the end of the century *and* the end of the presidential term (keep in mind the mythic quality of the six-year term), and both implied a new beginning and called for a new man. The public was ready to go out on a limb and make a great change. This might explain the youth vote going in an unconventional direction. Finally, there emerged the successful campaign of the PAN, during which the candidate took on irreverent positions, by suggesting that the PRI candidate was homosexual, nicknamed him "The Transvestite," and played the anti-political political game. He offended politicians by calling them *tepocatas* ("bugs") and dark spiders, notwithstanding the years Fox had spent in politics; on the other hand, his publicists understood the usefulness of manipulating people's emotions.

Vicente Fox had been a very aggressive congressman, and when he was governor of Guanajuato, he was strongly criticized for his particular penchant for travel, which he kept up as president. Nevertheless, the first jokes were benevolent, and even optimistic; it seemed the honeymoon period was coming full circle. The public had great expectations and high hopes that finally things would radically change with the defeat of the PRI. The old ailments would disappear (this, at least, was a common mistake among political science scholars), and independent of structural obstacles, the country would reinvent itself by means of a voting magic act. Humor reflected things this way:

> It turns out that our President Zedillo, nearly at the end of his term, without having resolved a single problem and overwhelmed by so much national crisis, delinquency, poverty, jails, fired judges, corrupt Mexicans, and violated the Constitution, etc., decides to send everything to hell, and forget for a long time this ungrateful Mexico that doesn't repay he who tries to do something for the nation. To do so, he impulsively decides to go to New York and submit himself to a treatment of being frozen cryogenically [hibernation by means of freezing] for fifty long years. He in fact goes through with it, and once the time has elapsed, he is awakened by a nurse dressed in white, who informs him that the treatment has been completed and that he is able to resume his normal activities.
>
> Zedillo, now fully rested after his *siesta*, heads for the airport. Since he is used to traveling only by the best means, he requests the first flight to Mexico City on the best airline, and the airline employee gives him the ticket. He proceeds to the departure area where he can see an airplane larger and more modern than the rest. On the side can be seen the words *Space Mexico*.

Disheartened, he asks if this has anything to do with the old airline Aeromexico, and the person in charge answers that it's a subsidiary of the most important space travel airline in the world: *Mexnasa*.

Surprised by the blossoming of the airline, he boards the mega airplane and takes his seat; when a stewardess passes by, he asks her at what time the plane arrives in Mexico and she says in thirty minutes.

Zedillo can't believe what he is hearing, and thinking he has gotten on the wrong plane, asks if the flight is the one from New York to Mexico:

"Yes, this is it," answers the stewardess, "The thing is that you are traveling on an *Azteca 5000*, the most advanced technology in aeronautics, built entirely in Mexico. It's the only airplane able to fly outside of orbit at a speed ten times the speed of sound."

So, Zedillo has a calm and short trip on *Space Mexico*, landing in Mexico City thirty minutes later. When he disembarks, he is surprised by the technological advances, and by the quality of service at the airport, and at a distance he sees something like a spaceship. With a proud smile he mentions to a fellow passenger how grandiose the airport is, who answers that it is the biggest and most modern one in the world.

Our friend heads toward the street, which is located on the first level of the four-level thoroughway. Suddenly, while waiting for a taxi, a levitating car without wheels, stops in front of him. . . . The national emblem and the letters HEM [*Hecho en México*, or Made in Mexico] could clearly be seen on the manufacturer's seal. He gets in and asks the driver to take him to the Government Palace, and the driver corrects him:

"You're referring to the Government Museum."

And Zedillo doubtfully asks:

"What, it's no longer the Government Palace?"

"Not anymore, it became too small, but next to it is the tallest building in the world, headquarters of government administration, should I take you there?"

"OK," answers Zedillo, who is infinitely astonished.

On the way he is conversing while looking from one side to the other, seeing three- and four-level highways, a spectacular electric train, and in the distance immense skyscrapers covering what were once uncomfortable viaducts. He sees the Xochimilco River with its crystalline waters, ducks, and swans, and people fishing at the edge. It all looks very picturesque, especially under a bright blue sky and no smog. Finally, the driver stops in front of an enormous skyscraper.

"We're here, sir," says the driver while the automatic door of the powerful car *Levitaaguila Aztec* [name of the car, meaning "levitating Aztec eagle"] opens up.

"Thank you very much. My, how Mexico has grown, hasn't it?"
"The most modern city in the world, sir."
"OK, how much do I owe you?"
"That will be three foxes, sir."

The optimistic outlook regarding Fox's arrival to power was so great that it was even reflected in the United States:

Francisco Labastida receives a telegram from George Bush that says: VICENTE FOX YOU.

The phonetic use of the new president's last name is very suggestive: "Fox" sounds like "fucks." In addition, it implies not only his victory but also the defeat of the other candidate—and this is the way in which many perceived the result of the election: the PAN didn't win; rather, the PRI lost! This was an erroneous yet powerful argument because ideas implanted in the mind of the people had many political implications.

For Fox's election, the *voto util* ("useful vote") promoted by a "leftist" group working in the Fox campaign was very important in dislodging the PRI from power. This political position meant that a vote for Cárdenas was a waste. The vote would go to the non-PRI candidate, and it was better yet that it should go to the PAN candidate in order to defeat the PRI. A common mistake was to think about taking the PRI out of power without eliminating its authoritarian support (I expanded this argument in Schmidt, 2005a). This was proven when Fox kept, among other appointees, a distinguished PRI[4] member as his personal secretary. Finally, it was a mistake to think that the defeat of the PRI alone would bring about the demise of the authoritarian system, without taking into account that a president from another party could use and take advantage of the features of that same system to succeed.

Fox was destined to fail in his effort to bury such a system, even if that had been his intention; maybe because of that he started very early on to lose the public's sympathy. This loss was exacerbated by the irritation caused by his excessive use of rhetoric, which turned out to be insulting and was considered to be disrespectful. For example, what stands out was his offer to use "head hunters" to hire the best people in the country for his cabinet. This provoked an avalanche of applications and résumés from people hoping to hop on the cart of change and from other unemployed people, when in the end the cabinet was formed by political commitments. It was also irritating that, from the beginning of his administration, he offered examples of his ignorance, disregard for culture and reading, and great inexperience for someone who claimed to establish himself as head of state. His mistakes became legendary, and he preserved them while trying to justify himself:

> Vicente Fox and Martita went to the gynecologist to get their *trompas* [*trompas* means both "mouth" and "tubes"].

There are several famous phrases that already today distinguish him in the annals of history. At a presentation in Madrid before the Royal Academy of Spanish Language, while reading a speech complimenting Latin American writers, the president spoke about José Luis, looked up in surprise, looked back down at the text, and continued, "José Luis Borgues." (He called the famous author Jorge Luis Borges by the wrong name). This became, and rightly so, a national scandal, and has been seen reflected in many other spheres in which the president, several years later, kept trying to minimize its importance, reminding the public even more of his uncouth ways when he apologized for the Borges mistake; he complained about why people made a fuss if he had a "lapsus lingus." The weekly publication *El Reto*, which is published in Ciudad Juárez, included a column called "Pitorreando en serio" ("Seriously Just Kidding") and relates to a chat between young people and "Don José Luis Borgues" (to which have been added the feminist Rabina Gran Tagora, Martita Fox, dixit). Nacho Jaime (2004:55) has a chapter called "Borgues: The Fourth Bard of Celaya," in which it is confirmed that a poet by that name did exist toward the end of the nineteenth century. He lived in Pungaraguato in the state of Guanajuato, and given that the president is from there, he should have mentioned it: "He speaks well of the poetic culture of Vicente Fox Quesada."[5]

A president who involuntarily inspires a great deal of humor also produces the emblematic phrase of his administration: *¿Y yo por qué?* ("And why me?"). That is how he answered when reporters asked him for an explanation of what he would do if an armed paramilitary group decided to defend the interests of TV Azteca, a group that took advantage of the 2004 December holiday to take over the facilities of channel 40 (CNI), with whom it had a serious legal difference. The joke referring to this is the following:

> It's the first day of school in the United States and the teacher introduces the new student, Suzuki, the son of a Japanese businessman to the sixth grade class. The teacher says:

"Let's begin by going over some American history. Who said, 'Give me liberty or give me death'?"

The class was quiet except for Suzuki:

"Patrick Henry said it, 1775."

"Very good. Who said, 'The government of the people, for the people should not perish from the face of the earth'?"

Again nobody answered except Suzuki:

"Abraham Lincoln, 1863."

Surprised, the teacher says, "Children you should be ashamed. Suzuki, who is new in the country, knows more about our history than you do."

When one child hears, he murmurs, "Fuck the damn Japanese!"

"Who said that?" asked the teacher.

Again Suzuki raised his hand and said:

"General McArthur, 1942, and Lee Iacocca, 1982."

The class quiets down and one of the kids says, "I'm going to throw up."

The teacher tries to see who the disrespectful child was. "Enough, who said that?"

"George Bush (the father) to the Japanese Prime Minister, 1991."

Furious, one of the students shouts from the back: "Suck me!"

Suzuki, almost jumping out of his chair says to the teacher:

"Bill Clinton to Monica Lewinsky, 1997."

The class becomes hysterical. The teacher faints. Chaos ensues while the students surround the unconscious teacher; one of them says:

"Don't blame me for this damn mess . . . !"

Suzuki raises his hand and says:

"Vicente Fox, October 28, 2002."

The dismal management of public relations and communication forced diverse changes in the social communication team due to the titanic responsibility of correcting all of the president's faux pas. Humor resolved this like so:

They call the spokesman for the president of the republic, Rubén Aguilar, "The Dawn," because he gets up early each day and clears everything up.

~

They call Fox "The Dog" because he only gets "it" with the swat of a newspaper.

The Presidency of the Republic didn't succeed in transmitting its message because its strategy was to saturate the media with presidential messages without considering that Fox's singsong is tiring, his syntax is poor, and his articulation of syllables is inadequate. All advantages are derailed when the president abandons the script in search of procuring a better personal image rather than promoting the image of the government and its actions. This is a substantial idea that the government has not understood. One event showing Fox's focus on his personal image took place on February 13, 2006, when the president gave an interview to Televisa's anchor Joaquín López Doriga, which lasted more than an hour. Nevertheless, only two themes emerged.

First, Fox defended Marta Fox's children, who were being investigated for illicit power plays by the House of Representatives, and he defended the presidential retirement package, because at his age, as he said, "It's damn tough to get a job." To hold on the one hand that jobs would be created, and on the other, that there were none for someone his age was incongruous and emphasized the fact that it wasn't an appropriate topic for discussion, considering what the country was going through at the time. What was highlighted in the end was the trivial management of power, which was absolutely selfish, and without important national perspectives. Demagoguery and lies produced the following jokes:

"How do you know when Fox is about to lie?"
"His lips begin to move and his moustache, too, and he raises his right eye."

~

Fox asks Pepito: "So you're the one who makes up the stories?"

"No, Mr. President, I'm the one who makes up the jokes; you're the one who makes up the stories."

Nearly from the beginning of his administration, when Fox plagiarized Franklin Roosevelt's phrase—"It is the duty of the President to propose and it is the privilege of Congress to dispose"—the government became characterized by its light management of the president's statements. In Fox's version, the president proposes and Congress disposes. But the phrase, a good one at that, turned out to be hollow rhetoric, because Fox never had the intention to back the federal proposal. Maybe because he is ignorant of the federalist theory, Fox lacks federal vocation. The transfer of power to the states and the support for checks and balances diminished his already intellectually challenged presidential administration.

Fox fails to understand that in a federal system, Congress implies balance, equilibrium, and a difference in representation, because legislative power emanates from the districts being represented. That is, it is more specific than executive power, whose wide national reach is more abstract. That is why the "privilege"—even though it's more accurate to say the *function*—of Congress should be to dispose, correct, or eliminate the initiatives driven by executive power, assuming they don't dare violate the Constitution, because that is what judicial power is there for—to make sure that it is not violated. In other words, it limits its potential overreach. But in that area, Fox also broke the federal pact. He got very close to Supreme Court judges to gain support for his personal goals (such as the illicit behavior against Andrés Manuel López Obrador), and this launched a feeling of suspicion about the neutrality showing the other branches to be submissive to the executive power, like in the good old authoritarian PRI days.

When Congress opposed some of Fox's proposals, pompously labeled as "structural reforms," the president mounted an incessant media offensive that offended different representatives, because a long and useless fight began on the part of the executive that would rise to the degree that the president would mount a campaign against Congress in the 2003 mid-term elections, and in turn, Congress would deny him permission to leave the country.[6]

As if his mistake about Borges' name wasn't irritating enough, Fox's ignorance of history, geography, and the Spanish language became the meat of the jokes about him. Notwithstanding his "interest" in mediating great conflicts such as that of the two Koreas, humor cut him down to size:

> Vicente Fox returned very excited from a trip to New York and he told his cabinet that while traveling by car, he had made many accords with the president of Afghanistan for the rebuilding of his country.
>
> Nobody wanted to tell him that the guy with the turban was the taxi driver.

It was very early on that rumors and jokes about the president's travels began to spread over the country. That is how the same joke the public had made about Zedillo became adapted to Fox.

> They call Vicente Fox Easter Week because they don't know if he'll come around in March or April.

It wasn't only his incompetence, but rather also that he portrayed the typical case of abandonment of post, for reasons of travel or health. Often mentioned was that he had an incurable disease, and it was said that he had adopted children because he was impotent as a result of a venereal disease (Loret de Mola, 2001). The fact is that the country was stuck; the lack of movement and leadership was foreboding of a certain ruinous situation:

> Vicente Fox, George Bush, and the Queen of England run into each other in hell. Bush was telling the Queen of England that there was a red telephone in hell and that he was going to talk to the devil to ask for permission to use it.
>
> Quickly he went and asked the devil for permission to call the United States to se how the country had fared since his departure.
>
> The devil approved the call and he spoke for two minutes. When he hung up, the devil told him that the cost for the call would be 3 million dollars; Bush made out a check and paid him.
>
> When she found out, the Queen of England wanted to do the same, so she called England and spoke for five minutes. The devil gave her a bill for ten million pounds, which she paid.
>
> Vicente Fox also felt like calling Mexico to see how the country had fared and so he spoke for three hours. When he hung up the devil told him that he owed thirty-five Mexican cents.
>
> Fox, having seen what it had cost the others, was dumbfounded, and so he asked why it was so cheap to call Mexico. The devil answered:
>
> "Look, dumb ass . . . with the reforms you approved, your new policies, your inexperience, the unemployment rate, Martha's stupidities, and the high cost of living, you left the place a living hell—and—from hell to hell it's a local call."

A joke that had already been said about Zedillo came back:

> They're going to change the national emblem to a seal instead of an eagle, because we're up to our neck in water yet we keep clapping.

And a joke that was made about López Obrador:

> Today the government announced that it's going to replace the national flag with a condom, because it portrays the government's *posture* more clearly.
>
> A condom resists inflation, halts production, destroys the next generation, and gives the people a sense of security while they're being screwed.

"Do you know who is going to get the prize for best magician in Mexico?"
"President Fox will, because from the one country he got, he made two."

"Why is Fox's policy so precise?"
"Because with every resolution he tells us Mexicans: *Precisely* nothing for you or for you or for you."

Inevitably, a climate of animosity grew against Fox as shown in this isomorphic joke about the economic crisis:

Fox's enemies have been discovered: me, you, him, her, we, they and them.

Vicente Fox insisted that close ties with the United States would aid in the national recovery, and that American growth would drag the Mexican economy along with it. He maintained that the signing of an immigration accord would relieve the pressures posed by a fleeing labor force. His actions to align himself with his neighbor to the north stemmed from this belief.

The binational agenda was reduced to reaching an immigration accord in exchange for any type of concession by Mexico. Among the concessions was a distancing from Cuba and offending Fidel Castro; a distancing from Latin America and a confrontation with Hugo Chávez and Nestor Kirchner; an opposition to continental energy projects led by Brazil, Venezuela, and Argentina; and later on, in association with Bolivia, with whose President Evo Morales there was also friction. In the meantime, Fox's government apathetically watched while border violence grew, and the number of Mexicans assassinated by U.S. border police increased. But the jokes kept on coming without delay:

At a meeting to discuss a solution to the problem of undocumented aliens, George W. Bush and Vicente Fox met after the so-called *Cumbres de Monterrey*.

Bush says, "*Little Vicente*, we can resolve the undocumented alien problem if you hand over *Calsonsin* [a character in Rius's *Los Supermachos*]."

Fox goes back to Mexico and looks for an Indian who resembles Calsonsin. When at last he finds him and takes him, Bush says, "No, my friend, maybe you didn't understand me, *Chente* [nickname for Vicente]: I want Cal-ifornia, Son-ora, and Sin-aloa."

Santiago Creel says to Fox:

"Hey, Chente, do you know that at the Monterrey summit the people changed your nickname from Tarzan to *Mesias*?"

Fox, inflating himself like a bullfrog answers, "Could it be that these hicks finally understood me?"

"Don't be an ass, Chente, they gave you that nickname at the meeting because you rocked our boss Bush this way and you rocked him that way." [Mesías (Mesiah) sounds as *mecías*, meaning "to rock like in a rocking chair."]

In a message to the nation Fox says, "Citizens, I have good news and bad news for you."

"What's the good one?"

"Our foreign debt has been settled."

"And the bad news?"

"We have seventy-two hours to leave the country."

The isomorphic joke ends with "and now let's sing the national anthem," and the people begin to sing the American national anthem. This joke has also reappeared:

Creel and Fox decide to go to the United States to negotiate the foreign debt with Bush, but as luck would have it, they arrive at the White House after a heavy rainstorm, and Fox, rancher that he is, raises his pant cuffs to not get wet in the puddles.

In the reception area, and seconds before Bush's arrival, Creel discovers that the president has forgotten to rearrange his silly looking pant cuffs.

"Sir," he whispers in his ear, "pull your pants down."

"Shit! Do we owe him that much?"

Just as his dependency on the United States was evident, there was much speculation about his personal dependency on Carlos Salinas de Gortari, and it was even maintained that thanks to this dependency, Raúl Salinas de Gortari was finally released from jail. The respective joke says:

"Why do they call Fox 'The Condom'?"

"Because he covers for baldy."

If Vicente Fox won the election, as Carlos Monsiváis says, because the people were tired of the PRI, or as Antonio Hermosa says, "It's not

Fox's fault that the Mexicans elected him," we can see that the immediate disenchantment and the impatience with Fox's silliness and inexperience became a joke:

> Vicente Fox was speaking to more than a million Opus Dei followers, in downtown Mexico City, when all of a sudden Jesus Christ appears descending slowly from the sky. When he arrives at Fox's side he whispers something in his ear.
>
> Then Fox faces the crowd and says:
>
> "Listen, comrades, Jesus Christ our partner here wants to say something to you!"
>
> Jesus Christ faces the well-protected bleachers, takes the microphone into his hand and says:
>
> "People of Mexico, this man who has an excellence like my own, hasn't he spent his time ceaselessly visiting different countries just I did in the towns of Judea?"
>
> The crowd responds:
>
> "Yessssssssssssssssssssssssssssssssssssssssssssss!"
>
> "Isn't it true that just in the same way as I multiplied bread and fish to feed everyone, this man created friends of Fox with the support of dark subsidies so that you would all have a good president?"
>
> The happy crowd answered:
>
> "Yessssssssssssssssssssssssssssssssssssssssssssss!"
>
> "Hasn't he legalized his union with Martita through matrimony and assigned Carlos Abascal, representative of the Catholic ultra-right, as secretary of labor to give you faith and security the way I did for you?"
>
> The enthused crowd screams:
>
> "Yessssssssssssssssssssssssssssssssssssssssssssss!"
>
> "Wasn't he betrayed by the Green Ecological Party in the bosom of Congress regarding the rejection of laws that would allow the country to progress, just as I did for Judas?"
>
> The incontrollable and frenetic crowd answers:
>
> "Yessssssssssssssssssssssssssssssssssssssssssssss!"
>
> "So then, why are you waiting to crucify the son of a bitch?"

The following joke is isomorphic to the one about the Argentine (see chapter 1) who knows who the son-of-a-bitch president is:

> Before so much criticism about his administration, Fox decides to stop the negative commentary and orders every citizen who criticizes him

arrested. Two Head of State Guards were outside the presidential mansion and one said to the other:

"What do you think of the situation in the country?"

The other guard decides to watch what he says:

"The same as you."

The guard who asked the question says, "I have to arrest you for insulting the president."

After sticking his foot in his mouth so much, one day, in his patent leather boots and all, President Vicente Fox *kicked the bucket.* Following this tragedy that made the whole world collapse, the INEGI decided to hold an inquest among Mexicans as to where the ideal place would be to bury the remains of such a prestigious character. The surveyor of public opinion for the INEGI, Juan N., went to visit Pepito at his home to ask him where the burial should take place, and the innocent child answered:

"Bury him anywhere except Jerusalem."

"Why not in Jerusalem?" he asked, surprised.

"To be sure that he won't be resurrected in three days."

As we have seen in previous chapters, jokes serve the purpose of getting revenge, and one of the ways of doing so is to emphasize the president's numerous faux pas:

Do you know why they call Fox the steak?
Because he is a piece of an ox [*buey*, which means "fool"].

But very soon the tone sharpens, and the term *pendejo* begins to be used, which in Mexico summarizes many opinions, but let's let the jokes speak for themselves:

There were several leader gathered at the Vatican and they greet the Pope.

Bush says, "It was an inspiring meeting, Your Holiness."

Fidel Castro says, "This meeting has been as well organized as we Cubans like to do."

And Vicente Fox says, "Your Excellency, I congratulate you, and please, give my regards to your wife."

The Pope asks his personal secretary, "Who is this dumb ass?"

"The same one who sent us a telegram the day the St. Louis Cardinals won."

During Fox's presidential campaign he is shown the propaganda. It's a poster of his face and the logo of the Green Party [a toucan] above it. Fox doesn't like it and he shouts:

"No way, damn poster, it's no good, take away the asinine animal from there!"

His advisors bring back the new poster to show only a toucan!

This is an isomorphic joke with another one that is applied to several personalities:

The president goes into a bar with a parrot on his shoulder, and when he approaches the bar, the bartender asks him, "Does the animal speak?"

The parrot shrugs its wings as if to say "I don't know."

The following joke is isomorphic to another one:

A black person goes into a bar with a parrot on his head. The bartender asks him, "Where did you get that animal?"

The parrot answers, "In Africa."

A man from Veracruz is walking along the boulevard when he finds a magic lamp. He rubs it and out comes a genie that offers to grant him one wish. The *veracruzano* asks for a highway from Veracruz to Spain with a toll of seventeen pesos. Obviously the genie gets upset and says that there's too much red tape involved, and he gives the man a hard time until he convinces him to make a different wish.

"Make Fox not be dumb anymore."

And the genie says, "How many lanes did you say you wanted your highway?"

One day Fox was off on a working tour in the Lancandon Jungle. When he gets to the Municipal Palace he begins to make promise upon promise to the people . . .

"And no citizen of the town will lack drinking water, no one will lack work, and all of the boys and girls will have a Playstation . . ."

At that moment an advisor approaches him and says, "Sir, don't you think that's a bit much? These children don't even eat . . ."

"Oh no," answers Fox, "if they don't eat, there's no Playstation!"

Bush, Fox, and Blair were in the nude in the White House sauna, discussing the best strategy to defeat terrorism. Suddenly a beep was heard. Bush touched his forearm and the beeping stopped. The others just stared, perplexed:

"It's my beeper," Bush says, "I have a microchip underneath the skin of my arm."

Minutes later, a telephone rings. Blair puts the palm of his hand to his ear. When he's finished talking, he explains:

"It's my cell phone. I have a microchip in my hand."

Fox, feeling completely out of place and lacking in technology, gets out of the sauna. A few minutes later he comes back with a piece of toilet paper hanging out of his rear end. Bush and Blair are surprised. Fox explains to them:

"I'm receiving a fax."

"Do you know why they call Fox the Sixty-Four?"

"Because he's eight times dumber than *El Chavo del Ocho*. [*El Chavo del Ocho* is a popular show aired by Televisa, in which the main character is dumb.]

This joke is recycled from a Columbian president, who was number 16, and de la Madrid, who was number 32, and as can be seen, the multiples increase with the years (Peña Nieto is 80). The following is an old joke, but it shouldn't surprise anybody that it comes back to Fox:

Fox arrives at a special meeting with his cabinet at 2:30 a.m.:

"Gentlemen, dark snakes, and *tepocatas*! I quit! I'm leaving this wretched, poverty-infested, EZLN-guerilla- and critic-filled country."

He took a breath, and before his astonished looking cabinet, he continued:

"I received a letter from Bush where he tells me that he is naming me Middle East Envoy."

Fox takes out a sealed envelope stamped *Top Secret* (like in the spy movies), and he tosses it into the middle of the office desk. Martita, who hasn't recovered from the surprise, takes the envelope, takes out the letter that contained the alleged offer, and holding in her laughter, says to the president:

"Hey, Chente, don't be ridiculous; this doesn't say that he is naming you Middle East Envoy. President Bush is sending an envoy to somewhat orient you, dumb ass!!!" [This joke had been made numerous times.]

And another recycled joke, from the days of López Mateos, follows:

On an official visit to the United States, President Vicente Fox is invited to tea with President Bush. During the meeting Fox asks him what his philosophy is regarding leadership, and Bush tells him that it's all about surrounding himself with intelligent people.

Then Fox asks him, "How do you know if they're intelligent or not?"

"I can grasp that right away by asking the right question," answers Bush, "Let me show you."

Bush picks up the phone, calls Colin Powell and says to him, "Mr. Secretary of State, I ask that you answer the following question: Your mother has one son, your father has one son, and this child is neither your brother nor your sister, who is it?"

Colin Powell answers immediately, "Obviously, it's me, Mr. President!"

"Right! Thank you, Mr. Powell," says Bush, hanging up the phone.

"Did you understand, Mr. Fox?"

"Of course . . . of course . . . thank you so much. Without a doubt, I'll do the same!"

Back in Mexico, Fox decides to try it out with his secretary of the interior. He calls him to the Presidential Mansion for an urgent matter and asks him:

"Let's see, Santiago Creel, if you can answer me this question."

"Of course Mr. President, what would you like to know?"

"Your mother has a son and so does your father, and this child is neither your brother nor your sister, who is it?"

Somewhat confused, Creel says that he would like to think it over and analyze it with his aides to be able to give an appropriate answer. Leaving the Mansion in a total panic, he calls a meeting with his advisors to analyze the question. Two week later Fox call him in to give him the answer. On his way to the mansion he runs into Labor Secretary Carlos Abascal.

"Carlos, I have a simple little question for you."

"Yes, tell me, Santiago."

"Your mother has a son, your father has a son, and this child is neither your brother nor your sister, who is it?"

Abascal thinks it over, consults with his group of aides, and after a while he answers, "Well, it's me . . ."

Having calmed down, Creel arrives at the Mansion.

Fox says to him, "So what's up, Santiago, do you have the answer?"

"Yes, Mr. President, I do, it's Abascal!"

And Fox says, "What a dumb ass! . . . It's Colin Powell!"

~

On one of his presidential tours, Fox's tiresome speech was interrupted by the penetrating sound of a donkey's braying:

"What's that?" asked the president.

"The echo," answered a voice in the audience.

The isomorphic version is as follows:

A mayor was in the middle of a town council meeting, when he suddenly let out a strident sneeze, and said:

"Excuse me, I sneezed like a donkey."

A peasant answered, "Yes, it was very strong [*re juerte*]."

~

"Why was Fox awarded two medals in Washington?"

"One for being a dumb ass and the other in case he loses the first."

Jokes indicate discontent within society. We have previously concluded that the argument suggesting that the president is a dumbass has most to do with inadequate decisions, but in Fox's case, with his public displays of ignorance, it is entirely possible that the argument has more of a connotation related to his lack of education and knowledge.

Fox and his wife made trivial use of their power. They systematically found themselves in the eye of the hurricane, such as, for example, when they became the governing "presidential couple," which unnecessarily opened up public opinion as to whether the spouse should be involved in fundamental political decisions. And much more occurred when they were shown to have a family plan for transcending the six-year term by having Mrs. Fox follow her husband as the next president. This became a great distraction from attention and political discussion, and a slew of very explicit jokes emerged:

A man goes into a costume shop:
"I want a priest's costume and a mask of Fox."
"What do you want it for?"
"To disguise myself as a reverend."
"A reverend?"
"A reverend son of a bitch!"

The isomorphic joke regarding the presidential style of initiating discussions with the masculine or feminine (*niño* ["boy"], *niña* ["girl"], etc.) goes:

"Why will Fox begin his next speeches by saying, 'brothers, sisters'?"
"So they don't say 'son of a whore' or 'son of a bitch,' which aren't exactly the same thing."

~

"Why do the birds flying over the presidential mansion do it looking up?"
"To not see so many dumb-asses!!!"

~

Fox went to the *El Mundo de Carlos V* [The World of Charles V] exhibition because he thought there would be a chocolate tasting [in Mexico, *Carlos V* is a chocolate brand].

~

Fox ordered for all of the ironworks surrounding the presidential mansion, to be removed, because he had heard on the radio that Mexicans were tired of so many *yerros* in the presidential mansion [play on words that sound alike: *yerro*, which means "blunder," and *hierro*, which means "iron"].

~

The residents who live close to Fox's ranch ordered the tripling of the fence of San Cristobal Ranch, because they don't want another ass of those to escape.

The presidential couple's religiosity also generated a commotion. On the one hand, the president elevated the role of the Church; he knelt before the Pope, which for many reflected a submission of sovereignty. The Vatican was pressured by the president to annul both his and Martha's marriages, and both ended up blowing a provoking kiss in St. Peter's Square, after the Pope refused to receive them as a couple, as they're not married by the Catholic Church. This joke ensued:

> Fox doesn't go to the Palace of Fine Arts anymore because his advisors stopped him from attending *public cult(ural) affairs.*

Playing with the theme of religion, combined with discontent with the administration, the following joke emerged:

> The Pope announced that he would be making a trip to Mexico because he wanted to see how in just a couple of years 50 million people repented.

As expected, the other half of the presidential couple also received her share of jokes, and though it isn't new that a first lady should become the butt of humor, in this case the jokes are very strong. As much as the story appears to be a soap opera script, it's a tragic one. Mrs. Marta Sahagún was in charge of public communication during the presidential campaign, and she sent signals of certain close ties with the candidate who later would become president. Newspaper stories reported a certain tension in the presidential mansion because there were rumors of a closer-than-working relationship with a woman, and that woman wanted to assume the role of first lady, even without having married the president. She also had conflict with one of the daughters, since the president was divorced. Finally, before an imminent article in the *New York Times*, the wedding between them was hurried along. The presidential couple's wedding coincided with the first anniversary celebration of the Fox triumph. Instead of using the date as a symbol for "liberation" from PRI authoritarianism, they turned it into a celebration of another big transformation: the marital status of the president.

This change led to how the first lady would spell her name, the *h* disappearing from "Martha," and once in Los Pinos, she began to imitate Eva Perón, and for a first project created a foundation called "Vámos Mexico" ("Let's Go, Mexico"), interpreted by many as "Vámos Marta" ("Let's Go, Marta"). Her charity politics were based on a great confusion between the management of public resources that would find their way to the society, and the pressure exerted on certain businessmen, because the request for donations came from the presidential residence. Jokes reflected social opinion:

> Martita Sahagún is the Mexican Evita because *todo el mundo la evita* [everybody avoids her—play on words: Evita is a name, and it means "to avoid"].

This was a joke that was also made about Pancho Villa:

Marta Sahagún speaks with her foundation treasurer because she wants to see the numbers regarding the Vamos Mexico Foundation Employees.

When she looks at the numbers, she reads, "Pedro, 3.00; Juan, 5.00; Vicente, 7.00 [etc., etc., etc.]. Total, 150.00 pesos."

Marta says, "And who is this son of a bitch Total that he should make so much money?"

Los Pinos is now called Sahagún City. [Sahagún being Fox's wife's last name and also the name of an industrial city in the state of Hidalgo.]

Why do they call Los Pinos "The Haunted Mansion?"
Because there's a woman with balls and a man without a head in there.

This same joke was told regarding Echeverría, whose wife also played an important role, but never that of protagonist as did Mrs. Marta, as Fox calls her.

Why do they call Marta Sahagún "La Lenguisqui Mexicana?"
Because so many of the things she poses to the president suck! [It is a play on words with (Monica) Lewinsky and Lenguinski (using *lengua*, meaning "tongue").]

Why do they call Martita "The Dalmatian?"
Because she's a spotted dog.

The first great scandal of the Fox administration was the excessive spending done to remodel some cottages on the grounds of Los Pinos. The subject garnering most attention was that of some four-hundred-dollar towels, equivalent to nearly one hundred days of minimum wage. The joke resolved it this way:

Why were the towels so expensive?
Because they're made of *pelo de Marta* [play on words with the first lady's name, which also means "sable"—so they were made of sable fur].

During the presidential term, there had been an ongoing debate as to the existing perception of reality within Los Pinos, as opposed to the reality within the country, since the numbers being handled by the president were very different from the ones handled by economists and society. That is why the term *Foxilandia* was coined—to explain that a separate reality, a separate "land," had been built within Los Pinos, different from the reality of the rest of the country. The joke evens things up this way:

> "Do you know why Marta Sahagún can't be governor of the Federal District?"
> "Because a minimum of a five-year residency in the city is required, and she lives in *Foxilandia*."

Fox's eldest daughter's protagonist role caught the attention of the public early on and was largely reflected when, on inauguration day, she handed her father a crucifix. This act no doubt horrified a nation accustomed to a strict public division between church and state. The jokes made at that time reflect misogyny and discrimination and responded thus:

> What do politicians do with their maids?
> Carlos Salinas de Gortari kills them.
> Cuauhtémoc Cárdenas makes them governors of the Federal District.
> Ernesto Zedillo marries them.
> Vicente Fox adopts them.

~

> Fox's daughter gets to a discothèque and the doorman says to her, "You can't come in."
> She answers, "You don't know who my father is."
> "You don't either."

Jokes kept track of Fox's lies,[7] though they were translated as foul-mouthed babblings:

> "Why did Marta say *yes* to Vicente?"
> "Because at his age he already had a reputation for being *long tongued* [this can be taken literally or it can mean 'to be a liar']."

Corruption couldn't be left out of joke subjects. Truthfully, since the very time of the election, the Friends of Fox chapter (the group in charge of fund-raising for the campaign, which apparently committed several illegal acts) was opened, but its members received the appropriate treatment in these cases: they were aided and abetted by the political majority. Nevertheless, jokes took care of the subject:

> According to the latest news the Pope has announced his wish to be buried in Mexico upon his death; do you know why?
>
> Well, to die like Jesus Christ, surrounded by thieves.

> In what way are the government and the mafia alike?
>
> In no way; the mafia is well organized.

Nor could recycled jokes be left out, such as those that used the testicle metaphor, in this case to suggest that Fox lacked manhood and daring:

> "Why do they call Fox 'Pan Bimbo' [the Mexican equivalent of Wonder Bread]?"
>
> "Because it's bleached, soft, and doesn't contain eggs."

> "Why do they call Fox the three-peso shake?"
>
> "Because the six-peso shake contains eggs."

Vicente Fox built his propaganda on claiming that his was the government of change. For him, it was essential that the public identify the PAN government as separate from that of the past, in order to generate a new society. He went to the extreme of having removed a portrait of Benito Juárez from the Los Pinos residence, and he abstained from attending political events that at one time may have supported the "Mexican-ness" and civic cultural events promoted by the PRI. One example is that the celebration of the promulgation of the Constitution was moved from Queretaro, where it had always been celebrated. To win a majority in his 2003 congressional campaign, he used this motto: "Take the brakes off change," and Pedro Siller invented the phrase: "Reverse is also change." Still, jokes had already gotten their say:

> At a medical world congress, a Jewish doctor says:
>
> "Medicine in Israel is so advanced that we can take off the testicles of one person, put them on another, and in six weeks he's out looking for work."

A German doctor says:

"That's nothing, in Germany we take out part of the brain of one person, put it in another, and in four weeks he's already out looking for work."

A Russian doctor says:

"That's nothing either, in Russia medicine is so advanced we take out half of one person's heart, put it in another, and in two weeks they're both looking for work."

To all of this, the Mexican doctor answers:

"You are all a bunch of dumb asses, because we in Mexico wanted to make a *change*, we took a brainless, heartless, and cowardly rancher and made him president, and now the whole damn country is looking for work!"

The subject of political immaturity tied with stupidity, and the following jokes portray this:

"Why does Fox cover himself in newspapers to sleep?"
"To see if that way he matures [*mature* and *ripen* are the same word in Spanish, and in Mexico one wraps fruits or vegetables in newspaper to help them ripen]."

~

Why do they call Fox "The Pigeon"?
Because he takes three steps and he shits [messes up].

~

Why do they call Fox "The Sperm"?
Because if he doesn't come out with a pull [as in pulling a fast one], he comes out with a suck [by doing something that sucks].

~

Why do they call Fox "The Christmas Tree Ornament"?
Because he decorates Los Pinos [literally, "the pines"].

~

They say that NASA is going to honor President Fox . . .
Because he lives on the moon.

~

They call Fox "Mission Impossible" . . .
Because he ended up without an airport and because after every mission he self-destructs without any help from the Taliban.

Can it perchance be considered that humor was totally different for a new administration? The answer is that jokes found it difficult to have a new dynamic. It seemed as though benevolent jokes had gone full circle from the "honeymoon period," yet we found the same elements of criticism as we found then. It was said that the president was dumb, and that there was corruption; maybe a new element was to characterize him as a liar of a president, alongside a protagonist wife filled with histrionics who still generated a good number of jokes. Some, as we have seen, are very aggressive, showing little tolerance and much social annoyance: it was thought that Fox had offered a lot and delivered little, though in reality he had offered little, but there were great expectations of him.

The joke summarizes the president as the center of power. We therefore decided to end the description of his jokes with a couple of jokes that capture Fox very well and made the rounds throughout his administration, though the first is recycled from another one that the reader will find in the text and that has many isomorphic versions:

Fox is traveling on his private jet with Chief Diego [Fernández de Ceballos] and Pacorro Gil. The captain of the aircraft is flying over Mexico City. All of a sudden Fox takes out his wallet and says, "I'm going to throw out a hundred-peso bill to make a family of Mexicans happy."

Diego answers, "Better yet, why don't you throw out two hundred-peso bills and make two Mexican families happy?"

To which Gil says, "Look, even better, throw out four fifty-peso bills and make four Mexican families happy."

And the pilot says, "Better yet, why don't the three of you sons of bitches jump out and make all of Mexico happy?"

This next joke has several isomorphic versions:

One day, very upset with humanity, God decides to bring the world to an end and brings together all of the world powers to inform them personally of his decision to finish humanity in twenty-four hours. God tells them:

"I have brought you together to let you know that I will put an end to humanity in twenty-four hours."

"But Sir . . ."

"No buts. That is the time limit. Earth will no longer exist. Therefore, go to your respective countries and let your people know so that they may put their things in order. You heard, you have just twenty-four hours."

The first to gather his people was Clinton in Washington, D.C., and in a national message he told them:

"My fellow Americans, I have good news and bad news for all of you. The good news is that God indeed exists. He has just spoken to me. But of course we all knew that already. The bad news is that this Great American Nation, with our beautiful dreams, will no longer exist in twenty-four hours. That is God's will!"

Fidel Castro, the saint, gathered the Cubans and told them:

"Compatriots, Cuban people, I have two pieces of bad news to report. The first is that God exists; yes, I saw him, I was there. I was wrong and deceived all this time. The second is that in just twenty-four hours this magnificent Cuban Revolution, for which we struggled so much, will cease to exist."

Finally, Vicente Fox gathers the Mexican people in one of his famous assembly transmissions on national TV and says:

"Mexicans, people of Mexico. Today, today, today is a special day for all of us because I have two pieces of good news to report to you. The first is that I am God's envoy, a messenger, a guide, a communicator of his credo, because I have spoken to him personally. The second piece of news is that in accordance with what I have promised throughout my campaign, in twenty-four hours . . . listen up, in twenty-four hours . . . there will no longer be unemployment, illiteracy. drug traffic, crime, bureaucratic corruption, water, transportation, or poverty problems in our country. And what is most spectacular, I will remove all taxes from goods and services. There will no longer be children on the streets, nor guerilla wars lasting more than fifteen minutes, nor hunger, nor misery!!! . . . MEXICANS, THE PAN FULFILLS ITS PROMISES; THE PORTAL HAS BEEN OPENED ONTO THE NEW MILLENIUM!!!"

The 2006 election set forth several alternatives: the ratification of the option of the PAN to continue for a longer period of time; the restoration of the PRI; or a third path which, when examined closely, may not truly have anything to do with a third path, because in the great political formulations (for example, the management of the macroeconomy), it was no different from previous ones. Even so, new ideas could be played around with, and optimistic thinking, such as thinking about whether a differently oriented government could begin to establish the base to destroy authoritarianism (or further reinforce it), even though many spokesmen for the alternative seemed to be made-over dinosaurs (old *priistas*).

Voting abstention was less than what was expected (41 percent); those who supported Fox, in only six years, had come to understand that in the hand of politicians, concepts such as change and reform were sufficiently empty so as to not be trustworthy (see the earlier jokes about those who are regretful). The election was resolved based on an introduction to fear. In this way, the vote reflected that the country's political map had changed, a great part of it being blue (the color of the PAN). Because of Madrazo's defect, the PRI was sunk; even in areas where PRI politicians were in power, the PAN was victorious. This could be interpreted as a vote for punishing those politicians, or possibly the vote was manipulated, as was later on accepted by Elba Esther Gordillo, the president for life of the teachers' labor union, who convinced different PRI governors to support Calderón, and as votes gained by a tactic to create fear in the people.[8] Felipe Calderón's transformation was notorious. He started out with a quiet campaign, which later turned into a loud scream against the dangers that Mexico faced. According to some analysts, this reflects the moment in the campaign in which the *YUNQUE*[9] gained its strength and the financiers took hold of the reins that supported Fox, deciding that they wanted the opportunity to have a second puppet. The Partido de la Revolución Democrática (PRD) saw itself dragged through a dirty game that it apparently didn't want to be a part of, but in which it eventually did participate.

The PRI understood that it was better off being the "free rider," going along for the ride while the other two parties tore each other apart, which increased a public preference for the PRI but didn't amount to enough votes to keep the PRI in the battle. The case is that we saw dirty politics and a lack of proposals, the few of which did exist being lost in the scandal. As time went on and more dirt was uncovered, the discourse became increasingly embittered. The parties didn't try to convince us that they had the best platforms, but rather that the opposing parties were not trustworthy. After Andrés Manuel López Obrador (also known as AMLO) uncovered the corruption linked to the Calderón families, especially the governmental contracts awarded to Calderón's brother-in-law,[10] who later became known as the *lethal* brother-in-law, the PAN expanded its coverage of trying to disqualify the other parties and warned the public that if AMLO won, the country would sink under heavy personal losses. At that time, demons were running rampant and the argument to vote for the bad party to avoid electing the worst one was adopted in order for people to choose the lesser of two evils. The electorate would have the opportunity to have regrets for the next six years.

What is interesting is that the joke was turned into a political instrument, breaking the cycle that proved it as a means of spontaneous social expression free from political and ideological ties. Assisted by the Internet, the 2006 election showed the difference between the verbal joke and the graphic joke; the joke became part of the PAN's dirty war. Jokes were launched like darts, creating messages intent on scaring the public: laugh at the crafty fellow, and be scared of him, because he'll make you lose your house. Most of the jokes were against López Obrador.

One message drawn from a body of jokes that erroneously used PEJE (another nickname for AMLO) in their subject line provides one key for the way these jokes had been handled, by adding at the end: "FORWARD THIS SO THAT THE REDNECK FROM THE PEJE DOESN'T WIN . . . [*sic*]." In fact, the attacks against AMLO became defined by a disdain for the lower class. AMLO compared himself to Benito Juárez, without realizing that in the end, Juárez was another *pinche* ("damn") Indian who didn't represent the aspirations of a bourgeois class that imagined itself to be closer to the French Empire or to the white Spanish conquerors than it was. It's one thing when "official" history builds the myth of equal opportunity on an impoverished Indian (though protected by the ruling class of the time) who rose to the highest political position, and another when the current mestizo ruling class looks sharply down on the Indians, should the lower class want to buy the mythical reincarnation. AMLO possibly didn't realize that those who could have become inspired by the myth were in the minority but financed campaigns, while those who perhaps felt offended to relive it were the ones who voted. One thing is a history book and another is to try to make history repeat itself. This argument is clearly seen in one of the jokes made about AMLO; its message in unmistakable:

> They call AMLO Whiskas because eight out of ten cats prefer him. [Whiskas is cat food; *cats* (*gatos*) is a derogatory term for low-level employees or the lower class.]

I've received several collections of jokes, nearly all of which are against AMLO. None are original—they all have a clear origin; they are attributed to several presidents, though many were made about Fox. This shows that the traditional mechanism to turn the joke into a societal instrument for attack and destruction has broken.

In the book, I concluded that with the Internet, youth discovers the political realm. It's obvious that the Internet is also a means for the usurpation of a social expression; there are jokes that are included in the list that may not clearly be applicable to specific subjects during AMLO's administration, such as the following:

> AMLO is a three-peso milkshake because he contains no eggs.

This is the exact opposite image of what the politician demonstrated, which very much irritated certain political personalities, foreseeing attacks and even lawlessness. We must note that AMLO's initials were also played around with, calling him MALO ("bad one"). He is the candidate most attacked by humor, given his early campaign and his notoriety. His proposal worried the ruling interests, which in some way, for the joke, and only for the joke, makes him subject to attack, just like Carlos Salinas (chapter 4), who very early on showed his power and therefore became the object of humoristic attack.

Even though Calderón was the object of few jokes, humor had already begun to establish its truth:

> A rich man goes to a car dealership and asks to buy the most expensive car with the most advanced technology.
>
> The salesman says to him,"We just got this one in. It's the prodigy of cars."
>
> The man asked the price and paid without bargaining. He left the dealership driving the car, and the first thing he did was to turn on the radio. No sound came out. Annoyed, he returned to the dealership and complained to the salesman:
>
> "You told me that this is the most sophisticated car, and yet the radio doesn't work."
>
> "So sorry," says the salesman, embarrassed. "I forgot to tell you that your car is so modern that the radio doesn't work with buttons; it works with the mere sound of your voice. Furthermore, it's programmed to please; it'll play any type of music you ask for."
>
> The man leaves again in the brilliant car, and facing the radio in a loud voice, he says:
>
> "Mozart music."
>
> To his surprise the radio asks him, "Leopold or Wolfgang Amadeus?"
>
> "Amadeus," he replies, full of surprise. And the notes to the Prague Symphony can be heard coming from the radio.
>
> Intrigued, the man says, "Iglesias."
>
> "Enrique or Julio?" asks the radio.
>
> "Julio," says the man.

He could hear the voice of Julio Iglesias singing "Hey." The man can't believe such modernity. To test the radio, he says, "Fernández."

"Vicente or Alejandro?" asks the voice.

"Vicente," he answers. Then the song "Too Bad You're Alien" could be heard.

At that moment, as the driver was moving ahead someone cut him off to make an illegal turn. And the owner of the new car nearly crashes with him.

Furiously, he shouts, "You stubborn ass!"

And the voice of the radio asks, "Fox, Creel, or Calderón?"

Fox won in what was probably the first fair contested election since the PRI was created, and many scholars expected or hoped a system revival would happen with the PRI defeated. They thought in the year 2000, democracy had finally arrived in Mexico—some thought it was a revolution—but instead they discovered that a folkloric and effective candidate did not make a good president, and national embarrassment spread when Fox broke protocol while talking with familiarity to the king of Spain, bragging about his boots and making terrible mistakes such as confusing the name of famous writer Jorge Luis Borges, something Mexican intellectuals could hardly forgive (but which political jokes addressed while taking good care of the renewed social frustration). The sexenio ended, and a mythical new "millennium" started with a more educated politician, married to an intelligent and prudent wife perceived by many as more capable than her husband—but the expectations did not produce a new perception because of serious accusations of electoral fraud and extended political protest. This was the first post-PRI rigged election (López, 2009), making people recognize the long life of *gatopardismo*—the reform of everything to change nothing; they sent PRI home but PAN will rig elections and exceed corruption—and the butt of the jokes was Calderón's alleged stupidity (*pendejismo*). This attribute seems to be a constant, regardless of differences among presidents, as we have seen in this book. An old joke was adapted to Calderón:

Calderón goes to the headquarters of the electoral authority, knocks on the door, and tells the guard:

"I want to be the next president of Mexico. What are the requirements?"

"Are you stupid, under the influence, or just crazy?"

"No, but if these are the requirements, I qualify."

A feeling of disappointment lingered.

A Boeing 747 was kidnaped with Calderón, Mouriño, Elba Esther Gordillo, Fox, Martha Sahagún-Fox, and the Bribiesca brothers. When the negotiators arrived, the first thing they heard from the kidnappers was:

"If you don't come out with our demands, we will release each one of them every two hours."

Juan Camilo Mouriño was a very close associate of the president and was rumored to be his dolphin for 2012. Elba Esther Gordillo[11] was the head of the powerful teachers' union, and she played a key role in Calderón's election, especially brokering support for him among a few PRI governors who shared her aversion to the PRI's candidate Roberto Madrazo. The Bribiesca brothers are the offspring of Martha Fox and were accused of influence peddling that made them extremely rich. The option of names included in the joke summarizes the resentment over those characters close to the president or enjoying presidential protection and accused of depredation.

Many of the Calderón jokes were adapted from other presidents, which is not unique, as we have shown in this book. A few examples that the reader will find the proper reference to in the text are:

Why Calderón is called "Mission Impossible?"

Because he auto-destructs after every time he delivers a message.

Why is Calderón called "The Redeemer"?

Because he has 100 million people that are regretful.

Why are *panistas* called seals?

Because they have water up to the neck but keep clapping.

The most criticized of Calderón's policies was the war against drugs, which resulted in human tragedy.[12] The number of casualties fluctuates depending on the source consulted, but even the lower numbers are shocking: in six years, between 70,000 and 150,000 people were killed; around 300,000 were displaced; and between 27,000 and 150,000 disappeared. Jokes treated this in the following way:

Calderón meets with the world's best security experts and tells them:
"After analyzing my security strategies, where is the mistake?"
One of the experts looks at the report, looks at Calderón, shakes his head, and says:
"In your DNA."

Violence took its toll and was felt very close to the presidential office. Camilo Mouriño, the powerful secretary of government (*gobernación*), and a later secretary of government, Francisco Blake, were killed in airplane accidents that were rumored to be assassinations. Debate over these accidents was settled with the following joke:

What did Mouriño tell Blake in heaven?
We would have been better off with López Obrador.

This was López Obrador's post-campaign slogan when we were leading demonstrations against political fraud; it acquired a stronger meaning when the casualties of the war on drugs increased and the economy did not pick up; among other things, Mexico in the year 2000 was the ninth economy in the world, and it fell into fourteenth place by 2012.

"Dad, please close your eyes," says his son to Calderón.
"Why?"
"People say when you close your eyes, we all will be happy."

Postscript

This book ends with the dozen years of PAN administrations—or whatever it is that they did. Even before the second Spanish edition was published, I was already being asked if I would deal with jokes about López Obrador (AMLO), maybe because people took for granted that he would win in 2006 and they assumed that he would have to be tested, which is what Catón did in his time—unfortunately for AMLO, who protested against him. Or maybe because some members of the economic elite, together with the PAN, displayed a nasty campaign against him and the political jokes could be a good complement—and that campaign did in fact did happen. It was natural that jokes were not made about Madrazo or Calderón, even though one joke did emerge that said that people in the United States were worried because Mexico was trying to recover the lost territories, with Madrazo and Montiel starting out by purchasing apartments one at a time.[1]

I resisted writing a chapter about the presidential candidates at the time near when I was finishing the book—though I did mention something in the conclusion—because it would not have been demonstrative of anything; nevertheless, a short time after the book was published, I started to receive emails with political jokes that convinced me that I should at least include a reflection in *this* edition of the book about what happened in the country in 2006 and its projection regarding political humor; I did all this in chapter 5.

The end of the 2006 presidential campaign turned into a great nightmare, primarily because, instead of having been an exercise to help define the future of the country, the election turned into a dirty game with negative side effects that endured for six years.

The 2012 election was tainted with accusations of electoral fraud, the old PRI was back to buying votes and manipulating the hopes and dreams of the masses—and even so, the jokes started before the election day on July 5.

Apparently, the transition from one president to the next in the last decade provides society with a different perspective regarding the former president, as we see reflected in the jokes, such as this one about Calderón and Peña Nieto:

> Peña Nieto and Calderón come to the barber shop at the same time. They sit side by, with a barber to each person's side, but don't speak a word.
>
> The barbers avoided any conversation, fearing it would end in an argument. Both finished shaving their customers at the same time; Peña's barber reached for the aftershave, but his customer gently touched his arm:
>
> "No, thank you, when my wife smells it, she will think I was in a whorehouse."
>
> The second barber asked Calderón, "Do you want aftershave?"
>
> "Of course! My wife doesn't know what a whorehouse smells like."

Peña Nieto, just like his two predecessors, did not enjoy a honeymoon regarding political jokes. His predecessor in this sense was Carlos Salinas de Gortari, whose nomination was a long-announced candidacy, since he was the powerful secretary of planning and budgeting in charge of public expenditure and social programs. While the political part of his ascending career was secured, apparently society reacted with humor because the mysterious presidential succession disappeared and Salinas was not such a good idea. If the new sexenio was supposed to renew hopes with Salinas, this didn't happen, and the undesired continuation of bad policies was in place and jokes evened the score.

As we saw with Salinas, a typical announced candidacy triggers a strong social response. Peña's candidacy was expected at least three years before his nomination; his activity as governor of the state of Mexico—with the support[2] of the TV network Televisa—was promoted all over the country; he intervened in state elections supporting his party's candidates for governor; and his influence shaped Congress in 2009, giving him a strong influence over the legislative agenda. The PRI was a key actor governing the country from 2009 to 2012, and he was a strong actor behind the scenes. Regardless of this influence, jokes apparently started when he attended the Guadalajara International Book Fair in 2012 to present his own book[3]; during a press conference, he was asked about the three books that influenced him the most, and he responded that he didn't remember, then added that for sure one of them was the Bible—from which he read only parts. Trying to fix this press-conference mess, he went on to mention a Carlos Fuentes book (*La silla del aguila*); however, he stated that Enrique Krauze wrote it—and it just so happened that Fuentes and Krauze disliked each other and the comparison made Fuentes so angry that he said Peña Nieto wasn't fit to be president. This event triggered many jokes and helped develop a theme that accompanied him during all of his campaign, and that has continued to accompany him throughout the beginning of his presidency:

> Su abuela le dijo:
> Si no lees darás Peña Nieto.
>
> His grandmother told him:
> If you don't read, people will be sorry for you, grandson.

The joke is lost in translation. *Peña* means "sorry," and *nieto* means "grandson."

Since that early moment in the campaign, he acquired a reputation for being stupid and ignorant,

> Peña Nieto is called Facebook
> He has a lot of face but no book

Many people say that he is only a puppet, and Carlos Salinas is the puppeteer, so of course Peña Nieto's intelligence became the central topic of jokes about him; at some point he began to be compared to the actress Ninel Conde, who shared a reputation for being stupid. See the web page with Ninel Conde jokes at http://hazmeelchingadofavor.com/2011/08/23/65-chistes-chistes-de-ninel-conde/.

> Ninel ¿Crees que México deba ser gobernado por una mujer?
> Claro, así como cuando estaba Guadalupe Victoria.
>
> Ninel, you think Mexico should be ruled by a woman?
> Of course, the same when Guadalupe Victoria ruled.

The female PAN candidate was named Josefina Vázquez Mota, and Guadalupe Victoria was Mexico's first president.[4]

> Ninel ¿Qué opinas de los narco corridos?
> Que pena que el desempleo haya alcanzado también a los narcos.
>
> Ninel, can you comment on narcocorridos?
> It is a pity that drug traffickers are fired.

The joke refers to the musical genre *narcocorridos*, similar to ballads that extol drug traffickers—but drug traffickers without jobs, since a *corrido* is a person who has been fired.

Some of the Ninel Conde jokes were adapted to Peña Nieto, or vice versa.

Peña's campaign was marred with scandals; he had a confrontation with students at the Universidad Iberoamericana that triggered a social movement (#yosoy132) asking him to resign as candidate and requesting democratization of the mass media. His daughter reacted improperly to a critique of her father in the social media world by retweeting a tweet of her boyfriend calling her father's critics *pendejos* and *prole* (a derogatory term for working men, *proletarios*, that has been expanded to indicate all poor people).

> José Luis Torre (@JojoTorre) tweeted: @Pau_95Pena . . . un saludo a toda la bola de pendejos, que forman parte de la prole y solo critican a quien envidian! . . .

Jokes then focused on Peña's daughter. A Pepito joke was adapted:

> In a very exclusive school where there are no poor students (*proles*), the daughters of Slim, Azcárraga, and Peña had a conversational class and needed to use the words "I suppose."
>
> Slim's daughter said, "I heard the helicopter and I supposed my father was going to work."
>
> Azcárraga's daughter said, "I heard someone who was giving instructions to the airport characters complain because of Peña's lack of knowledge."

The Facebook page (http://www.facebook.com/pages/Los-chistes-de-Pe%C3%B1a-Nieto-y-su-hija/267292879987360) complains of censorship, though these complaints are likely not visible.

Conclusion

Pleasure is absolute while it lasts.

—VLADIMIR JANKELEVITCH

There is no situation so bad that it can't get worse.

—GEORGE BERNARD SHAW

In politics, as in almost everything, there are degrees of what is deplorable.

—HÉCTOR SUBIRATS

The study of political jokes implies an effort into "reading" politics with different eyes, since the latter has not only become an underground game but also the view of *Rashomon* (a film by Kurosawa whose title means "The Gate"), in which political truth is made known, depending on whom you listen to and where you are located; the joke is one more of these testimonials.

I was tempted to write a chapter of jokes about Mexico's presidential candidates, but it would have been very slanted, because jokes were not made for all of them, and because existing jokes are insufficient to measure true popular opinion.

For example, let's look at two jokes. The first has to do with two scandals attributed to the administration of López Obrador (AMLO) as head of government of the Federal District, suggesting that he was an accomplice with his finance minister (Ponce) in the poor management of his position, which included trips to Las Vegas to gamble, and the other pertains to the suspicious events related to one of his main political operators (Bejarano), who was forced to resign and was jailed after he was taped accepting a huge cash donation:

> AMLO, Ponce, and Bejarano were having dinner, and Ponce says worriedly:
> "I left the safe open in my office."
> AMLO says, "Don't worry, the three of us are here."

This joke was published by Catón, undoubtedly one of the most prominent humorists in the national press, leading AMLO (who seems to have little tolerance for having his image torpedoed by jokes) to complain about the joke. Of course, if this joke was harsh, López Obrador worked a lot on his image, especially as an honest man, so the joke was on the target at one of his sensible areas, but after his response, maybe he understood that a ruler can't fool around with a humorist of Catón's stature. Catón's response in his column the day after the politician's rebuff was a reminder of what humorists can and should do in a country that enjoys some remaining liberty regarding freedom of expression.

In a political move, Roberto Madrazo adapted a joke to fit AMLO. This was rather strange because one politician adapting a joke to another politician had not been seen.

On the other hand, around February 2006, a joke positive to AMLO began to circulate:

> Roberto Madrazo calls his wife and says:
>
> "My love, get ready because tonight you're going to sleep with Mexico's future president."
>
> And she answers, "Is Andrés Manuel really coming over?"

The 2006 election took place during a general disqualification of politicians. The country of change reverted in more than one sense. The continuity of the PAN would surely bring more of the same, which is saying a lot because that is how it has been for nearly three decades. The reorganization of the PRI was preceded by great scandals of corruption and influence trafficking (Governors Arturo Montiel from the state of Mexico, Ulises Ruiz from Oaxaca, and Mario Marin from the state of Puebla). What's left is the country of PRD. "Hope" is not trusted because in the party, not only can't the tribes come to an agreement—each day they pulverize each other more and more, leading the families who control the party to fall for the temptations of corruption and rampant nepotism. The Bonsai Parties, as they were named by Luis Javier Garrido, don't grow but are open to big business, as reflected by the Green Party, and seemingly by the Peasant Alternative Social Democrats, and the members of the New Alliance, who haven't been able to shed the image of being an instrument in the hands of the biggest winner of all, the leader of the teachers' union, Elba Esther Gordillo. The turbulent post-electoral process is an indisputable sign of how far Mexico is from democracy and how fragile are its processes; the institutions that were supposed to carry the citizens' voice (the Electoral Federal Institute, or IFE) were unveiled as party instruments and voluntarily or involuntarily undermined the small but costly steps toward political credibility.

One of the greatest constants in Mexican political humor is corruption, and the fact that the Mexican political system suffers from a lack of true ethical values. Velasco Piña (2005:77) is drastic: "a type of pyramid whose climb implies a loss of direct proportional integrity according to the height attained; the higher the hierarchy, the higher the dejection." According to our thesis, humor, and in this case, specifically the joke, reflect that which is bothering society; at this juncture, it seems there is no doubt that Mexicans are fed up with politicians' lack of ethical behavior, and consequently the distortion that politics have suffered.

There's no doubt that time heals wounds, and in relation to politics, the years allow society to see historical events with different eyes. With the advent of Salinas's administration, some begin to see Echeverría in a better light, and with Fox's administration, there are those who nostalgically dream for a return of the PRI. Echeverría himself told me, when I delivered a copy of my book *El deterioro del presidencialismo mexicano* (*The Deterioration of the Mexican Presidency*), that if I kept up the same theme, I should write about his successor. Of course he later ordered my book's circulation to be stopped and launched a tough political persecution toward me, which urged my exit from the country. He is still seen as the cause of the catastrophe, but humor remains as the witness of what society thought of presidents in their time and the general state of mind regarding the national leadership.

Jokes leave an indelible mark in the plumage of politicians, altering the image created by official history. Until now, the establishment has managed to control the formal historic retelling, but it hasn't been able to stop the resurgence of jokes and their subduing power. Ernesto Zedillo and Vicente Fox were the recipients of jokes that many thought to be extinct, with which we can confirm the thesis that society can rummage through its historical memory to get even with politicians.

Nowadays, with more political parties, more open means of communication, more Mexican international visibility, and more international scrutiny of Mexico, Mexicans have more instruments at hand to influence the political system; nevertheless, they keep getting even with politics and politicians by means of hearty laughter while continuing to abstain from voting; abstention in 2006 reached an unusually low 41 percent.

Political humor is an act of transgression that undermines the rituals, symbols, and values of politicians, and it is an instrument to get even with politicians. Politics, when defined as *real politik*, are conducted behind closed doors, and behind the scenes in an underground world that provokes social frustration that is overcome with humor. Political jokes send messages to politicians regarding aspects about them or their activities that are troublesome to society. And these messages try to correct without destabilizing the government.

Mexican political culture shows a defenseless society that feels inferior with respect to politicians. The Mexican character reflects how society has adapted to a traumatic history, and how it has assimilated with humor. Mexicans, in their rejection of authority, have turned the president (the symbol of highest power) into a target for jokes. They themselves are untrusting; they project this in political institutions, such as political parties, by refusing to trust in them. Thus, the majority of political participation is still informal and is expressed by means of humor, especially through jokes.

1. When we speak about "the Mexican," or Mexicans, we usually refer to the masculine.[1] One could assume that Mexicans—men *and* women—have the same defects or qualities; nevertheless, aside from the chauvinistic aspects, we must recognize that most authors refer only to the man. A list of characteristics clearly corresponds to a society dominated by men whose influence is reflected in the culture. There is a joke that Argentines like to tell to make fun of Mexican *machismo*:

> A Mexican runs into an Argentine and says to him, "In Mexico, we are all machos!"
>
> And the Argentine responds, "In Argentina, we are half machos and half female."

The conventional idiomatic denomination in Spanish to speak about gender in the plural, *mexicanos*, is masculine; it doesn't differentiate the genders. This perhaps expresses masculine preeminence, and the lack of equality between the genders. In Argentina, "macho" means man.

2. It is risky and unfair to characterize all Mexicans as if there were no economic, social, regional, or cultural differences between them. In fact, this is one of the most important negative aspects of making the stereotype. When we generalize, we attribute undeserved negative characteristics to people. To all of them, we apologize in advance. Nevertheless, the Mexican described and analyzed throughout this book corresponds to the accepted identified image of what has been conceived as "the Mexican" based on the research of what he's like and why he behaves the way he does, to be able to determine his characteristics. This is not a trial or exoneration, nor is it about burning a group of Mexicans at the stake. When Samuel Ramos completed his pioneer research about "the Mexican" in 1934, he expected

that such effort would help "the Mexican" mature, since he apparently got stuck in an adolescent phase that he must still overcome, the same as his failure to solve the great national problems of the last one hundred years.

This analysis is not an effort to degrade or offend the victims of humor. On the contrary, to some extent it is guided by Ramos's same optimistic spirit. I hope that this contribution helps break the ties and chains that bind Mexicans to a traumatic past that only offers them a bleak future.

This research about political jokes is an attempt to rescue information and valuable analysis regarding a greatly ignored social phenomenon. It attempts to contribute from a societal perspective to the completion of existing paradigms that explain the relationship between the State and society.

Society participates by means of formal processes (such as elections) but also in informal processes (such as through political jokes). The openness of the political system determines the type of consensus or dissention that exists, manifesting itself in guerrilla warfare, rebellions, civil disobedience, or political humor, not necessarily in that order.

The political game is mysterious and underground. It only rises to the surface to satisfy the needs of politicians, which can be reduced to the maintenance of power and the encouragement of social acceptance. This latter one is crucial for the survival of the political system and for that, politicians have to satisfy two vital factors traditionally identified by political science: consensus and legitimacy. But politicians have to deal with another largely ignored factor by political science: the mystification of the image of politicians and the powerful influence over society of that image and its symbols.

In general, society doesn't have many peaceful instruments to confront political power. In this book, political humor has been considered as part of society's attempt to even out the situation, to get even, and finally to claim victory over politicians.

With humor, we are left with the impression that society has consciously decided to remain at the same level as politicians. But society is not something abstract; it is a web of extremely complex relationships and interactions. Within this heterogeneity, the dominating sector is the elite, who also respond with humor to political frustrations.

To speak of political participation by way of humor isn't to say that it is the only way open or available for the elite, but it is one in which the elite exercise certain domination while creating their own symbols and values that will have an impact on public opinion. The flow of lore between the elite and the people explains how they communicate with each other and why certain humoristic forms and themes last for long periods of time.

Certain political practices emerge within a social class[2] and become instruments of other classes; some political practices appear with greater frequency in one social class than in others, even though they are present and are used by other classes. Political jokes are created for certain characters (celebrities), but some are adapted from nonpolitical jokes. Illustrating the way in which social classes communicate with each other and adapt to the cultural, social, and political practices of one another is one of the challenges for future studies. The study of jokes suggests that the historical memory lies with the elite, and that it can determine, and weaken, the heroic and nonheroic construction of values and political symbols.

Political humor can be the result of many fortuitous occurrences, of multiple causes and coincidences that the social scientist tries to see as a product of a great social order whose laws we don't yet understand because maybe they don't exist, even though more than a few scholars will perhaps tear their hair out due to not finding them. Even though we may conclude that society gets even with politicians, society's revenge is neither necessarily planned nor predetermined. Independently of the result, this behavior is generated spontaneously to correct the aspects in politics that trouble society. The conscious tendency to balance the sociopolitical inequalities could very well be more of an intellectual exercise than a genuine social expression. It's difficult to think that sociopolitical reactions are the result of a preconceived and planned process. The "final result" frequently occurs due to many fortuitous circumstances. It's difficult for society to consciously plan its revenge on politicians. But furthermore, we should give credit to society for its ability to stand up against the political suffocation of democracy and other oppressions. If it does this laughing, all the better, because this shows that its creativity has not been quashed by politicians and their megalomaniac designs.

We should give more weight to hedonism and research humor simply as the search for pleasure. What is relevant is that, with political humor, individual acts turn into collective action because they reflect social opinion. It is clear that we should think of a new social action model and not in the one that politicians intend to create or control vertically. This is how jokes transcend the strictly personal to gain a relevant political opinion for all of society.

The importance of the joke depends on the political system. If the system is open and democratic, the impact of the joke is relatively low, but if the system is closed, with restricted liberties, the joke can play a delegitimizing role.

The way in which society relates with power is a fascinating subject for research, and humor is a good instrument for understanding society's perception of power because it's a free and sovereign form of expression. Generally, we have a clear idea of the relationship between government and society, and our challenge now is to understand the relationship between society and government. For this, we should look for unconventional information sources, especially those that emerge with the liberties that society tears from politicians. This research goes in the direction of elucidating where Mexican society (which has been under authoritarian regimes for more than five hundred years) has conquered its own areas of expression and participation. I truly believe that the research into political humor contributes to the knowledge of human nature.

If there is yet much to do to understand the psychological, political, and social implications of political humor, its analysis in Mexico allows us to generalize about several tendencies that have existed for decades.

Jokes that occur over and over in Mexico are those that focus on corruption and the president, and there is no change after a new party (such as the PAN) assumes power. This demonstrates that the concentration of power and abuse, and the resulting disturbance of values and ethics in politics, is what most troubles Mexican society.

Humor concentrates on personal characteristics and ethical behavior on the part of politicians. Humoristic discourse indicates the type of critique that society is making when it demands honesty and higher moral standards from its leaders. We have also seen that it comments on cultural values and on *machismo*, not only in relation to power but also with respect to women or within a couple.

Mexican politicians don't use the joke as a political instrument. They still very much depend on the solemnity of power. Nevertheless, humor makes fun of this solemnity and minimizes the importance of political events. As time has gone by, presidents have become the most vulnerable victims of humoristic jabs, and jokes have acquired a sharper and bitter tone. A correlation can almost be made between the gravity of the economic crisis and the sharpness of the jokes, because democratic progress did not cause a "softening" effect in humor.

Since the politician who arrived at the presidency had bureaucratic merits, the joke began to disrespect him and not allow him to breathe, but, truthfully, we should acknowledge that the quality of government that these characters have had has left much to be desired. And even the PRI, which was the administrative party and efficient government model, has suffered the disgrace of having been turned into a secretary of state that competes for political control with other secretaries. On occasion, it even seems that the PRI gets in its own way. Society resents this, and not only has it yanked its monopoly of power, but also, with jokes, it has stripped politicians of the sweetness of being loved and even idolized.

If jokes about Echeverría were strong, with the passing of new administrations they have become bloody. The case of de la Madrid is very unique. Jokes massacred him, but perhaps his low profile and not having made enormous mistakes gave him the advantage of being able to continue to travel throughout Mexico without being assaulted or insulted. He even continued to be a public official, acting as director of the publishing company Fondo de Cultura Económica, the agency that, after having reached national glory, is now considered pitiful. But this, in the end, is the history of the Mexican government in the last forty years.

It's not surprising, therefore, that jokes didn't allow Zedillo to breathe, nor did they give him any respite. In the same way in which humor maintained that Gamboa Patrón was the true president because de la Madrid didn't even realize that he was president, and in which Salinas extended his power for two administrations, even though he tried to reach the all-time record of three (and he possibly reached it), all merit has been taken away from Zedillo. If the devaluation devalued him along with the peso, political humor didn't allow him to proudly show off the presidential stash. The opportunity to put the country on the path to democracy and progress was missed by Fox. His impoverished intellect, his lack of knowledge, his vulgar and tricky mentality, and his lack of ability to become a statesman did not allow the country to take advantage of the occasion to make the leap forward; on the contrary, with him, the factors that blocked democratic progress were reinforced, as was the system of privilege and inequality. Jokes attacked these elements without mercy. Calderón has had a legitimacy deficit and introduced the country to a bloody war against drug traffickers (from 70,000 to 250,000 casualties in six years) and was unable to overturn the economic crisis. At the end of the Calderón administration, we have seen recycled jokes, perhaps due to the fact that the Internet is helping to recover historical memory, and because research is emerging that brings jokes to light that would otherwise have been lost. This book is also dedicated to this purpose.

"The country made a 360 degree turnaround," a politician said, trying to appear wise and to exemplify the great advances that had been reached—not realizing that, in reality, it hadn't moved nor progressed. It is yet to be seen if Mexico will emerge from the mire and if the next president will have the means to embark on the great task of progress and advancement. For the time being, humor has begun to show its lack of faith.

One word about social media and political jokes in the twenty-first century: as already mentioned in the book, the Internet has changed the language, visualization, and even scope of political jokes. The networking taking place through social media has expanded communication among different people, facilitating communication among different generations and different countries and giving a new perspective on the impact of political jokes. The effect is stronger in countries with limited freedom, however, and thus the content of the jokes themselves is not new; many are recycled. I haven't seen new jokes on Twitter or Facebook, but I have seen some old jokes in emails and on Facebook, and certainly in a fair number of blogs and on Web pages. Yet it is too early to know if these forms of media will replace oral communication or if both of them will merely complement it.

Anonymity plays an important role in jokes, and as long as social media will continue to help keep anonymity, humor's destructive power over the image of the politician might even increase and help level up the relationship between society and politicians—but further research is required.

I finished the second edition of the Spanish version of this book right on time for the 2006 election; at the time, the jokes only reflected a Fox joke including Calderón and Creel, the two contenders for the PAN nomination. For the second edition, I was interested in how the jokes reflected the *alternancia*, as the switching from one dominant party to a new choice is called in Mexico. For the English edition we have the opportunity to observe two PAN administrations and analyze the idea of whether society used different symbols and language to evaluate a different political party in power. There is not much change for the PRI and PAN presidents' jokes; in essence, all jokes focus on the same issues: stupidity, corruption, and specific topics motivated by historical junctures and personal characteristics, as is explained in the book. I hope the English reader has enjoyed reading about this society's expression as much as I did doing the research and writing the book.

Acknowledgments

First, I must thank all those whose ingenuity creates jokes for the benefit of humanity and who keep jokes alive by the magic of telling them.

Since I became interested in political humor as a subject for research, many people—including my colleagues—have gone to the trouble and pleasure of telling me jokes. This is not an altruistic act, because an interchange was established, in which I've ended up being a sort of joke-distribution warehouse. Though there are many out there like me, I must recognize that it has been the most beneficial scholarly interchange that I've experienced. I most sincerely acknowledge all those who have exchanged jokes with me.

I must thank Roberto Moreno de Los Arcos (R.I.P.) for giving me one of the books I've most enjoyed. On a certain occasion, while discussing my project on political humor, he told me that I'd never understand the Mexican without first reading the first Mexican police novel. Immediately, he gave me *El complot mongol* (*The Mongolian Conspiracy*) by Rafael Bernal, and I realize that Roberto was right. Now, I give copies of this marvelous novel to my friends. The story is about a federal policeman who collaborates with the CIA and the KGB to resolve a Mongolian conspiracy with Chinese Mexicans who want to assassinate the president of the United States during his visit to Mexico. The plot develops in Mexico City's Chinatown on Dolores Street. I recommend this book to those interested in Mexican literature and folklore.

As I wrote this book, I gained from several conversations I had with James W. Wilkie, who urged me to collect and translate jokes after having used them to explain the conflict between Echeverría and business owners in my book that was published by the University of Arizona Press, *The Deterioration of the Mexican Presidency*. Wilkie has consistently sent me articles about humor, especially articles published in Los Angeles, and he made different commentaries on several previous versions of this book.

I thank Gustavo V. Segade from San Diego State University because he helped clarify several ideas.

Several colleagues read parts or all of the manuscript, among them James Platter, Brian Loveman, Alexandro Segade, Ricardo León, Antonio Hermosa, and Carlos Spector. I am tempted to blame them and other colleagues for helping me build this book, but I would rather assume individual responsibility for possible mistakes or poor translations.

Maybe there is some truth to the idea that humor runs in the Jewish people. I come from a typical and large Jewish family (five brothers and one sister) and the house was full of mischievous behavior and jokes.

I must mention my children Noa and Adam, who have assumed the very important responsibility of reminding me that jokes weren't made for the sole purpose of being studied. And Rosie, who was always there enjoying my laughter even though at some point she didn't believe I was writing a book.

And last, many thanks to the two anonymous readers for their valuable comments, and to the staff of the University of Arizona Press, who helped with the task of making clear a complex bicultural translation. Special thanks to Kristen Buckles for her interest in extending the knowledge on Mexico, and to Amanda Piell for her editorial help.

Notes

Prologue

1. I made a preliminary analysis in *Mexico encadenado: El Legado de Zedillo y los retos de Fox*, Colibrí, 2001.

2. Recently, I discovered that a history student used my book to write his dissertation and publish a book. In August 2013, after wide protests, he was fired from his full-time position at the School of Philosophy at UNAM; however, the dean refused to introduce my letter to the file, since I requested to remove the Ph.D. degree and she was the main adviser.

Introduction

1. Regarding the nineteenth century, Sergio Fernández (in González Ramírez, 1974) says, "The Mexican people, in spite of their rancor or maybe due to it, laughed more and better. He the ridiculer and with incredible rage liberated his passions as he tipped outside of himself. In the struggle he gambled his life and for that the very inside of that game of his was death, price of his revolutionary spirit."

2. The result was a book called *El deterioro del presidencialismo Mexicano: Los años de Luis Echeverría*, Editores Asociados Mexicanos, S. A. de C. V., 1986.

3. See, for example, my book on ethnic jokes (Schmidt, 2006).

4. From my collection of anecdotes. When I was nominated for the Scientific Research Academy Award, one of the jury members asked, "Why give Samuel the award, since he only collects jokes?"

5. During a conversation with Luis Donaldo Colosio, I asked him what his nickname was, and he refused to tell me.

Chapter 1

1. This also affects publishers. For example, the publisher of the first version of this book insisted that it was necessary to prove that the book was a serious enough work to go to a publishing house, and he proposed that it should be titled *Humor en serio* (*Serious Humor*). Another title could have been *We Laugh at Politicians Because They Laugh at Us*, but this is probably not commercial enough.

2. The volume of cartoons by Trino called *Fabulas de policias y ladrones* may give the impression that the cartoons are not political because they concentrate on assailants and often specifically on bank robbers, even though they certainly *are* political, since their central theme is the police.

3. For a long time it was suggested to me that I should write a book about Mexican political jokes so that I could become rich. I finally wrote this book (Schmidt, 1996), but neither the publisher nor myself has become rich because of it.

4. "While the serious individual tends to be solemn and anxious about how things may turn out, the individual with a rich sense of humor tends to be more relaxed, less disappointed by failure, and in general happier" (Morreall, 1983:122).

5. Refer to an excellent discussion on this theme in Eco (1989).

6. "Since each of our childhoods as with the childhood of civilization, our hostile impulses toward our brethren are subject to limits and progressive repression as that of our sexual impulses" (Freud, 1973:91). From my collection of anecdotes: On a certain occasion while dining in the home of an Israeli diplomat in Mexico City, I met an official from the Mexican president's press office. When he asked me about my work, I told him that I researched political humor. He stated that under no circumstances would he allow the telling of jokes regarding President de la Madrid. But he then changed his mind, saying that since what I did was scholarly, I should after all recount a few of those jokes. Later on, he asked me to provide him with a study regarding jokes about the president; however, he refused to pay for the service, so it never came to fruition. It's one thing that I laugh at the president; it's another that I should work for free for him.

7. Here, all political jokes have been handled in the same manner; nevertheless, a great distinction must be made between what is written for television—for such programs as *Lechuga and Salinas*, *The Tonight Show with Jay Leno*, *The Late Show with David Letterman*, *Jimmy Kimmel Live!*, *The Daily Show with Jon Stewart*, and Stephen Colbert's *The Colbert Report*—and those that are told by people in general.

8. According to Udall (1988:xv–xvi), this idea is attributed to an advisor of President James Garfield.

9. This joke has been told about Fidel Castro and Hugo Chávez. It is also very interesting that it was told about Nestor Kirchner. He was a democratically elected president with a strong orientation toward social democracy. This reaffirms our thesis presented further on: that the political joke is part of elitelore and it is a kind of social critique.

10. A makeup artist from a certain television station told me that the personalities, who leave their make-up on after their interviews, are in fact politicians. There are stories about politicians who alter their shoes to seem taller than others, or who flex their knees to look the same height as their bosses in photographs. These people shouldn't be bothered by differences in height, since power is what counts, but appearance is important in politics.

There is a delicious scene in Charlie Chaplin's 1940 movie *The Great Dictator*, in which Mussolini and Hitler are seen together in a barbershop and each one adjusts his chair to seem to be taller than the other. The movie in general discusses how dictators try to show themselves as superior beings. On the subject, the movie *De Undertag*—which depicts Hitler's final moments—shows him as an ill-tempered neurotic.

11. When I was doing the research for this book at UCLA's Research Library, it surprised me that there were so few computerized references for works on humor, yet when I looked under satire, I found a very long list, in several languages. Obviously, this resulted from a misunderstanding of the concept of satire on the part of librarians. I discuss definitions and concepts further on in this chapter.

12. "Any type of good research begins with what is better known, and from there as if from the lowest step on a staircase to the highest, it leads us to the comprehension of the most ardent and difficult ones" (Joubert, 2002:39). This quote was written in the sixteenth century.

13. These same reasons for omission are valid for political humor in radio, television, and theater. They lack spontaneity, they are managed with great care, and—in some cases—they are even censored.

14. For a definition of the cartoon, see A.D. (1960), CIESPAL (1990), Pruneda (1958), Rius (1984), Freud (1973), Fernández in González Ramírez (1974), and the taxonomy of humor in this chapter.

15. In July of 1988, under the auspices of the Department of Communications of the School of Political Science of the UNAM, I organized a series of lectures about political humor. At the first session were present cartoonists Magú and El Fisgón from *La Jornada*. The conference was very well attended, to the degree that there were people outside of the conference room. Both cartoonists did a humoristic presentation regarding their relationship with Carlos Salinas de Gortari. The presentation alluded to aggression toward freedom of the press and to corruption of journalists. After that lengthy first session, students gathered around the cartoonists to ask them to autograph the cartoon of the day. This seemed like an unusual occurrence at a school where the faculty is utterly solemn ideologically. On the day of the presentation on political humor analysis, the number of people in the audience was greatly diminished from the number who had attended the cartoonists' presentation.

16. The term "humor" derives from the Latin *humor*, or more appropriately *umor*, which means liquid (*Encyclopedia Britannica*, 1990:145).

17. "When humoristic discernment awakens it grows incrementally and then decreases. These changes in the awakening are associated with the positive emotion of happiness are accompanied by several degrees of laughter and smiles [. . .] most humor contains elements of distortion regarding personal knowledge of the world [. . .] humor is disrupted when these roles revert" (McGhee, 1985:371–372).

18. "In an abstract sense [humor] is the capacity to perceive or express the entertaining aspects of a situation. Plato (and also Thomas Hobbes) maintain that when we laugh about people or situations it makes us feel superior" (Goldenson, 1984:415). Lipman (1993) analyzes the role that humor played during the Holocaust.

19. I haven't found any evidence of political jokes originating among the lower class.

20. Here I refer to television programs that show people suffering from this type of accident, or better said, in which practical jokes that generate ridiculous situations are made popular in many countries.

21. *Sketch* can also be translated to mean "a short work"—a note or a short narration.

22. The nickname Nikito Nipongo is a joke in and of itself and brings to mind a popular saying: "Nor does he hit a pitch, nor does he catch, nor does he allow you to bat." Since the administration of José López Portillo, the presidential cabinet has been identified by political program categories, such as the one herein mentioned formally: the economic cabinet.

23. I thank Ricardo Vigueras for pointing this out.

24. Regarding evil, see Becker's (1977) wonderful analysis.

25. Because of that, Amartya Sen (1981) considers totalitarian regimes incapable of avoiding famine.

26. Sibley (1963:9) uses the concept within the context of opposition to violence.

27. Sharp (1970) classifies nonviolent resistance according to the type of social grievance involved.

28. On the Day of the Dead, skulls are very elaborately made. The skull is a written parody for a specific character, in general a politician. In no case are the skulls looking to offend politicians, even when they refer to the death of such a figure. Newspapers publish skulls referring to politicians—and on occasion it happens that, in certain institutions, someone makes the skull of the year as if honoring a special character.

29. Some theoretical considerations of this study are consistent with Mexico, which is the object of the study. Schutz (1977) recognizes a similar geographic deviation in his study.

30. President of Bolivia. First presidency April 15, 1952 to August 6, 1956. Second presidency August 6, 1960, to August 6, 1964. Third presidency August 6, 1964, to November 4, 1964. Fourth presidency August 6, 1985, to August 6, 1989.

31. Providing sayings on the brevity of jokes, Freud (1973:12) gives the following quotes: "The brevity is the body and soul of all jokes, and we could even say that it is what constitutes it precisely" (Jean Paul, *Vorschule der Aesthetik*, I, paragraph 45); "Since brevity is the soul of wit and extensiveness is its body and ornate exterior, it should be brief" (Shakespeare, *Hamlet*, Act II, sec. II, said by Polonius); "The joke says what it ought to say, not always in few words, but in less than are necessary; that is, in words which according to strict logic or to the current manner of thinking and expression, are not sufficient" (Lipps, 90).

The Internet is changing the expression of humor. Jokes that, before the Internet, were primarily (or solely) shared verbally are now being written down and circulated profusely; jokes are being illustrated more than ever before; and many jokes are even being enriched with sound. It's possible that the wide circulation of jokes on the Internet demonstrates that the Web's circulation reaches several age groups; still, up until the beginning of the twenty-first century, this continues to be the space for communication of the elite (see Schmidt, 2003).

32. Some political poems I have collected about Mexico are extremely long. When I have lectured on political humor and I have read these poems, they always seem heavy. The truth is that in some way it would be an exaggeration to say that one might go around carrying in one's pocket a sheet of paper with poetry written on it, and that reading it to anybody would guarantee their time and attention just because the poems are long. I have seen very lengthy poems attempting to be humorous hung on some walls in governmental offices, but I doubt that given their reach they would have many attentive readers at all, which in fact questions their effectiveness.

33. Sharing something in the personal arena, I will say that when I came back from completing my post-doctorate at UCLA, some of my opponents at the university put out a story that said I worked for the CIA. This is another one of the political accusations in Latin American countries. It wasn't until after several years, when the U.S. embassy invited me to a committee for the selection of scholarship recipients and the embassy paid for my work on the committee, that I was able to return to the UNAM with the check to prove that in reality the government of this country had paid me—not specifically the CIA. After that, the attacks regarding me working for the CIA ended.

34. See Martre's 1972 novel that talks about this subject.

35. This paragraph was taken from James Stradberg's translation (Norton Public Library, 1960).

36. Vives says: "Happiness purifies the blood, ensures health, refreshes joviality and a nice color to the complexion, prolongs life, sharpens wit, rejuvenates the body, it invigorates it and adapts it for any purpose" (Moody, 1978:32).

37. According to Schutz (1977:160–161), Lincoln was famous for inserting clever anecdotes or jokes at the end of a rough discussion. For example, we have the following: An abolitionist delegation arrived demanding the emancipation of slaves before the time that he thought it would be practical and realistic. So then he asked, "How many legs would a sheep have if we called the tail a leg?" They answered, "Five." "You are wrong," said Lincoln. "Calling a leg a tail doesn't make it so." In this simple way, he proved to them the fallacy of their position instead of using twenty syllogisms.

38. People expect their leaders to be the best, but the media can improve images. When Bella started to work for the Ullstein brothers in Germany, her editor gave this advice: "A society reporter doesn't write realistically. Remember that each ambassador is a beauty, each minister is an excellent politician, in fact, the best in the world; every new arrival to diplomatic service is always the most brilliant star in the ministry of foreign relations" (Metcalfe, 1988:69).

39. It is interesting that I was told this joke in Mexico City.

40. I've worked on the concept of the relative autonomy of the State in Schmidt (1988), considering that the State has the ability to become independent from society; that is, it is able to unhook itself from the immediate interests of the dominating class, establishing an autonomic project, which allows the heads of the state to reproduce themselves as the governing elite, for which they formulate a specific project which can oppose certain social interests, even though without negating the essence of the system that in capitalism is the protection of private property. Federico Engels (Marx and Engels, 1969:738) does an analysis about the autonomy of the State in a letter to Konrad Schmidt.

41. This joke is quite old, even though in 1985, after the earthquake in Mexico City, it reappeared with Reagan sending the telegram to de la Madrid.

Rojas and Esparza (1985) picked up an isomorphic joke: A minister sent a telegram to a commander in a military zone: "We foretell seismic movement with the epicenter within the territory under your control. Take measures." Two days later the answer comes: "Seismic movement suppressed. Epicenter and three more executed."

Another joke is told with a similar play on words: "Orders: arrest captain Fuentes with major secrecy. Memorandum: captain Fuentes arrested. We are still looking for major secrecy."

In Rojas and Esparza's essay, there's a compilation of jokes told outside of the elite of which 4 out of the 155 are political jokes.

42. It is recommended to see the movie *La Ley de Herodes* by Louis Estrada (1999) because it deals with this principle. The synopsis of the movie according to a relevant web page (http://cinemexicano.mty.itesm.mx/peliculas/ley_herodes.html) says that in 1949, during the administration of Miguel Alemán, the corrupt mayor of San Pedro de los Saguaros is lynched and decapitated by the indigenous population that lives in that place. Come election time, when the governor is not willing to jeopardize his position due to a political scandal, he therefore orders his government secretary, Mr. López, to name a new mayor for San Pedro. López decides that the most qualified is Juan

Vargas, an inoffensive and loyal member of the party who surely will not be as corrupt as his predecessor, but the new mayor "opens his eyes" and with difficulty overcomes his predecessor's actions to the degree of a political juggler who outlives his patrons to embroil himself politically.

43. Democracy has to do with equality, which introduces the economy into the debate, the wellbeing and quality of life, aspects which in some way I broach in this essay when speaking about economic aspects that sharpen the tone of jokes. A review on this problem may be found in Cansino (2010).

44. Some of the themes confronted by the analysis of the quality of democracy are the stable institutional structure, which permits freedom and equality; the rule of law, accountability, and responsiveness to social wishes; and the effective control of political institutions (Morlino 2005). See in general the dossier in *Metapolitica* in volume 8, 39 (January–February 2005).

45. Suarez was contracted by the government television station afterwards. This helps confuse the role of censorship and how it is applied; the truth is that Suarez never came back to tell a presidential political joke.

46. In the United States abstention has gone from 13 percent in 1848 to 39.1 percent in 1984 (Wilkie and Lorey, 1987:900) and 43 percent in 1988 (Stanley and Niemi, 1990:80–81). This last figure could be substantially larger if we add the 33 percent of voters that were kept from registering. In Mexico it passed from 0.1 percent in 1861 to 32.2 percent in 1982 (Wilkie and Lorey, 1987:820) and to 66.6 percent in 1988 (Schmidt, 1990b). In both countries, the numbers refer to presidential elections. For municipal elections in the United States, abstention could surpass 80 percent.

47. Traditionally there exists the expectation that Mexican students will participate politically, but Nahmad (1987) suggests that Echeverría's government decided to create a technical high school system (Colegio de Bachilleres) to depoliticize high schools.

48. This is not a contradiction, but rather one understands that the elite is one of the means of political humor and people in general look to the powerful. In 1984, with a colleague, we conducted a Delphi exercise in Mexico City, including a group of members of the elite. We asked them, "If you are in an accident involving a person of influence and he was at fault, what are the chances that you will win the case?" The majority, including public servants, answered that they had no chance of winning, recognizing that there is always somebody more powerful. This reflects a culture of inequality.

49. Scott (1990:86) develops this idea of resistance even though he doesn't consider humor.

50. In the case of television jokes, they can be seen as a response to the political needs of an entity. This forces us to ask ourselves to what point do writers, editors, producers, and conductors enjoy autonomy, and what amount of autonomy they enjoy. See an interesting discussion about soap operas (*telenovelas*) and their role in constructing identity (Uribe, 2009).

51. A great example, even though in a fiction book on the reaction of power against humor, can be seen in Kundera (1986:41), where the State destroys the political and professional life of a Czech student who sends a telegram to another student playing a joke which he thought was cute. The text of the telegram was: "Optimism is the opiate of the people! The Holy Ghost stinks of idiocy! Long live Trotsky!" In two lines the author, through humor, destroys a Marxist principle, a communist leader, and the

solemnity that one is supposed to have for members of a political party; as an answer, political power destroys the witty one.

52. Soviet humorist Mijail Zhvanetski says: "The only thing that has saved us all of these years is humor and jokes. Humor has played the role of opposition, and anyone who wanted to know what we were thinking could have found it in humor. This is a country, where you can't tell the people that they were wrong, you have to be witty and say it through humor" (Bonet, 1987).

53. This same joke is told on the border between Mexico and the United States. The Mexican dog comes to the United States to eat, and the American goes to Mexico to bark. This concept is especially suggestive because the United States presumes to be the most advanced democracy in the world.

54. "The jokes obviously can be told about a dictator" (Banc and Dundees, 1986:157–58). There exist versions of the joke about Franco, Hitler, Fidel Castro, and one who was even about de la Madrid when he visited Cuba.

55. On one occasion, I observed a confrontation between political figures constrained by their corresponding moral behavior. During a student conflict at the UNAM in 1986, students organized a political debate with university authorities. The sessions took place in an auditorium with more than a thousand people present, mostly students, and were transmitted live by Radio University over a period of several weeks. The students were very aggressive and insulting, while the authorities kept the composure required by their role. What would have been the outcome if one of the functionaries had been sarcastic or witty?

56. For Newell and Rubio (1984), consensus is the central element in understanding Mexican political stability.

57. A legend has been woven surrounding this woman regarding the power that a woman can have thanks to her beauty. She was the girlfriend of one of the most well-known student leaders in 1968; then she became the daughter-in-law of Luis Echeverría, and she became secretary of tourism under López Portillo. There is the rumor in Mexico that she was Echeverría's and López Portillo's lover. This supposed romance was the subject of many jokes, even though it may not have been the worst part of López Portillo's administration. While some looked down on this, others viewed the relationship and the fact that she was named as part of the presidential cabinet as a step of courage and machismo.

58. The series of legends about the mayor of Lagos, a small town in Jalisco, are attributed to the envy of the inhabitants of the nearby towns, even though some can be traced all the way to Germany (De Alba, 1991).

59. During a visit to Los Angeles in 1980, I went to two comedy clubs, in which comedians switched every twenty minutes. One of these places was in Manhattan Beach, where many young people went to the beach to live out their California dream. After an hour and a half, I had heard only one political joke. The other place was in Hollywood. After two hours, I had heard only three political jokes. It is very common to go to parties and in several hours of jokes, nobody tells even one single political joke.

At one time, Radio Mil combined jokes in their programming during the day, but I didn't hear one single political joke there, either.

60. Regarding elitelore, see Wilkie (1973), Herrera-Sobek (1979), and Wilkie and Manell-Kinberg (1981).

61. Television programs that penetrate into the nooks and crannies of the personal lives of artists are very popular. Why not think that the joke can do the job with respect to politicians—maybe because television would not dare to produce anything of this type?
62. This argument is based on the Freudian economic concept (Freud, 1973).
63. This was my focus when I analyzed the political jokes during the Echeverría administration (Schmidt, 1991a).

Chapter 2

1. "Political mockery is the indispensable condiment of our everyday gossip. The Mexican who doesn't smile, who doesn't make a joke at the expense of the government or who doesn't boo some politician in the bunch, is a specimen which surely lives in a zoological era very distinct from ours" (Homero, 1974:31).
2. There are psychologists who specialize in the management of sorrow, affliction, bitterness, condolence, pain, suffering, sadness, feelings that are normally associated with death.
3. I use the underground concept in the same sense as I did in chapter 1.
4. I had the opportunity of participating in a campaign in which a singer had been invited to perform who attracted thirty thousand people—free, of course—to a politician's event. The politician was conscious of the fact that most of the people hadn't gone to see him, but it was important to take advantage of the opportunity to send a message to so many people. That same politician lost the election due to reasons too complex to describe here; the point is that the multitudes who attended the political/musical didn't have political intentions; for them, simply attending a free concert did not sway them politically.
5. The people from Monterrey have a reputation for being stingy, and the jokes concentrate on that subject; for example, a child in Monterrey says to his father: "Dad, can I watch television?" and the father answers, "Yes my son, but don't turn it on."
6. Paz's analysis of the Mexican can be considered negative, but he was one of the few Mexican officials who protested the student repression in 1968, resigning as ambassador for India, which without a doubt demonstrated different personal values.
7. "Mexicans, even those from the city, are not used to and don't trust in studies of their personality" (Díaz Guerrero, 1961:71). None of the opinion polls into the 1988 presidential election approached the results of the same (De la Peña, 1988); in the year 2000, only one poll was correct, and even though political inquiry has improved, there is a long way to go until they turn into a completely trustworthy instrument.
8. Gumaro Morones (1980)—a pseudonym for Marco Murray and Guillermo Farber—attempted to analyze the Mexican by way of irony and ended up writing a moral discourse, which seems to happen frequently with this type of book. The rumored history is that one of the authors used a pseudonym because he was a researcher well known at the UNAM, but he turned out to be identified and forced to resign from the university, which, according to rumor, he did, and later on he was rehabilitated.
9. It seems that not even fiction is safe from censorship. *La sombra del caudillo*, by Martin Luis Guzmán, was censored, and the movie, which was made based on the same, was canned for almost thirty years.
10. Regarding the mestizo, see Basave (1992), and regarding the colonial inheritance in Latin America, see Stein (1970) and Wiarda (1983).

11. In his psychological study of the albur, Álvarez Díaz de León (1976) finds association with sex and concludes that the associations regard or stem from passive homosexuality.

12. The national indigenous institute, using language as a criteria to identify a people, warns that more than nineteen Indian people are in danger of disappearing. If nothing changes, in the course of one generation—or, that is, by the year 2020—there will only be thirty-three Indian pueblos left, and that is even with the assertion that after the twentieth century there would supposedly be political preservation of the indigenous.

13. Bartra (1987:178) concludes that slang, which he considers a dialect, which emerges in popular colonies, is defensive and establishes a barrier that keeps foreigners from understanding conversation. See Aguilar's (1989) slang dictionary.

14. For Basave (1992:19), the Creoles, Spaniards born in New Spain, expropriated the indigenous past.

15. Cantinflas is perhaps the most popular comic of the twentieth century. Bartra (1987:chap. 18) argues that Cantinflas's humor illustrates the relationship between the State and society.

16. In April of 1987, I saw an episode of the popular television series *¿Qué nos pasa?*, in which two men fool a woman, stealing from her car while they pretend to repair it. Since she has no money to pay, they accept her driver's license as a guarantee with the promise that she will return to pay. Without knowing that she has been robbed, she happily says, "I fooled them, the license had expired." This is a common story in Mexico where everybody fools the other. For me, the best summary of this condition is the end of a monologue by Manolo Fabregas at the end of the movie *Mecánica nacional*: "Everybody screws everybody, and that is the democratic equilibrium." Sometimes we can see this in real life: on the 12 of August of 1987, I heard on the radio that a Mexican woman had been disqualified from the 10,000-meter race, apparently for reasons not justified, by a judge who incidentally was the father of a woman who, thanks to the disqualification, won the gold medal. In view of the scandal that ensued, the radio announcer said: "Okay, but the winner also has merits."

17. "The history of Mexico is one of false recounting or arbitrarily evoked at least by the whim of unpleasant power. A free and unpleasant power [. . .] the greatest incarnation of that power is Antonio López de Santa Anna [. . .] whims of that style we call today the Mexican presidency" (Aguilar Camin, 1991:45–46).

18. I translated *vivencial* as "behavioral."

19. It's interesting that the PAN continues insisting on blaming the PRI for all the bad things that have happened—without assuming, very conveniently, that in the last seventeen years its members have been accomplices in the most ruinous decisions for the country, which go from the approval of FOBAPROA (the bank rescue program) all the way to the incineration of electoral ballots, which would have shown the claimed electoral fraud of Carlos Salinas.

20. Regarding women, see an analysis with strong misogynist tones in Paz (1986).

21. See Cansino's discussion (2004, especially chapter 4, "El evangelio de la transicion") regarding the scholars who got a hold of the history of the transition to democracy to increase the fruits of debate and of course the politically created situation.

22. *Fregar* means *estropear*, or "to attack," "to ruin something," "to rub strongly," and also "to clean with energy." Someone *friegas* the floor. A *friega* of alcohol turns out to

be a remedy for problems provoked by cold weather or wind. But, when somebody says that I *fregue'd* him, it means that the other one had the poorer outcome in the situation. One Mexican tries to *fregar* another Mexican, the government, or anybody in general.

23. On one occasion, I compiled with the late Jorge Gil (R.I.P.), professor of engineering, and with David Mejía, expert in software development, what we considered the laws of Mexican dialectics. Take into account that dialectics in Mexico—especially as developed in a university with a strong Marxist influence, such as the UNAM, during several decades—is something like a Decalogue of thought. The laws are as follows:

*One thing is one thing and another thing is another thing.
*When you can't anymore, you can't anymore.
*The one who knows, knows.
*Yes, but no.
*First things first.
*Tomorrow.
*We'll talk later.
*What is "fallen, is fallen."
*What is written, written is; what is said, said is. [This is the only law that has a known author, Jorge de la Vega Dominguez, who was president of the national executive of the PRI at the time of its creation.]
*What is not allowed is neither prohibited.
*If we don't like the same wine, we have tasted two.
*If it is short, is not very tall.

24. There is an anecdote that illustrates this: When Andre Breton visited Mexico to attend a convention of surrealists, he called on a carpenter to make a table for him. He demonstrated what he wanted with a drawing. When he received the table, it was exactly the way he had drawn it, with some legs shorter than the others—because the table had been made according to the perspective in which it had been drawn. It is said that Breton commented, "We Europeans invented surrealism, the Mexicans live it." Angelina Muñiz-Huberman (2005:189) tells us of another anecdote regarding this observation: "From this statue [*Carlos IV of Spain* or *The Little Horsey*—as it is known in Mexico City, *El caballito*] after attempting several times and being confronted with the impossibility of crossing the street, was like Andre Breton, in an ontological sea, it occurred to her to affirm, with all seriousness, that Mexico was a surrealistic country." Within this same context, it is often said that if Franz Kafka had lived in Mexico, he would have been no more noteworthy than any other author, or maybe he would not have even written.

25. It will be interesting to see the social and cultural impacts of the law passed in 2006 that eliminates three-day weekends and forces Mexican national holidays to be celebrated on the Monday closest to the date of the holiday.

26. See the application of this concept in the poem to López Portillo in chapter 4, page 149.

27. See a sarcastic version in the movie *El mil usos* (Roberto G. Rivera [1981])—though the movie is better known for the acting job done by Héctor Suárez.

28. "I heard inside of me the words of Jesus: 'Don't worry about tomorrow, tomorrow will have its own worrisome situations. Today has its own sufferings'" (Kundera,

1986:232). It wouldn't be surprising that Mexicans should interpret tomorrow in a sense opposite of Kundera's, saying: "Don't worry about today, it has enough of its own ailments; tomorrow one will have to worry about oneself." Ramos (1962:65) established this in the following manner: "In Mexico, each person is worried about immediate problems. He works for today and tomorrow but never for afterwards."

29. It is common to allegorically hear the question regarding the difference between a bucket full of crabs from Mexico and one full of crabs from a different country—the Mexican bucket lacks a cover and the crabs don't escape because, just as soon as one crab starts to climb, the others pull it down.

30. It is hard to translate *pendejo* into English. The translation may mean "dumb person," "stupid person," "dumbass," or "fool"; however, I think the closest meaning is "doltish person." Because of its many possible exact translations, I will use the Spanish word in the rest of the book, and depending on the context will use stupid and idiot.

31. The 1985 earthquake that caused more than ten thousand people to die put de la Madrid's government to the test and proved that it was incompetent in handling a tragedy, with little ability to react quickly to an emergency of that magnitude.

32. Ortega (1992:99, 312–13) narrates a fictitious visit to Mexico City from someone who has lived in Los Angeles for forty years. The narrator writes, "This city scares me; even though Los Angeles is one of the most violent cities in the United States, here, in addition to violence, there is a lack of authority and lies, many lies. You can't believe anyone and that causes distrust and fear." Further on, the character adds, "Why live in a country where everything is fiction?"

33. Being a student of political science at the UNAM, a constitutional history professor asked which government was worse in the sense of its laws—a government of lawyers or one of military members. Of course, most of the students responded "one of military members," to which the professor responded to the negative: "The military person doesn't understand the laws but still tries to respect them, but the lawyer knows how to break them and doesn't respect them."

Of course the military person simply puts down the laws and ignores them, but the example is still interesting.

34. In 1988, an economist was elected president. Even when he had a doctorate in political science, he continued using his *licenciado* (B.A.), which in common and current perception is associated with being a lawyer.

35. In Mexico, they still call Spaniards *gachupines*, an offensive term created by the indigenous population during the conquest because they were wearing iron spurs (Santa María, 1942:7).

36. Many anecdotes, though they reflect real images, are illegitimate. Some are invented by the elite to weaken the image of politicians, and others are invented by politicians to improve their image.

37. In this area, Spota's novel *Casi el paraiso* (1967) is required reading. In it, the son of a prostitute impersonates a noble Italian man and sees that all doors are opened for him in Mexico.

38. A version of this anecdote is attributed to the Rockefellers. David Rockefeller took one of his poor relatives around New York for a week. At the end of that time, the relative asked the rich one if he was going to help him, to which he responded that he already had. He said that if, after a week of having been seen with him, his relative couldn't improve his situation, nothing would help him.

39. I thank Dr. Abraham Katz for his comments on this point.

40. See a cartoon about the cliché that revolution has done justice to the people, in Rius (1966, 1989, 1992).

41. One of the more surprising aspects of corruption is its dimension. Ayala (1984:84) says, "Javier Coello Trejo, an official who was in charge of most of the corruption cases at the attorney general's office in the republic, declared that the arrests during the presidential period of de la Madrid brought in eleven million pesos to the government, and even so he thought that this number represented barely 1 percent of what had been stolen by public officials during that administration." "In his sixth State of the Union, Miguel de la Madrid indicated that the federal government recovered nineteen million five hundred thousand pesos during the investigation of 1,571 lawsuits against public servants" (*Excelsior*, September 8, 1988:4).

42. The Benito Juárez myth should be deconstructed. He was a Zapotec Indian who rose to power due to his marriage into a powerful criollo family.

43. I once participated in a meeting at a café in downtown Mexico City with a group of small business owners who complained about the current government corruption, and I said, "Excuse me, do you pay your taxes? They looked at me as if I were a strange creature, but the conclusion was obvious: They were just as corrupt as the officials—everybody fools everybody, so who can throw the first stone?

44. The rationale to not hire a lawyer, other than due to a lack of trust, is reflected in the saying, "You're better off with a poor outcome than with a good fight."

45. I thank Héctor Subirats, perhaps the best philosophical economist of Mexico today (even though he doesn't live in the country—or possibly *because* of it) for catching my attention with this quote, apparently from George Bernard Shaw: "There is no situation so bad that it can't get worse."

46. The following is a typical lawyer joke that is possibly the source of the one about the Mexicans: "More and more laboratories are using lawyers instead of rats for their experiments because: 1. There are more lawyers available. 2. Rats look better. 3. The lab technicians never developed feelings for the lawyers. 4. There are some things that not even rats would dare to do" (Barallier 1922:22).

47. See the magnificent essay by Pablo Vila (2000) regarding the building of the border identity and how the Mexican reacts when settled on the American side of the border.

Chapter 3

1. This last one refers to his comment that he would defend the peso like a dog, after which his nickname became "El Perro" (The Dog). See chapter 4 regarding this event. The theme of the Nobel Prize and the destruction of the value of money was applied to the dictator Tito, as was mentioned in chapter 1.

2. In Schmidt (1986), I analyzed the political context of the Echeverría jokes.

3. There is a useful collection in Gallo (1987).

4. What can illustrate this is the experience of Rius and the systematic governmental harassment and aggression that led him to abandon some of his projects, such as his comic books.

5. There are those who feel that the PRIAN must be given its place as the long alliance between the PRI and PAN.

6. The United States followed a policy of isolation from Europe under the Monroe Doctrine. This protected the country from European colonization and allowed it to consolidate as a nation. Afterward, the country's struggle against ideology produced hatred of communism, which has now been amplified toward immigration. All of that might be in search of a new national identity that invented the theory of the *melting pot*, even though someone ironically has stated that the true melting pot is a metal pot in a microwave; this has permitted the ideological homogenization of its society.

7. Unlike in the United States—where people use the symbols on the country's flag for diverse purposes, including in designs on clothing—in Mexico, the use of national symbols is legally restricted and supervised by the military, that is, the repressive arm par excellence. Haven't you asked yourself: *If we were liberated, would we make underwear out of our country's flags—and if we did that, would anything happen?*

8. The anti-hero anecdotes that demystify the hero are popular in many countries. A Russian one tells the story regarding a hero of the sixteenth century, Ivan Susanin, who was captured by Polish troops. He was forced to lead the Poles through a forest, where they killed him—but then the troops were unable to find their way out of the forest and died themselves. One joke about this story says that the tragedy of Ivan Susanin is that he got lost and couldn't find his way out of the forest. (I thank Professor Vladik Kreinovich for this anecdote). Several Soviet jokes cited in this book refer to the anti-hero.

9. That is to say that there is explained the origin of the *mordida* (bribe) and robbery, and "gouging the nail" means to steal or pickpocket.

10. This joke is also attributed to a Jewish gangster (Telushkin, 1992:67).

11. This is one of Fuentes's main arguments (1978), and it is seen with many political events. For example, on September 21, 2005, a helicopter crash killed Mexico's secretary of public safety, and no matter how much the government insisted this incident was an accident, many people rumored it to have been an attack. Similarly, on November 4, 2008, a plane crash killed the secretary of the interior, a close associate to President Calderón, and it also was rumored to be the result of sabotage. A large percentage of people believe in government conspiracies.

12. On January 1, 1994, an indigenous revolt in Chiapas established as a central point on the agenda the negotiation regarding the autonomy for indigenous villages, though there are communities in Oaxaca that have enjoyed that status for a long time.

13. The debate regarding the relationship between geography and patriotism is not over. In Europe it plays an important role, and this partially explains the growing importance that regions have in the new economic and political order of Europe (Petschen, 1992). There is also the open debate regarding the creation of a single European nationality after the creation of the European Union (De Federico, 2004; García Faroldi, 2004).

14. This method of establishing territorial boundaries is not exclusively Mexican. In other parts of the world, youth gangs behave in much the same way. In many cities in the United States, for example, freeway overpasses and walls are covered with code messages belonging to gangs.

15. In literature, political culture is used as civic culture. For me, political culture is how the individual sees himself in front of political power, how political power sees the individual, how the individual sees other individuals, and how political power sees other political actors.

16. Discovering national objectives by picturing one's country in the future is an important element of Mexican political dialogue. See Ortiz Pinchetti (1990).

17. Pacts signed since the government of de la Madrid are an exception and have had doubtful economic results—as well as *disastrous* social results.

18. It has always seemed interesting to me that somebody by the last name of Pérez, which is a Spanish-Jewish last name, should ask Schmidt, who is a Polish Jew, "Hey, your last name isn't Mexican, is it?"

19. Let's repeat here the words of Muñiz-Huberman (2005:190) that we cited in chapter 2: "The advantage of living in Mexico is that Mexico doesn't exist. Mexico is what each person invents. Mexico is Mexico. All of the Mexicos that could be wished for, present. Past. Future. The Mexico that will be perfect the day that it is inaugurated. An imaginary country."

20. Minogue's thesis (1995:19) is that politics for the Romans was to love one's country, and patriotism guided that passion.

21. Newell and Rubio (1984) both conclude that a consensus is needed, though for different reasons.

22. See De Mora (1980), especially the chapter that begins, "To confess a robbery that he hadn't committed, they submitted him to torture."

23. Here are some interesting graffiti quotes found in Mexican bathrooms (taken from Jiménez, 1980:122–23):

Quizo alcanzar la victoria el traidor de Victoriano ¡Como si victoria y ano fuesen igual en la historia!	He wanted to attain victory Victoriano the traitor As if Victory and anus Were the same throughout history

~

Viva Francisco Madero Sentado en este agujero.	Long live Francisco Madero Sitting in this *agujero* [hole].

24. Perhaps the rejection is due to the idea that Rodolfo Neri Vela, the first Mexican astronaut, was rumored to be a governmental favorite during the process of selection. This idea was reinforced when he was elected by the PRI as a stand-in senator in 1988. Consequently, his merits were made to seem doubtful.

25. Udall (1988:214) tells the same joke about a candidate who visits an Indian reservation.

26. During the government of Miguel de la Madrid, this joke was revived and adapted to say "the presidency of moral renovation."

27. I thank Álvaro Echeverría Zuno for telling me this joke.

28. According to Freud (1973), saving money is one of the basic comic elements.

29. This is the opinion of economist Luis Pazos; see his interview with Ortiz Pinchetti (1990).

30. Regarding the theory of modernization, see Eisenstadt (1970) and Feierabend, Feierabend, and Nesvold (1969).

31. These details don't coincide with those in chapter 1 because I am referring to details in different years. The difference between them should show that there is less voter abstention in presidential elections than there is in the election of members of Congress; in 1970 it was presidential and in 1979 it was for members of Congress. This

phenomenon appears regarding local versus national elections in the United States, where voter abstention is much more common in local elections than in national ones—in local elections, voter abstention can be as high as 80 percent.

32. In an unusual Mexican political event, ex-president Miguel de la Madrid acknowledged in a televised interview in September of 2005 that the PRI had lost the election.

33. Downs (1973) suggests that the vote can be seen as having an economic value; that is, when the individual votes, he is investing his asset and expects a gain. In the case of Mexico, electoral behavior suggests that the vote has been devalued and that the small gain, if there is one, is derived from the investment and doesn't stimulate voting. I applied this economic-value approach in a study of elections on the border of Mexico and the United States between 1962 and 1988 (Schmidt, 1990b). Another explanation of the value of the vote might be that Mexicans don't know how to use their assets in order to invest them.

Chapter 4

1. I thank the distinguished late historian Horacio Labastida (R.I.P.), for having commented to me the importance of patrimony in the Mexican political system. Labastida had a very important role in Mexican politics: he was a senator, the rector of the University of Puebla, and the president of IEPES, a study-center part of the PRI.

2. In 1838, France demanded payment for damages inflicted upon French citizens during the Mexican revolts. Many of the damages were exaggerated; for example, a French baker claimed damages for cakes lost during a riot. That is why it is called the War of the Cakes.

The French attacked Veracruz by cannon, and in these combats, Santa Anna was injured and lost a leg. With no money to pay for nor to organize a defense, Mexico solicited new loans and paid France an unjust and exaggerated amount.

3. See a retelling from the American perspective in Michener (1985, chapter 8). Historians suggest that Santa Anna was irresponsible, and it is maintained that he may have been in bed with a lover instead of leading the battle of the Alamo, which was crucial in that war. Enrique Serna (2001:235–36) relates the event this way: "My sleep is interrupted by the sound of weapons. Upon awakening, with surprise, I see that the enemy has entered the encampment. I have no time to put on my boots. I put my hand on my saber and leave running, looking for a horse, between the whistling bullets that sting the skin. What happened with the guard of *Castrillon*? I had orders to report the most minor enemy movement. When I pass by his tent I see him agonizing with a fan of playing cards between his fingers, his head reclined on a crate that acted as an improvised game table. He has a gash in his back, and on his side are the bodies of two other players. Too late to get mad at him. I tried to organize the defense but I can't make myself hear in the tumult. Possessed by fear, the older recruits let themselves be killed in cold blood without making use of their weapons. Others flee toward the small brook that's outside the woods, where the shooters from Houston hunt them like rabbits [. . .]." I thank Pedro Siller, who showed me this source. Santa Anna lost his wooden leg at the battle of El Alamo.

4. That same joke was done about Spanish dictator Francisco Franco. This suggests that the joke could have origins in Spain and could have been taken to Mexico by refugees of the 1936 civil war—or, possibly, the Spaniards heard it in Mexico and adapted it to fit Franco.

5. Among the many critiques about those who prospered under the blanket of the revolution, we have those by Fuentes (1962) and Rius (1992).

6. This same joke was applied to Marta Sahagún de Fox.

7. There is a similar Russian joke in which the car is offered to a minister after he has visited the automotive plant. The car is offered for five rubles and he says that with such a low price he would like to buy two.

8. I don't allude here to the final rebellions, such as that of Almazán (1940) or Padilla (1946), which were motivated by electoral fraud because they weren't able to derail the system that was becoming consolidated.

9. In 1982, James and Edna Wilkie and I got together with Miguel Alemán and invited him to Los Angeles to an interview on a program of oral histories of Latin American leaders. The program was directed by Professor James Wilkie at the University of California at Los Angeles. Just a few minutes after the interview and conversation had begun, and without us asking, Alemán commented, "Look, they say that I was corrupt. How could I have stolen money if the entire budget for the government of Veracruz was only three hundred million pesos?" The accusation of corruption against Alemán refers to his presidential term and his term as governor. Clearly he was worried about the impact that the accusation would have on his image in history.

10. Title of a novel by José Rubén Romero.

11. Mexican poet (1918–2000).

12. According to Julio Hernández López, author of the column "Astillero" that is published in *La Jornada*, there are several authors associated with this epigram. Citing someone anonymous, López's column says the epigram was a remnant that appeared in 1964 and that it "was probably written by Renato Leduc; appeared in a memorable one-time publication: a flying leaf like the ones in the *posadas* assigned with the permission of Leduc, Rius and surely other journalists whose names I don't remember" (http://www.jornada.unam.mx/2005/09/05/index.php?section=opinion&article=006o1pol).

13. They protect the president; their function is similar to that of the Secret Service.

14. This was the chorus of the song "Amante Bandido" that Miguel Bose made popular in 1982.

15. The devaluation in those years reached the following percentages:

Echeverría, 81 percent.
López Portillo, 562 percent.
De la Madrid, 1,555 percent.
Salinas, 36 percent.
Zedillo, 180 percent.

16. Later on, López Portillo maintained that in Mexico, a presidential term is judged by the parity of the peso. This explains why what is simply an adjustment of monetary value is blamed on the president; it also perhaps explains why Carlos Salinas—in his great egotism and his wish to go down in history as the greatest president of Mexico—refused to devaluate, leaving a fiscal time bomb to Zedillo.

17. Velasco Piña (2005:100) defined technocrats in the following manner: "It was a generation of children educated in private schools with post-graduate diplomas from American universities, without any experience in the inner workings of the party, and only on the merits of bureaucratic positions attained."

18. The last two nicknames appeared in an article in the *Los Angeles Times*, December 20, 1987, p. 20, and the subject returns with Fox.

19. Spiro Agnew was the subject of a previous form of this joke that described Agnew's brain as the size of a walnut—which, with *nuts* held as slang for testicles, may be interpreted as saying that the U.S. vice president thought with his testicles instead of with his brain.

20. I've already mentioned the similarities between Mexican and Soviet humor. Here is another example of some of these isomorphic jokes:

> A train stops due to the lack of tracks. How do the Soviet leaders respond?
>
> Lenin calls the Subbotnik, or volunteers without pay, and the passengers build the track.
>
> Stalin orders the engineers killed and gives the passengers twenty-four hours to build the track.
>
> Khruschev orders the rear tracks removed and has them put in front.
>
> Brezhnev says, "Let's draw the curtains, let's move the train slowly from side to side, and let's pretend that it's moving."

21. Even though de la Madrid was born in Colima, he was considered to be from Mexico City because he left his native Colima when he was two years of age. Apparently, he never intended to establish political contacts with that state. His bureaucratic career was made in the federal district.

22. In a conversation with Manuel J. Clouthier in San Diego, presidential candidate of the PAN in that election, he told me that Cárdenas won the election and that they had stolen 5 million votes from him that they had given to Salinas; that is, the PRI candidate had ended up in third place. Velasco Piña (2005:111) repeats this version.

23. This joke was adapted to López Obrador and its probable origin is from the nineteenth century attributed to people from the Polish city of Chelm, who were stigmatized as idiots.

> A Jew from Chelm visits the main synagogue in Warsaw and hears the director of the synagogue (*Shammes*) say the following riddle:
>
> "Who is the son of my father who is not my brother?"
>
> Nobody answers.
>
> "It's me," exclaims the *Shammes*.
>
> The Jew from Chelm is very impressed, and when he goes back home, he visits the synagogue, and after the prayer service he asks, "Who is the son of my father and mother, but is not my brother?"
>
> Nobody knows. So, the Jew from Chelm answers:
>
> "The *Shammes* from Warsaw." (Telushkin, 1992:59)

24. In 1963, Mexico had 30 million impoverished citizens. This number increased to 55 million in 1991, nearly 67 percent of the total population of the country. It wasn't expected that *Solidaridad* would reduce the number of poor people in absolute terms (Balboa Reyna, 1991:4–5) and it didn't do so. In 1993, the CEPAL reported a diminishing percentage of people in extreme poverty from 1988 to 1992 (Sainz, 1993),

but the truth is that after thousands of millions of dollars spent on *Solidaridad* and the specific program for peasants, *Procampo*, the poor people of Mexico were equally poor, or more so, than before. But, the PRI won the election in 1994 on the promise of poverty relief. From then on, part of the extreme poverty has been reduced thanks to statistical manipulation.

25. One time I asked a Mexican undersecretary if he would go to a meeting in the United States, and he answered: "I don't like the gringos, I'm going to send one of my directors."

26. There is serious doubt if Telmex can explain the source of all the cash that has allowed Mr. Slim to become a multi-billionaire, or if there is another source of money.

27. Rául Salinas spent ten years in jail, accused of murder and unexplained financial gain; in 2013, he was exonerated and all his assets were returned to him.

Chapter 5

1. A politician told me that Zedillo confirmed in private the he didn't want to be president and he almost got his wish.

2. I went into detail in the original explanation regarding homosexuality in Mexican political humor (see Schmidt, 2005).

3. The mistake of December (1994) hastened the devaluation, provoked a usurious interest rate, and caused great pay problems for millions of Mexicans. Faced with this desolate picture, the government created a rescue program that would end up costing more than one hundred thousand million dollars, and on which many have enriched themselves, including Fox's wife's children (Hernández and Quintero, 2005).

4. With the defeat of the PRI many politicians came out of the ideological closet. Some have gone to the PRD and others to the PAN, parties where their hearts truly were to begin with. This issue will have to be analyzed in another section.

5. Fox wasn't the only one to show the magnitude of his ignorance. At a public meeting in 2005, his wife quoted words from the famous feminist Rabina Gran Tagora (Rabindranath Tagore, who became a feminist author).

6. Congress must authorize presidential travel abroad, but the law changed in 2008.

7. In 2001, I published the book *Mexico encadenado. El legado de Zedillo y los retos de Fox* (Mexico, Colibri). The editor attempted to make a co-edition with the National Polytechnic Institute, which objected that I should say that Fox was a liar. The editor changed the words "a liar" to the word "fickle," and yet the institution bowed out of the project, saying you don't "bite the hand that feeds you." I believe nothing more needs to be said regarding the new Mexican democratic culture.

8. López (2009) demonstrates electoral fraud using mathematical models.

9. An extreme right movement that became very powerful with the PAN administrations starting with Vicente Fox.

10. During the Carlos Salinas administration, the concept of "uncomfortable brother" became popular, since it portrayed the corrupt brother who benefitted from the family relation. It was applied to governors such as Francisco Barrio in Chihuahua and expanded to other relatives, such as in this case to Calderón's relative.

11. In the year 2013, she was jailed by Enrique Peña Nieto in a very well-orchestrated maneuver that distanced the union from the PRI and distanced her from the president.

12. I summarized the outcome of the policy in Schmidt (2012).

Postscript

1. Roberto Madrazo was the PRI presidential candidate in the year 2006; Arturo Montiel, governor of the state of Mexico, bought apartments in Florida, and the purchase became a scandal.

2. This support was very well paid; one journalist from the UK send me a copy of an invoice for one million pesos (about 80,000 dollars) to pay journalists López Doriga and Beteta to make positive remarks about the governor. This apparently is not exclusive to one state, and as Picato (2010) states, the policy of having journalists or newspapers on the governmental payroll started with Porfirio Díaz at the beginning of the twentieth century.

3. It became a fashion for politicians to write books; however, many people suspect they are not the real authors. The three major candidates (PAN, PRI, PRD) in 2012 had written books.

4. It is not uncommon for a male in Mexico to be named Guadalupe, honoring the Virgin of Guadalupe.

Conclusion

1. I thank Gustavo Segade for having guided me in this aspect of the analysis.

2. "The emergence of a political party clearly implies that the masses should be taken into account by the political elite" (LaPalambara and Myron, 1966:4).

Bibliography

Acevedo, Esther. 2000. *La caricatura política en México en el siglo XIX.* México, D.F.: Circulo de Arte.

A. D. 1960. *La caricatura política argentina.* Buenos Aires: EUDEBA.

Adler-Lomnitz, Larissa, and Marisol Pérez-Lizaur. 1987. *A Mexican Elite Family.* Princeton: Princeton University Press.

Aguilar Camín, Héctor. 1991. *La guerra de Galio.* México, D.F.: Cal y Arena.

Aguilar de la Parra, Octavio. 1971. *Las mil anécdotas y un comentario.* México, D.F.: Costa Amic.

Aguilar Melantzón, Ricardo. 1989. *Glosario del caló de Cd. Juárez.* Las Cruces: New Mexico State University.

Agustín, José. 1986. *Cerca del fuego.* México, D.F.: Plaza y Janés.

Alcántara, Narda. 2000. *The Power Network in Mexico (1920–2000): A Network Model of Kinship, Marriage and Loyalty Ties among the Ruling Elite.* Irvine, CA: University of California, Irvine. PhD dissertation.

Almond, Gabriel, and Sydney Verba. 1963. *The Civic Culture, Political Attitudes and Democracy in Five Nations.* Princeton: Princeton University Press.

Álvarez, Griselda. 1992. *Cuesta arriba. Memorias de la primera gobernadora.* México, D.F.: Fondo de Cultura Económica.

Álvarez Díaz de León, Germán. 1976. *Una nota acerca de los albures.* México, D.F.: Facultad de Psicología, UNAM.

Asimov, Isaac. 1971. *Isaac Asimov's Treasury of Humor.* Boston: Houghton Mifflin Co.

Ayala Anguiano, Armando. 1984. *JLP: Secretos de un sexenio.* México, D.F.: Grijalbo.

Balboa Reyna, Flor de María. 1991. "Antes de que la verdad irrumpa . . . ." *La Jornada,* México, D.F., Aug. 30. Sección Laboral 4–5.

Banc, C., and Alan Dundes. 1986. *First Prize: Fifteen Years!* Cranbury, NJ: Associated University Press.

———. 1990. *You Call This Living?* Athens and London: The University of Georgia Press.

Barajas Durán, Rafael. 2007. *El país de "el llorón de Icamole."* México, D.F.: Fondo de Cultura Económica.

———. 2005. *El país de "El Ahuizote."* México, D.F.: Fondo de Cultura Económica.

Bartra, Armando, and Juan Manuel Aurrecoechea. 1988. *Puros cuentos: La historia de la historieta en México.* México, D.F.: Consejo Nacional para la Cultura y las Artes, Dirección General de Publicaciones; Dirección General de Culturas Populares, Museo Nacional de Culturas Populares; Grijalbo.

Bartra, Roger. 1987. *La jaula de la melancolía. Identidad y metamorfosis del mexicano.* México, D.F.: Grijalbo.

Basave, Agustín. 1992. *México mestizo. Análisis del nacionalismo mexicano en torno a la mestizofilia de Andrés Molina Enríquez*. México, D.F.: Fondo de Cultura Económica.
Becker, Ernest. 1977. *La lucha contra el mal*. México, D.F.: Fondo de Cultura Económica.
Beezley, William H. 1987. *Judas at the Jockey Club*. Lincoln: University of Nebraska Press.
———. 1985. "Recent Mexican Political Humor." *Journal of Latin American Lore* 11:2.
Bejar Navarro, Raúl. 1968. *El mito del mexicano*. México, D.F.: Facultad de Ciencias Políticas y Sociales, UNAM.
Bergson, Henri. 1973. *La risa*. Madrid: Espasa Calpe.
Booth, John A., and Mitchell A. Seligson. 1994. "Paths to Democracy and the Political Culture of Costa Rica, Mexico and Nicaragua," in Diamond, Larry (ed.), *Political Culture and Democracy in Developing Cultures*. Boulder and London: Lynne Rienner.
———. 1984. "The Political Culture of Authoritarianism in Mexico: A Reexamination." *Latin American Research Review* 19:1, 106–124.
Bonet, Pilar. 1987. "Juvenal en Moscú." *El País*, Oct. 4.
Borah, Woodrow. 1977. *New Spain's Century of Depression*. Arden: Arden Library.
Brallier, Jess M. 1992. *Lawyers and Other Reptiles*. Chicago: Contemporary Books.
Camp, Roderic. 1992. *Generals in the Palacio. The Military in Modern Mexico*. New York: Oxford University Press.
Campbell, Howard. 1994. *Zapotec Renaissance: Ethnic Politics and Cultural Revivalism in Southern Mexico*. Albuquerque: University of New Mexico Press.
Canar, Israel Tzvi. 1974. *Abdija anitzjit*. Tel Aviv: Boostan.
Cansino, César. 2010. *La revuelta silenciosa. Democracia, espacio público y ciudadanía en América Latina*. Puebla: Benemerita Universidad Autónoma de Puebla.
———. 2004. *El desafío democrático. La transformación del Estado en el México postautoritario*. México, D.F.: Cuadernos de Metapolítica.
Carrasco, Pedro. 1976. *El catolicismo popular de los tarascos*. México, D.F.: Sep-setentas.
Ceceña, José Luis. 1970. *México en la órbita imperial*. México, D.F.: El Caballito.
Center for Media and Public Affairs. 1990. *Media Monitor*. Washington, D.C.
CIESPAL. 1990. *Caricatura*, Quito, Ecuador: QUIPUS.
Cisneros, Enrique. n.d. (possibly 1986). *Si me permiten actuar*. México, D.F.: CLETA.
Cockroft, James D. 1983. *Mexico, Class Formation, Capital Accumulation and The State*. New York: Monthly Review Press.
Cohen, Ted. 1999. *Jokes: Philosophical Thoughts on Joking Matters*. Chicago and London: Chicago University Press.
Cohn, Haim. 2004. *The Trial and Death of Jesus*. Old Saybrook, CT: Konecky and Konecky.
Correa, Guillermo. 1983. "Infantería, tanquetas, helicópteros y paracaidistas en los combates de Ocosingo." *Proceso*, México, D.F., no. 866, June 7.
Coronado, Rodolfo. 1984. *La picaresca. Antología del ingenio mexicano*. México, D.F.: EDAMEX.
Covo Torres, Javier. 1987. *Gandhi en Ayunas*. México, D.F.: Dante.
Critchley, Simon. 2002. *On Humour*. London and New York: Routledge.
Crouch, Colin. 2004. *Posdemocracia*. México, D.F.: Taurus.
De Alba, Alfonso. 1991. *El Alcalde de Lagos*. Guadalajara, Jalisco: Hexágono. 8th edition.

de Federico de la Rúa, Ainhoa. 2004. "Los espacios sociales de la transnacionalidad. Una tipología de la integración relacional de los migrantes." *Araucaria*, año 6, no. 12.

de la Peña, Ricardo. 1988. "Del impacto político de los sondeos de opinión." *El Cotidiano* 25. Sept.–Oct., pp. 29–41.

de Mora, Juan Miguel. 1980. *Si tienes miedo*. México, D.F.: EDAMEX.

Dehesa, German. 1988. *Tapadeus II*, México, D.F.: mimeografiado.

———. 1982. *Y despues . . . actuaremos nosotros. Pastorela para tiempos de crisis*. México, D.F.: Gatopardo.

Delumeau, Jean. 2002. *El miedo en Occidente*. Madrid: Taurus

Díaz de León, Francisco. 1985. *Gahona y Posada, grabadores mexicanos*. México, D.F.: Fondo de Cultura Económica.

Díaz del Castillo, Bernal. 1985. *Verdadera crónica de la conquista de la Nueva España*. Madrid: Espasa-Calpe.

Díaz Guerrero, Rogelio. 1961. *Estudios de psicología del mexicano*. México, D.F.: Antigua Libreria Robredo.

Díaz Serrano, Jorge. 1989. *Yo, Jorge Díaz Serrano*. México, D.F.: Planeta.

Diccionario hispánico universal. 1964. México, D.F.: W.M. Jackson, Inc.

Dole, Bob. 1998. *Great Political Wit*. New York: Doubleday.

Downs, Anthony. 1973. *Teoría económica de la democracia*. Madrid: Aguilar.

Durón Ruiz, Ramón. 1992. *El filósofo de Güémez*. México, D.F.: Logos Editorial.

Eastman, Max. 1972. *The Sense of Humor*. New York: Octagon Books.

Eco, Umberto. 1989. *En nombre de la rosa*. México, D.F.: Lumen.

Eisenstadt, Shmuel. 1970. *Ensayos sobre el cambio social y la modernización*. Madrid: Tecnos.

Eliade, Mircea. 1985. *Mito y realidad*. Barcelona: Labor; English translation, 1963. *Myth and Reality*. New York: Harper.

Espino, Fidel. 1989. *Cuando las manos hablaron. Clavillazo*. México, D.F.: Diana.

Feierabend, I., R. Feierabend, and B. Nesvold. 1969. "Social Change and Political Violence: Cross National Patterns," in Graham, Hugh D., and T. Gurr (eds.), *Violence in America: Historical and Comparative Perspectives. A Report to the National Commission on the Causes and Prevention of Violence*. New York: Signet Books.

Flota, Marco Antonio. 1985. *Tumbagrillos. Primer diccionario para tecnócratas apolíticos y para políticos atecnócratas*. México, D.F.: Diana.

Foster, David. 1989. *From Mafalda to Los Supermachos*. Boulder: Lynne Rienner.

Freud, Sigmund. 1973. *El chiste y su relación con lo inconsciente*. Madrid: Alianza.

———. 1961. "Humour," in *The Standard Edition of the Complete Psychological Works of Sigmund Freud*. London: The Hogarth Press. Vol. XXI.

Fuentes, Carlos. 1993. *El naranjo*. México, D.F.: Alfaguara.

———. 1978. *La región mas transparente*. México, D.F.: Fondo de Cultura Económica.

———. 1962. *La Muerte de Artemio Cruz*. México, D.F.: Fondo de Cultura Económica.

Fultz, Barbara (ed.). 1970. *The Naked Emperor*. New York: Pegasus.

Gallo, Miguel Angel. 1987. *La sátira política mexicana*. México, D.F.: Quinto Sol.

Gally, Héctor. 1982. *Humor a primera vista*. México, D.F.: Gernika.

García Faroldi, Livia. 2004. "Apoyo a la Unión Europea y difusión de una identidad europea a través de las redes personales." *Araucaria*, año 6, no. 12.

García-Robles, Jorge. 1985. *Que transa con las bandas?* México, D.F.: Posada.

Gardner, Gerald. 1986. *All the Presidents' Wits*. New York: Beech Tree Books.
Gil, Jorge, Samuel Schmidt, and Jorge Castro. 1993. "Red de un ex-presidente mexicano." *Revista Mexicana de Sociología*, no. 3.
Goldberg, Carey. 1990. "Hey, That's Funny, Mikhail! Now Did You Hear the One About . . ." *Los Angeles Times*, Nov. 28.
Goldenson, Robert (ed.). 1984. *Longman Dictionary of Psychology and Psychiatry*. New York: Longman.
Gómez Hermanos. 1987. *Chistes colorados*. México, D.F.
———. 1985. *Chistes groseros*. México, D.F.
González, Edward, and David Ronfeldt. (1986). *Castro, Cuba and the World*. Santa Monica: The RAND Corporation.
González Meza, José Luis, and Walter López Koehl (eds.). 1987. *Un asesino en la presidencia?* México, D.F.
González Ramírez, Manuel. 1974. *La caricatura política*. México, D.F.: Fondo de Cultura Económica.
Haddad, Gerard. 1985. *El hijo ilegítimo. Fuentes talmúdicas del psicoanálisis*. Jerusalem: Semana.
Hall, Edward T. 1973. *The Silent Language*. New York: Doubleday and Co.
Heller, Joseph, and Speed Vogel. 1986. *No Laughing Matter*. New York: Putnam.
Hernández, Anabel, and Areli Quintero. 2005. *La familia presidencial*. México, D.F. Grijalbo.
Hernández M., Alberto, and Luis Narro R. (eds.). 1987. *Cómo somos los mexicanos*. México, D.F.: Centro de Estudios Educativos, A.C.-CREA.
Herrera-Sobek, María. 1979. *The Bracero Experience. Elitelore versus Folklore*. Los Angeles: University of California Press, UCLA Latin American Center Publications.
Hiriart, Hugo. 1982. *El Universo de Posada: Estetica de la obsolescencia*. México, D.F.: Martin Casillas/Secretaria de Educación Pública.
Homero, Elmer. 1974. *El despiporre intelectual*. México, D.F.: Editores asociados.
Howe, Irving. 1951. "The Nature of Jewish Laughter." *American Mercury* 32:326.
Hugo, Víctor. 1989. *Los miserables*. México, D.F.: Porrúa. Originally published in 1862.
Iturriaga, José. 1951. *La estructura social y cultural del mexicano*. México, D.F.: Fondo de Cultura Económica.
Jaime, Nacho. 2004. *El día en que la inmortalidad estuvo a punto de dejar de ser una exclusiva del cangrejo*. México, D.F.: Urdimbre.
Jankelevitch, Vladimir. 1982. *La ironía*. Madrid: Taurus.
Jiménez, Armando. 1960. *Picardía Mexicana*. México, D.F.: Libro Mex.
Johnson, John J. 1980. *Latin America in Caricature*. Austin: University of Texas Press.
Joubert, Laurent. 2002. *Tratado de la risa*. Madrid: Asociación Española de Neuropsiquiatría.
King, Nancy. 1991. *A Cartoon History of United States Foreign Policy: From 1945 to the Present*. New York: Pharos Books.
Kishtainy, Khalid. 1985. *Arab Political Humor*. London: Quartet Books.
Kirschen, Yaakov. n.d. *Israel's Comic Strip Dry Bones*. Tel Aviv: Cherryfield Associates.
Knight, Alan. 1994. "Cardenismo: Juggernaut or Jalopy." *Journal of Latin American Studies* 26, part 1:73–107.
Kundera, Milan. 1987. *El libro de la risa y el olvido*. México, D.F.: Seix Barral.
———. 1986. *La broma*. México, D.F.: Seix Barral.

LaPalombara, Joseph, and Myron Weiner. 1966. *Political Parties and Political Development*. Princeton: Princeton University Press.
Lauerhass, Ludwig, Jr. 1979. "Who was Getúlio? Theme and Variations in Brazilian Political Lore." *Journal of Latin American Lore* 5:2, 273–290.
Le Bon, Adam, and Boyer Rogers. 2005. *Seduced by Hitler*. New York: Barnes and Noble Books.
Le Clézio, J. M. G. 1992. *El sueño mexicano. O el pensamiento interrumpido*. México, D.F.: Fondo de Cultura Económica.
Levine, Jacob. 1968. "Humor," in David L. Sills (ed.), *International Encyclopedia of the Social Sciences*. New York: Macmillan Co. and the Free Press.
Linares, Arturo. 1976. *Como el mexicano no hay dos*. México, D.F.: Posada.
Lipman, Steve. 1993. *Laughter in Hell: The Use of Humor during the Holocaust*. Northvale, NJ: Jason Aronson, Inc.
Lipovetsky, Gilles. 1987. *La era del vacío*. Spain: Anagrama.
Lomas, Juan. 1975. *Protesta y chiste político*. México, D.F.: Posada.
Lomeli, Antonio. 1975. *Anecdotario político mexicano*. México, D.F.: Costa Amic.
Lomnitz, Larissa. 1987. *Como sobreviven los marginados*. México, D.F.: Siglo XXI.
———. 1984. "Un modelo de la estructura de poder en el México urbano," in Walton, John (ed.), *Ciudades y sistemas urbanos. Economía informal y desorden espacial*. Buenos Aires: CLACSO.
López, Jorge. 2009. *2006. ¿Fraude electoral?* Chihuahua: Doble Hélice.
Lorey, David. 1993. *United States-Mexico Border Statistics Since 1900*. Los Angeles: UCLA Latin American Center Publications, UCLA Program on Mexico, University of California.
Loret de Mola, Rafael. 2001. *Los cómplices*. México, D.F.: Océano.
Lukes, Stephen, and Itzhak Galnoor. 1985. *No Laughing Matter: A Collection of Political Jokes*. London: Routledge & Kegan Paul.
Manoff, Robert. 1987. "Dissecting Glasnost." *Same World/Freeze Focus*, Autumn.
Martínez Nateras, Arturo. 1986. *El secuestro de Lucio Cabañas*. Madrid: Altalena.
Martínez Ríos, Jorge. 1970. *El perfil de México en 1980*. México, D.F.: Siglo XXI.
Martínez, Sanjuana. 1995. "De los Salinas no puedo hablar; es cosa de ellos; nosotros somos Castañon Ríos Zertuche, familia Decente." *Proceso*. No. 996, Diciembre 4.
Martré, Gonzalo. 1972. *Los símbolos transparentes*. México, D.F.: Collin y Asociados.
McGhee, Paul. 1985. "Psychology of Humour," in Kuper, Adam, and Jessica Kuper (eds.), *The Social Science Encyclopedia*. London: Routledge & KeganPaul.
Mejía Prieto, Jorge. 1992. *¡A que risa me dan los políticos!* México, D.F.: Planeta.
Metcalfe, Philip. 1988. *1933*. New York: Harper & Row.
Michener, James A. 1985. *Texas*. New York: Fawcett Crest.
Minogue, Kenneth. 1995. *Politics: A Very Short Introduction*. Oxford: Oxford University Press.
Monroy, Oscar. 1967. *El mexicano enano un mal de nuestro tiempo*. México, D.F.: Epoca.
Moody, Raymond. 1978. *Laugh after Laugh: The Healing Power of Humor*. Jacksonville, FL: Headwaters Press.
Morlino, Leonardo. 2005. "Calidad de la democracia. Notas para su discusión." *Metapolítica* 8:39, 89–108.
Morones, Gumaro. 1980. *El mexicano: ¡Diseñado por el enemigo!* México, D.F.: V Siglos.
Morreall, John. 1983. *Taking Laughter Seriously*. Albany: State University of New York.

Munro, Edmonson. 1959. *The Mexican Truck Driver*. New Orleans: Tulane University, Middle American Research Institute.

Muñiz-Huberman, Angelina. 2005. *El Sefaradí romántico. La azarosa vida de Mateo Alemán II*. México, D.F.: Plaza y Janés.

Nahmad, Abraham. 1987. *El sistema universitario de educación media superior y la política de educación del estado*. México, D.F.: UNAM, Facultad de Ciencias Políticas y Sociales. MA thesis.

Naranjo. 1976. *La escena política*. México, D.F.: Author's edition for the Partido Mexicano de los Trabajadores.

Newell, Roberto, and Luis Rubio. 1984. *Mexico's Dilemma: The Political Origins of Economic Crisis*. Boulder: Westview.

Nilsen, Don L. F. 1990. "The Social Functions of Political Humor." *Journal of Political Culture* 24:3, 35–47.

Nipongo, Nikito. 1985. "Perlas Japonesas." *Excelsior*, Oct. 17.

Ochoa Sandy, Gerardo. 1990. "Berrinches del poder acaban con periódicos o con periodistas." *Proceso*, No. 709, June 4.

Oreg. 1991. "Horoscopolítico." *Diario 29*, May 6.

Ortega, Gregorio. 1992. *Estado de gracia*. México, D.F.: Planeta.

Ortiz, Francisco. 2002. *Comprender a la gente. Por qué ganó Fox*. México, D.F.: Aguilar Nuevo Siglo.

Ortiz Pinchetti, José Agustín. 1990. *La Democracia que viene*. México, D.F.: Grijalbo.

Padgett, L. Vincent. 1976. *The Mexican Political System*. Atlanta: Houghton Mifflin Co.

Paulos, John Allen. 2000. *I Think, Therefore I Laugh*. New York: Columbia University Press.

———. 1982. *Mathematics and Humor*. Chicago and London: Chicago University Press.

Paz, Octavio. 1986. *El laberinto de la soledad*. México, D.F.: Fondo de Cultura Económica.

———. 1979. "Reflections. Mexico and the United States." *The New Yorker*, September 13.

Paz-Rudy, Daniel. 1990. *Ríanse, no los voy a defraudar*. Buenos Aires, Argentina: Ediciones de la Flor.

Petschen, Santiago. 1992. *La Europa de las regiones*. Barcelona, España: Institut d'Estudis Autonòmics.

Phillips, Bob. 1981. *The Last of the Good Clean Joke Books*. Eugene, OR: Harvest House Publishers.

Pitchford, Henry Grady. 1960. *The Social Functions of Humor*. Emory University. Ph.D dissertation.

Plunket, Robert. 1983. *In Search of Warren Harding*. New York: Laurel.

Portilla, Jorge. 1984. *Fenomenología del relajo y otros ensayos*, México, D.F.: Fondo de Cultura Económica.

Provine, Robert E. 2001. *Laughter*. New York: Penguin Books.

Pruneda, Salvador. 1958. *La caricatura como arma política*. México, D.F.: Instituto Nacional de Estudios Históricos de la Revolución Mexicana.

Quino. 1989. *Potentes, prepotentes e impotentes*. Buenos Aires: Ediciones de la Flor.

Ramírez, Ignacio. 1987. "El nuevo sketch de Palillo: Para que vea que no somos dejados." *Proceso*, Dec. 7.

Ramón y Rivera, Luis Felipe. 1982. "La Risa en el Folklore Venezolano." *Artesanía y Folklore de Venezuela* VII:39.

Ramos, Samuel. 1934. *The Profile of Man and Culture in Mexico*. Austin: University of Texas Press.

Reding, Andrew. 1988. "Favorite Son." *Mother Jones*, November, pp. 34–37, 44–45.

Reyna, José. 1980. *Raza Humor. Chicano Joke Tradition in Texas*. San Antonio, TX: Penca Books.

Richmond, Douglas. 1988. "Crisis in Mexico: Luis Echeverría and López Portillo, 1970–1982." *Journal of Third World Studies* 5:1.

Rius. 1992. *La Revolucioncita Mexicana*. México, D.F.: Posada.

———. 1989. *¿Quién ganó la Revolución Mexicana?*, México, D.F.: Posada.

———. 1984. *Un siglo de caricatura en México*. México, D.F.: Grijalbo.

———. 1966. *Los supermachos*. México, D.F.: Meridiano.

Rojas, Alicia, and Rodolfo Esparza. 1985. *Enseñanza, aprendizaje, comicidad*. México, D.F.: UNAM, Fac. de Psicología.

Ronfeldt, David. 1998. *The Zapatista Social Netwar in Mexico*. Santa Monica: The RAND Corporation.

———. 1987. *Questions and Cautions about Mexico's Future*. Santa Monica: The RAND Corporation.

———. 1985. *The Modern Mexican Military: Implications for México's Stability and Security*. Santa Monica: The RAND Corporation.

Rothenstein, Julian (ed.). 1989. *Messenger of Mortality*. London: Redstone Press.

Rubio, Luis, and Francisco Gil Díaz. 1987. *A Mexican Response*. New York: Priority Press Publications.

Rubio, Luis, et al. 1988. *La conversión industrial en México. Alternativas para el futuro*. México, D.F.: IBAFIN-Diana.

Ruiz Harrel, Rafael. 1986. *Exaltación de ineptitudes*. México, D.F.: Posada.

Rodríguez Estrada, Mauro, and Patricia Ramírez-Buendía. 1992. *Psicología del* mexicano *en el trabajo*. México, D.F.: McGraw-Hill.

Runes, Dagobert. 1983. *Dictionary of Philosophy*. New York: Philosophical Library.

Sainz, Pedro. 1993. *Informe sobre la magnitud y evolución de la pobreza en México en el período 1984–1992*. México, D.F.: CEPAL/INEGI. Mimeo.

Salgado, Antonio. 1986. *Humor negro a la mexicana. La risa del mexicano*. México, D.F.: Libra.

———. 1986a. *Lo mejor del humorismo mexicano*. México, D.F.: Libra.

———. 1986b. *¡Salucita Compadre!* México, D.F.: Libra.

Sanders, Sol. 1988. *México. Caos a la vista*. México, D.F.: EDAMEX.

Santamaría, Francisco J. 1942. *Diccionario General de Americanismos*. México, D.F.: Pedro Robredo.

Scherer, Julio. 1990. *El Poder. Historias de familia*. México, D.F.: Grijalbo.

———. 1986. *Los presidentes*. México, D.F.: Grijalbo.

Scherer, Julio, and Carlos Monsiváis. 1999. *Parte de guerra Tlatelolco 1968*. México, D.F.: Aguilar Nuevo Siglo.

Schmidt, Samuel. 2012. *México: Estado suplantado*. PROFMEX 17.5.

———. 2006. *Chistes étnicos. La risa de todos contra todos*. México, D.F.: Punto de Lectura.

———. 2005. "La homosexualidad en el humor político mexicano." *Revista electrónica de estudios latinoamericanos* 3, no. 10, Jan.–Mar.
———. 2005a. *México. La nueva gobernabilidad.* México, D.F.: CEPCOM-Anzuelo.
———. 2003. *Los grandes problemas nacionales.* México, D.F.: Taurus.
———. 1995. "Los chistes de Salinas." *Revista Nueva Antropología.*
———. 1992. "Humor y política: Algunas consideraciones teóricas y una reflexión sobre México." *Revista Mexicana de Sociología* 1.
———. 1990a. "Elitelore in Politics: Humor vs. Mexico's Presidents." *Journal of Latin American Lore,* 16:1.
———. 1990b. "Votación y Elecciones en la frontera México-Estados Unidos: Revisando las tendencias electorales." *Estudios Fronterizos* 21.
———. 1991a. "La Red de Poder y la Estabilidad Política en México." 39th Annual Rocky Mountain Council for Latin American Studies. Flagstaff, AZ. February 21–23.
———. 1991b. *The Deterioration of the Mexican Presidency.* Tucson: University of Arizona Press.
———. 1988. *La autonomía relativa del Estado.* México, D.F.: Quinto Sol.
———. 1986. *El deterioro del presidencialismo mexicano.* México, D.F.: EDAMEX.
———. 1977. *La reforma democratica de López Portillo.* México, D.F.: Facultad de Ciencias Políticas y Sociales, UNAM.
Schmidt, Samuel, James Wilkie, and Manuel Esparza (eds.). 1988. *Estudios Cuantitativos sobre la historia de México.* México, D.F.: Instituto de Investigaciones Históricas, UNAM.
Schmidt, Samuel, and Jorge Gil. 1991. "Mexico: The Network Behind Power." *Review of Latin American Studies* 3:2.
Schutz, Charles. 1977. *Political Humor.* Rutherford, NJ: Fairleigh Dickinson University Press.
Scott, James C. 1990. *Domination and the Arts of Resistance,* New Haven and London: Yale University Press.
Sen, Amartya. 1981. *Poverty and Famines: An Essay on Entitlement and Deprivation.* Oxford: Clarendon Press; New York: Oxford University Press.
Serna, Enrique. 2001. *El seductor de la patria.* México, D.F.: Ed. Joaquín Mortiz.
Serrano, Irma y Elisa Robledo. 1978. *A calzon amarrado.* México, D.F.: Distribuidora Sayrols de Publicaciones.
Sharp, Gene. 1970. *Exploring Nonviolent Alternatives.* Boston: Extending Horizons.
Sibley, Mulford Q. (ed.). 1963. *The Quiet Battle: Writings on the Theory and Practice of Non-Violent Resistance.* Boston: Beacon Press.
Solares, Ignacio. 2005. *La invasión.* México, D.F. Alfaguara.
Spota, Luis. 1967. *Casi el paraíso.* México, D.F.: Diana.
Stanley, Harold W., and Richard G. Niemi. 1990. *Vital Statistics on American Politics.* Washington, D.C.: CQ Press. Second edition.
Stein, Stanley J., and Barbara H. 1970. *The Colonial Heritage of Latin America: Essays on Economic Development in Perspective.* New York: Oxford University Press.
Suárez, Luis. 1984. *Echeverría en el sexenio de López Portillo.* México, D.F.: Grijalbo.
Teichman, Judith A. 1988. *Policymaking in Mexico: From Boom to Crisis.* Boston: Allen & Unwin.
Telushkin, Joseph. 1992. *Jewish Humor: What the Best Jewish Jokes Say about the Jews.* New York: William Morrow and Co.

Torres-Rivas, Edelberto. 1993. "America Latina. Gobernabilidad y democracia en sociedades en crisis." *Nueva Sociedad*, no. 128: 88–101.

Trochim, Michael R. 1987. "Humor as a Response to Repression. The Orange Question and the Birth of the Brazilian Republic." *New World* 2:1–2.

Trueba Lara, José Luis. "La corrupción como arma política." *Página Uno*. México, D.F.: Uno mas Uno.

Trujillo Barriga, Ana Bertha. 1990. *La Caricatura Política en México*. México, D.F.: UNAM, Facultad de Ciencias Políticas y Sociales. B.A. thesis.

Udall, Mo. 1988. *Too Funny to Be President*. New York: Henry Holt and Company.

University of Chicago. 1990. *The New Encyclopædia Britannica*. Chicago: University of Chicago.

Uribe, Ana. 2009. *Mi México imaginado: Telenovelas, televisión y migrantes*. México, D.F.: El Colegio de la Frontera Norte, Universidad de Colima, M.A. Porrúa.

Velasco Piña, Antonio. 2005. *Círculo negro*. México, D.F.: Punto de lectura.

Vila, Pablo. 2000. *Crossing Borders, Reinforcing Borders*. Austin: University of Texas Press.

Villa, Rosa Helia. 1999. *Itinerario de una pasión*. México, D.F.: Plaza y Janés.

Viuti. 1982. *No pido la palabra*. Buenos Aires: Ediciones de la Flor.

Whitehead, Lawrence. 1980. "La política económica de Echeverría: ¿Que salió mal y por qué?" *Foro Internacional* 20:3.

Wiarda, Howard J. 1986. "Social Change, Political Development and the Latin American Tradition," in Klaren, Peter F., and Thomas J. Bossert (eds.), *Promise of Development. Theories of Change in Latin America*. New York: Westview.

Williams, Nick. 1987. "Political Humor Is No Joke in South Korea." *Los Angeles Times*, September 13.

Wilkie, James. 1984. "The Historical View of Octavio Paz: A Critique of the Washington Address." *New Scholar* 9:1–2.

———. 1973. *Elitelore*. Los Angeles: UCLA, Latin American Center Publications.

Wilkie, James, and David Lorey (eds.). 1987. *Statistical Abstract of Latin America*. Los Angeles: UCLA, Latin American Center Publications, vol. 25.

Wilkie, James, David Lorey, and Enrique Ochoa (eds.). 1988. *Statistical Abstract of Latin America*. Los Angeles: UCLA, Latin American Center Publications, vol. 26.

Wilkie, James, and Monica Menell-Kinberg. 1981. "Evita: From Elitelore to Folklore." *Journal of Latin American Lore* 7:1, 99–140.

Zaid, Gabriel. 1987. *La economía presidencial*. México, D.F.: Vuelta.

Zuno, José. 1961. *Historia de la caricatura en México*. Guadalajara, n.p.

———. 1958. *Posada y la ironía plástica*. México, D.F.: Biblioteca de Autores Jalisciences Modernos.

Zweig, Stefan. 1958. *Fouche: El genio tenebroso*. Barcelona: Ed. Juventud.

Index

About the Author

Samuel Schmidt has taught at different universities in the United States and Mexico. He is the associate director of the journal *Araucaria,* and the director of the weekly *El Reto*. He received his PhD in political science from the Universidad Nacional Autónoma de México in 1973 and did postdoctoral work in history at the University of California, Los Angeles, in 1982. He has written numerous books, including *Los Grandes problemas nacionales* (Miguel Angel Porrua, 2010), *En la mira. Chiste politico en México* (Taurus, 2006), *Chistes étnicos. La risa de todos contra todos* (Punto de lectura, 2006), *Las grandes soluciones nacionales* (Aguilar Nuevo siglo, 2005), and *The Deterioration of the Mexican Presidency: The Years of Luis Echeverría* (University of Arizona Press, 1991).

